Confessions of Love

The Ambiguities of Greek *Eros* and Latin *Caritas*

Edited by Craig J. N. de Paulo,
Bernhardt Blumenthal,
Catherine Conroy de Paulo,
Patrick A. Messina, and Leonid Rudnytzky

PETER LANG
New York • Washington, D.C./Baltimore • Bern
Frankfurt • Berlin • Brussels • Vienna • Oxford

Library of Congress Cataloging-in-Publication Data

Confessions of love: the ambiguities of Greek eros and Latin caritas /
edited by Craig J. N. de Paulo ... [et al.].
p. cm. — (American university studies VII: Theology and religion; v. 310)
Includes bibliographical references and index.
1. Love—History. 2. Love—Religious aspects—Christianity—
History of doctrines. I. De Paulo, Craig J. N.
BD436.C589   241′.4—dc22   2010046757
ISBN 978-1-4331-1184-6
ISSN 0740-0446

Bibliographic information published by **Die Deutsche Nationalbibliothek**.
Die Deutsche Nationalbibliothek lists this publication in the "Deutsche
Nationalbibliografie"; detailed bibliographic data is available
on the Internet at http://dnb.d-nb.de/.

Cover image: "The Ecstasy of St. Theresa" by Gian Lorenzo Bernini
in the Chiesa della Vittoria in Rome, Italy.

The paper in this book meets the guidelines for permanence and durability
of the Committee on Production Guidelines for Book Longevity
of the Council of Library Resources.

Printed in Germany

Confessions of Love

AMERICAN UNIVERSITY STUDIES

SERIES VII
THEOLOGY AND RELIGION

VOL. 310

PETER LANG
New York • Washington, D.C./Baltimore • Bern
Frankfurt • Berlin • Brussels • Vienna • Oxford

Dedicated to

**Our *Alma Mater*,
La Salle University,
and to all of the Christian Brothers
who have taught there over the years.**

Contents

Acknowledgments

First of all, we would like to express our sincere gratitude to Dr. Wayne Huss, Professor of History and Chair of the Division of Humanities at Gwynedd Mercy College, for his gracious support and encouragement. We would also like to thank Dr. Lisa McGarry, Interim Dean of the School of Arts and Sciences at Gwynedd Mercy College, for her gracious support of our scholarly endeavors. We are most grateful to Dr. Denise Wilbur, formerly the Vice President for Academic Affairs at Gwynedd Mercy College, for her kind encouragement and the generous research grant her Office awarded in support of this project. We must also acknowledge the kindness of Dr. Kathleen Owens, President of Gwynedd Mercy College, and Dr. Robert Funk, Acting Vice President for Academic Affairs at the College.

We must also acknowledge our sincere thanks to the contributors of this volume, and especially to the Rev. Professor Roland Teske, S.J. and Professor Phillip Cary.

Finally, we gratefully acknowledge the support and encouragement of the Rev. Dr. William J. Geisler, whose learned conversation greatly contributed to this volume.

Foreword

Craig J. N. de Paulo

What could be closer to philosophy than the experience of love? Of course, the very word philosophy is founded upon the two Greek terms *"philia"* (love) and *"sophia"* (wisdom) since it is the "love of wisdom." How interesting that, unlike other disciplines and sciences, the word philosophy does not use the Greek term *"logos"* as a suffix in order to indicate that it is a discipline of reason that "studies" some topic. Despite its exulted position among the Greeks, or perhaps because of it, philosophy is most of all, a love. And, unlike all the other disciplines, it does not love anything in particular since it is in love with wisdom, which involves all things. It could also be said that there is a kind of symmetry to love and wisdom since both appear to be infinite, something observed by Plato in his magnificent *Symposium* where the great philosopher argues that the ascent of the soul begins with its craving (*eros*) for beauty, which moves the soul from the beauty of a body to the beauty of bodies in general, to the beauty of a soul, to the beauty of ideas and onward to wisdom and philosophic ecstasy. As Plato points out, by having Socrates scandalize his company, love is also an experience of coming to understand one's neediness or lack; and since *eros* lacks, it cannot be a god! But, the fall of *eros* from divinity, in Plato's reckoning, leads to the near deification of his mentor and his ancient love. Indeed, the

Greeks viewed philosophy as divine activity. So, returning to Plato's dialogue on love, we discover that it is the philosopher who is very aware of his or her lack of wisdom, and the one who *craves* what he or she lacks, namely wisdom.

So powerful an experience this was and remains, that philosophy has frequently inspired love between master and disciple, as with Socrates and Plato, for instance. It has also fathered many great friendships throughout the ages, which has inspired schools like Plato's Academy and Aristotle's Lyceum, communities like Augustine's in Fifth-century Roman North Africa and, to some extent, the early Christian monasteries and also the first universities in medieval Europe.

But, let us return to love again. Aside from the powerful experience of love that we find in ancient, classical Greece, it was the rise of the Christianity no doubt that brought the credibility of love to its summit where God is revealed as love (*agape*) and the teaching of Jesus in the New Testament *Gospels* will boldly command the ancient world "to love God and love one's neighbor." And, who would have thought then that a religion dedicated to love and meekness would conquer the mighty Roman Empire and convert it as well? Needless to say, Christianity's message of love changed the ancient world — indeed, the whole world — so that today we may speak of human and civil rights, the freedom of religion, care for the poor, the sick and the disabled, all of which are directly the result of love. Nevertheless, poverty, neglect and war continue to plague the world, and the tender message of love is often assailed by those who are more enamored with power. Of course, this is quite simply of war of loves. As the Apostle Paul has written, "The flesh lusts against the spirit, and the spirit against the flesh." But, perhaps, Augustine of Hippo put it more clearly, by his powerful description of the spiritual warfare that exists, both cosmically and in our hearts, between the city of God and the city of man? And, are these two loves not also too very different *confessions*?

This volume is rightly entitled "Confessions of Love: The Ambiguities of Greek *Eros* and Latin *Caritas*" because there appears to be a kind of battle between these two ancient loves for the place of divinity. In *Eros*, there is the memory of the pagan god and its chaotic love, but it is also the love preferred by Christian mystics and thinkers like Origen, Pseudo-Dionysius and Marsilio Ficino to mention a few, in their discussion of God. Yet, the New Testament writers neglected *eros* in preference for *agape* in their description of God. Thus, in the West, Greek *agape* is translated into the Latin *caritas*, but many scholars would argue that *caritas* would be soulless without its philosophical connection to the more sensual *eros*.

Finally, what could be more timely than a collection of essays on the topic of love at a time in history when we seem to be losing our humanity more and more? The so-called advances in technology have resulted, for instance, in online classrooms that do away with the natural relationship between the teacher and the student, and so what love could possibly result from this? Cell phones seem to ring everywhere in the world today, on the street, in the park, interrupting our conversations and even our worship; and virtual conversations and cell phone calls often take precedence over real conversations in the presence of actual persons, our friends, our family and colleagues. Students today do "google" searches instead of research in the dusty stacks, finding books and journal articles, in libraries. The question is, however, can this kind of "research" inspire love for a book, or a discipline? Our relations with one another have deformed into virtual encounters through email, instant messaging, texting and even sexting!

So, following Augustine who wrote, that we can find "truth through love," our volume is focused on the question of love in order to find truth. Thus, our love is always a kind of confession of some truth. What are *our* confessions of love today? And, what do our loves *confess*?

Introduction

Craig J. N. de Paulo and Leonid Rudnytzky

THE RETURN OF EROS IN THE WEST

Without a doubt, love is something very near to us, and yet it remains a mystery. While love is clearly the most appealing of all things, it also reveals our vulnerability, which can turn the rapture of bliss quite quickly into intense sorrow and despair. As Socrates indicates, recalling the words of the Oracle at Delphi in Plato's *Symposium*, love (*eros*) is something wealthy and impoverished, something utterly needy and ultimately rich, and something that fulfills us, while remaining a consuming desire. What could be more simple, more tender and more ambiguous than love?

While the experience of love is often ecstatic, intense and ultimately transcendental, it is also, perhaps, the most common of happenings. Further, love is not only an experience between persons, but also an experience that persons have with other living things such as animals and nature. We can also love music, art, literature, philosophy, poetry, history, and mathematics, for instance, with profound intensity, turning our natural *libido* into a spiritual and deeply interior romance with these disciplines and their histories, texts and ideas. Of course, this is an elite type of love, which inevitably enkindles only a few, especially since this love begins with an intellectual apprehension and knowledge of the other, which seems endless, and only deepens the affections of the lover. In this case, while the beloved (such as philosophy) is unmoved, it has the capacity to move the lover forever. So, the philosopher, as we know, is a "lover of wisdom" whose involvement with philosophy is always between reason and love, throwing the will into play with the intellect, making the philosopher question even *himself*. To the philosopher, it is not mere ideas that he or she loves, but something *real* in his or her relentless search for being. It might be said that the only thing that could further intensify such an experience of love would be to share it, as a teacher does with a student—that is, a real teacher with a real student, or, perhaps, with another lover of the same discipline, where two scholars can enjoy each other's company in their common love for wisdom. Nevertheless, such a love—a scholar's love—is always and inevitably a singular kind of love whose commitment is often unintelligible to most, yet it is this peculiar love, and these lovers in particular, that constitute the hope of their disciplines, preserving them and helping them to endure the neglect of generations and the contempt of a materialistic society.

Another intense, and much overlooked love today, is the love of friendship, termed *"philia"* in ancient Greek. As Aristotle writes in his *Nichomachean Ethics*, true friendship is a rare experience since there are so few good men. True or perfect friendship, for Aristotle, is a state of blessedness, a gift from the gods, reserved for serious men of virtue. Following Socrates' lead in Plato's *Symposium*, where the old sage denies the advances of the lovely Alcibiades, Aristotle purifies the *philia* between men, preferring the intellectual bond of their souls instead of one that might also include the love of bodies, which was common in Ancient Greece, as exemplified by the relationship between the great warrior, Achilles, and his lover, Patroclus. In Classical Latin literature, too, we can also cite Cicero's *De Amicitia*, his captivating treatise in praise of friendship, which describes in great detail the romance and spiritual depth of this profound love between men of virtue. Yet, even this noble love, as unique as it may be, can also turn for the worse, as St. Augustine forlornly warns us, "How often do we mistake a friend for an enemy, and an enemy for a friend."

So profound is this experience that the Evangelist St. John finds no word more apt to describe God than love (*agape*). Needless to say, in the *Gospel of St. John*, the teaching of Jesus is focused on the two-fold meaning of love: *agape* is the love of God *and* the love of one's neighbor. Jesus himself taught, "What you do for the least among you, you do for me," which reveals the imperative of love in the Christian community in addition to the notion that love of others is a divine act. And, as for terminology, we find that the Johannine *agape* is translated into the Latin "*caritas*" by St. Jerome, which develops and even converts, one might say, the old pagan Roman term into a new Christian one that will reign over all other kinds of love for the entire history of the Church in the West.

Probably because of the Latinization of the Church and its liturgy on the Italian peninsula beginning around the fourth century, the Ancient Greek loves of *eros, philia* and *agape* were abandoned in the West in favor of Latin terms like *amor, caritas, cupiditas, amicitia*, etc. But, what of *eros*? What happened to erotic love? In the Augustinian tradition, which has dominated the Latin Church ever since the fifth century, *eros* is essentially confused with lust (*concupiscentia*) and doomed in its association with the biblical fall of Adam and Eve; and therefore, conceived as evil desire. Aside from mention in some of the Greek tradition of the Church, such as Origen, St. Gregory of Nyssa, Pseudo-Dionysius and the Medieval mystics, in the West *eros* becomes associated more with paganism until a brief revival in Florence during the Italian Renaissance, with figures like Marsilio Ficino, commenting on Plato's great dialogue on love. In point of fact, however, the experience of *eros* has never left us. One can easily see it in the monastic ideal throughout the Middle Ages; and of course, in the scholar's love that moved Scholasticism into being. Nevertheless, the term *eros* was lost in Western discussion in favor of the Latin and seemingly more noble and grace-filled *caritas*, something perhaps akin to what happened to philosophy in its subjugation to theology during the centuries between Albertus Magnus and someone like the Jesuit theologian Karl Rahner. Ironically, it appears that *eros* has been rehabilitated by none other than a pope—Benedict XVI, in fact, has restored the ecclesiastical credibility of

Greek *eros* in his first Encyclical, *Deus Caritas Est*.[1] In this work, in his apparent desire to reconcile the disparity between the Greek and Latin traditions, the pontiff argues that God is *eros* as much as *caritas*.[2] Thus, *eros* returns to the West not only as a divine love, but as God Himself.

EROS, AMBIGUITY AND CHRISTIANITY

Now any classical scholar would affirm that the term *eros* is certainly an equivocal term, which can be used for divine love, friendship and sexual love. The ambiguity of *eros* is certainly intriguing, which makes this ancient term particularly appealing in a postmodern context. Thus, our retrieval of *eros*—and particularly within theology—is definitely controversial. It was Anders Nygren, in his well-known work, *Agape and Eros: A Study of the Christian Idea of Love*, who in 1932, had argued that *eros* was essentially a pagan love.[3] More recently, the Dominican theologian Fergus Kerr has also argued that (platonic) eroticism "has had fateful effects in the development of Christian spirituality and asceticism."[4] Without doubt, the restoration of *eros* reveals one of the central tensions in the Western Mind—that is, the convergence of Jewish and Greek thought that appears in the New Testament Gospels, the Letters of St. Paul and in theological themes and concepts further developed by the great Augustine of Hippo. Further, since the term *"eros"* is not used explicitly by the evangelists to describe God or divine love, some scholars may well argue that the restoration of this term might return us to a pre-Christian context. As such, in ancient Greek, pagan literature and philosophy, *eros* can describe everything from the sacred to the profane, from the love of wine to the divine, heterosexual, homosexual or bi-sexual love. In fact, the term could also be viewed as an attempt to return to the pagan orgiastic. Thus, the use of *eros* in Western discourse remains ambiguous; and therefore, an intriguing problem for Christianity, especially with regard to the Augustinian tradition and its fundamental dichotomy of love: with *caritas,* on the one hand, and *concupiscentia,* on the other. Thus, the question remains: can the Western mind ever reconcile these two ancient loves, Greek *eros* and Latin *caritas*?

EASTERN (BYZANTINE) EROS

There is no doubt, however, that our recent retrieval of the term *eros* has been imported to the West from the East—that is, as we have already seen, from the ancient Greek tradition. Yet, this time, with Benedict XVI's retrieval of *eros*, we must focus primarily on the early Greek Christian heritage and its place within Byzantine Christianity. Here, we find in Christian orthodoxy and in Greek Christianity in general a greater openness and appreciation for the term *eros* simply because it belongs to this cultural and linguistic heritage. Whereas, in the Western Latin tradition, *eros* experiences a definite fall from grace, so to speak, translating it almost exclusively with terms like *libido, concupiscentia,* and even *perversio* without any mention of its more divine, elusive and mysterious origins. Aside from philosophical and artistic attempts during the Italian Renaissance to rehabilitate it, *eros* has almost always been confused with sensual sin in the Western Church. Perhaps, *eros* was simply too erotic for the West and especially for our beloved Augustine, who struggled so much with it in his own spiritual journey? And, without *eros*, the West has long contended that our loves seem to be more pure and more neatly divided up into intelligible parts, good love and bad love. Unfortunately, this division in love may also neglect to capture the existential connection between our own human longings and our divine aspirations for a love greater than ourselves, which leads us to question whether our own capacity for love, even when it is fallen, can be converted to something better? Or, is it rather that our love is simply doomed for failure, for pride and perversity, and we require a higher love and divine assistance to turn our fallen love away from ourselves and to the other? But, the ancient Greek philosophers would certainly reply, "What love could be higher than *eros*?" And, so, we must now question again if these loves are, indeed, so completely different, belonging to two different worlds and arising from two fundamentally different desires and aspirations, as Augustine powerfully describes by his use of the two cities—the city of God and the city of man? But, is there any connection between these two cities and these two

loves? Where would *eros* be in this Augustinian schema of love?
Is it simply condemned to the perverse love of the city of man?
Or, can it somehow be conceived as a bridge between these two
worlds and their two loves, as Benedict seems to suggest? Again,
Greek *eros* is equivocal; and therefore, it is an ambiguous experience. It can be everyday love and it certainly has the potential for
divine love, as Plato, Plotinus and Gregory of Nyssa will affirm.
Nevertheless, terms have histories and they belong to their own
cultural, philosophical and historical contexts so when we employ
a Greek term like *eros* within the Western (i.e. Latin) tradition we
are inevitably left with ambiguity. And, since we cannot change
history, this current retrieval of *eros* points us toward the future
and a new direction for philosophical speculation requiring a new
synthesis of Greek thought and Christianity, which we already see
bearing fruit within Catholic moral theology and also in the recent
development of the theology of the body and specifically with regard to the contemporary theology of marriage and conjugal love
and its newfound appreciation for pleasure. Needless to say,
however, this development is a departure from the ancient apos-
tolic and patristic tradition that associated pleasure with paganism. Yet, in this new synthesis, we find that the sensual pleasure
associated with conjugal love belongs to that *eros* that connects us,
and specifically the married couple, to God, who is love itself.
However, Augustine along with many of the Fathers of the
Church would certainly question whether this pleasure is a fruit
from above or below despite its noble association? Thus, our retrieval of *eros* provides us with a new kind of methodology
whereby in our turning back to the Greek term, we may also be
retrieving some of the ancient Hebrew assumptions about love
and marriage. Again, we find ourselves surrounded by ambiguity
since the Hebrew idea of conjugal love is, to a great extent, abandoned by the Apostle St. Paul, who greatly inspires the Christian
patristic tradition.

    So, in the end, the question of *eros* appears to be a problem for
the West *again*, and Western philosophers and theologians will
have to continue to wrestle with it. And, despite modern attempts
to import *eros* into Western discourse by philosophy, psycho-
analysis, art, music and literature, *eros* remains very Eastern and

exotic to us in the West. *Eros* is attractive *and* elusive. It opens up old wounds and ancient controversies, and it throws us face to face with our fundamental assumptions and provokes us to question the mysterious realm of love in all of its ambiguity. Ultimately, it seems, any attempt to define *eros* inevitably leads us to the experience of mysticism, which has also been a great problem for the West in its insatiable desire to grasp all things with the *mind*. Nevertheless, in a word, *eros* leaves us breathless and speechless in our desire to love, and fully content with the experience of beauty in our pursuit of the truth.

REVISITING ANCIENT EROS AND ITS LITERARY AND MYTHOLOGICAL GENEALOGY

EROS AND THANATOS

"Agnosco veteris vestigia flammae" – "I recognize the vestiges of an old flame." These words uttered by Aeneas to Dido upon their initial encounter, reveal the powerful, primeval force of *eros* and its connection with *libido*. Aeneas senses, or rather recognizes the unquestionable, all-consuming power of love which leaves an indelible imprint on the human soul and which is intrinsically intertwined with sexual attraction. The reference to flame is, of course, of special significance; it is both a reminder of a past consuming erotic encounter as well as a foreshadowing of Dido's ultimate demise through immolation. Thus, *eros* and *thanatos* are often inextricably linked together forming a special dimension to human love and sexuality.

This relationship between love and death and its ultimate consummation in fire is found in many literary works. In his mystical period, Goethe set it a lasting monument in his poetry, especially in the two ballads, written partially in praise of the old pagan religion and as a condemnation of excessive Christian asceticism: *"Die Braut von Korinth"* and *"Der Gott und die Bajadere,"* in which the flames bring about the end of life, the promise of ultimate salvation and, in the latter, divinity. The ubiquitous *Liebestod* motif popularized by Wagner in his operas, is another example of the love-death connection, which, *mutatis mutandis*, in a more vulgar version, is found in the French expression for orgasm: *"le petit mort."* But perhaps the most poignant poetic capturing of the love-death relationship and its intrinsic connection to beauty has been achieved by Goethe's epigone, August Count von Platen-Hallermünde (1796-1835). Von Platen was an ardent admirer of the Greeks, especially of Pindar, and a lover of classical literature, whose own poetic oeuvre is characterized by remarkable lucidity, restraint and harmony. His poem "Tristan" (1825), of which we offer here the first stanza in the original as well as in a rather prosaic translation, is a good example of semiotic encoding in the *eros-thanatos* relationship:

> Wer die Schönheit angeschaut mit Augen
> Ist dem Tode schon anheimgegeben,
> Wird für keinen Dienst auf Erden taugen,
> Und doch wird er vor dem Tode beben,
> Wer die Schönheit angeschaut mit Augen!
> He who beheld Beauty with his eyes
> Is already doomed to death.
> No longer will he be of any use on this earth,
> And yet he will tremble in the face of death,
> He who beheld Beauty with his eyes!

Eros and Ecstacy

Of course, not all manifestations of love in European letters have this deathlike Dionysian nature as first expostulated by Friedrich Nietzsche. Sometimes the Apollonian view, initially conceived by Johann Joachim Winckelmann (1717-1768) in his dictum that underlying all of Greek art is "a noble simplicity and a quiet grandeur," takes the upper hand. The Austrian poet Hugo von Hofmannsthal (1874-1929) in his brief yet incomparably powerful poem *"Die Beiden"* ("The Two"), offered here in a plain prose translation taken from *The Penguin Book of German Verse* (first published in 1957), is an excellent example of this Apollonian attribute of *eros*:

> She carried the cup in her hand – her chin and mouth were like its rim –

Her gait was so light and assured, not a drop spilled out of the cup.
His hand was equally light and firm; he rode on a young horse,
And with a careless movement he made it stand still, quivering.
But when he was to take the light cup from her hand,
it was too heavy for both of them; for both trembled so much that no hand
found the other hand, and dark wine flowed on the ground.

Another example of the Apollonian nature of *eros* is found in Boris Pasternak's Nobel prize winning novel *Dr. Zhivago* (1957). Here *eros* enables the two lovers, Zhivago and Lara, to escape, albeit momentarily, the sufferings and ravages of war which is destroying their world. In a typically romantic manner (and *eros*, lest we forget, finds in Romanticism its most popular expression), the two lovers experience fleeting moments of peace and tranquility. They become a part of the cosmos, a link in the great chain of being, which makes them impervious to the violence and ugliness surrounding them. *Eros*, in its Apollonian incarnation, is not simply unbridled passion that robs people of tranquility driving them to destruction; rather it is the source of beauty and salvation:

They loved each other, not driven by necessity, by the 'blaze of passion' often falsely ascribed to love. They loved each other because everything around them willed it, the trees and the clouds and the sky over their heads and the earth at their feet. Perhaps their surrounding world, the strangers they met in the street, the wide expanses they saw on their walks, the rooms in which they lived or met, took more delight in their love than they themselves did. Ah, that was just what had united them and had made them so akin! Never, never even in their moments of richest and wildest happiness, were they unaware of a sublime joy in the total design of the universe, a feeling that they themselves were a part of that whole, an element in the beauty of the cosmos.[5]

Eros becomes a powerful antidote to the evils of ideological depravity that attempt to restructure the world. Love is the inner sanctum of lovers, a fortress in which they become unassailable: "Their love was great. Most people experience love without becoming aware of the extraordinary nature of this emotion. But to them – and this made them exceptional – the moments when passion visited their doomed human existence like a breath of eternity were moments of revelation, of continually new discoveries about themselves and life."[6]

This power of *eros* to change the individual and his world is also fittingly captured by Mario Puzo in his bestseller *The Godfather* when Michael Corleone first encounters Apollonia:

> he found himself standing, his heart pounding in his chest; he felt a little dizzy. The blood was surging through his body, through all its extremities and pounding against the tips of his fingers, the tips of his toes. All the perfumes of the island came rushing in on the wind, orange, lemon blossoms, grapes, flowers. It seemed as if his body had sprung away from him out of himself.[7]

Eros often strikes like a thunderbolt (a word used by the Puzo himself in describing this event, p. 334) and its effects are life-changing and ever-lasting. Indeed, the two quoted passages, taken from authors from two different worlds, demonstrate this power of *eros* not only to change human beings, but also to change their perception of their surroundings, indeed to change the nature surrounding them and the world in which they live.

SOME ANCIENT TALES OF *EROS*

While these selected passages provide us with revealing glimpses into the power of *eros*, its beguiling ambiguity and its ubiquity in literature, they offer little information on its genesis and origins. And indeed, the origins of *eros* are shrouded in mystery. Born of Chaos, *Eros* in his primal and primeval incarnation is the Greek god of love. He is not mentioned in Homer, but Hesiod refers to him as the fairest of divine entities whose allure is irresistible to both gods and humans. According to Hesiod, *Eros* is not merely a god who evokes deep passion and unbridled sexual frenzy, but a primordial force, which forms and reforms the world by uniting its disparate inner elements. There are also a number of other tales in later Greek lore which present him as a son of Aphrodite by Ares or Hermes, the youngest among the gods, willful, capricious and often cruel. However, perhaps the best known story about him appears in "*Eros* and *Psyche*" found in Apuleius' book *Metamorphoses*, which dates to the second century.

Briefly told, this story begins with *Psyche*, the youngest of three daughters of a royal couple. Her beauty is such that people believe her to be an incarnation of Aphrodite. However, her beauty is also a curse; it inhibits suitors from asking for her hand in marriage and invokes the wrath of the gods upon her. Her father consults the oracle of Apollo and is told that that she must be placed on a mountaintop as a sacrifice to a horrifying monster-serpent. She is saved from this terrible fate by a gentle wind that carries her to safety. Walking in the woods she finds a magnificent, magic palace. A voice tells her that she is to be married. A magic wedding feast is held, and her bridegroom, *Eros*, whom she cannot see but only feel, visits her after midnight. Following a passionate night, he leaves her before sunrise. *Psyche* lives in the castle enjoying the moments of love but longing for human companionship. Her husband continues his nocturnal visits but never reveals himself to her. She begs him to allow her to see her sisters. He relents but orders her never to tell them anything about him, informing her that she is pregnant and that their child will be a god if she keeps their secret. She enjoys the subsequent visit of her sisters, tells them of her happiness and gives them precious gifts but, in responding to their prying, tells them contradictory stories about her husband. They become suspicious and envious suspecting that she has never seen him and that he may be a god. On their third visit they convince her that, as predicted by the oracle, her husband is a monster who will devour her and her child. The following night, *Psyche* does look at her husband when he is asleep and is overwhelmed by his beauty. She suffers terrible pangs of remorse and attempts unsuccessfully to kill herself. *Eros* awakens and tries to fly away. She clings to him; they soar into the sky but eventually his strength ebbs and they come down to earth. *Eros* informs *Psyche* that he has disobeyed Aphrodite's command by marrying her instead of making her fall in love with an unworthy mortal man. He tells her that he will leave her and punish her sisters for what they have done. *Psyche* is terribly distraught, she attempts suicide but is saved by Pan, who urges her to live and to try to regain *Eros'* love. She tricks her sisters into believing that they have a chance of marrying *Eros*, and both sisters die in their respective attempts to get to his magical palace.

Psyche continues her search for *Eros*, but is captured and brought before Aphrodite who, having found out about her liaison with *Eros*, wants to punish her. She orders *Psyche* to perform four impossible tasks that would defy the strength of Hercules. With the help of her own ingenuity and that of some kindly natural forces, as well as Zeus, who is beholden to *Eros*, *Psyche* is able to pass Aphrodite's first three tests. The fourth and most demanding task sends her to Hades to get some of Persephone's beauty salve. Once again, *Psyche* is ready to commit suicide. She mounts the tower from which she intends to leap to her death. But the friendly tower instructs her how to enter the underworld safely and get the box containing the precious ointments. The tower also warns her not to look into the box. Psyche follows the instructions and manages to get the required item. However, once again, overcome by curiosity, she opens it and, as a result, falls into a deadly sleep. This time *Eros* himself comes to her rescue by awakening her from the lethal slumber.

The story has a happy ending. Zeus allows the wedding of *Eros* and *Psyche* to take place. Aphrodite grudgingly approves of the match, and *Psyche* by marrying *Eros* becomes a goddess. The result of their union is a daughter called *Voluptas*.

There are numerous variants of this tale. *Psyche* and *Eros* motifs flower during the age of Romanticism. It has fueled the imagination of hundreds (if not thousands of poets, dramatists and novelists.) The tale has also a great significance on modern psychology. Numerous literary scholars, philosophers, theologians, social thinkers and psychologists, among them Freud and Jung, have offered diverse and challenging interpretations of its meaning in trying to delve more deeply into the vagaries of the human soul. *Eros* in its innumerable *hypostases*, incarnations and disguises will forever remain a fascinating and inexhaustible subject for scholars of all disciplines. Our present volume is but a modest contribution to a better understanding of human love and its transcendent dimensions.

A HERMENEUTICS OF AMBIGUITY IN SEARCH OF SENSUALITY AND EROTICISM

As our previously published volume, *Ambiguity in the Western Mind*, pointed out the significance of the *concept of ambiguity* as a hermeneutical means back into some of the great books throughout the ages, this volume also uses the concept of ambiguity in its focus on love and specifically in its retrieval of the Greek term *eros* and the Latin term *caritas*. While our English term "love" may be more ambiguous than the ancient Greek term and the ancient Latin term, English love may also have become meaningless. By contrast, *eros* and *caritas* both have rich traditions; and as we have seen, through our hermeneutics of ambiguity in both our volumes, *eros* was not left to die in antiquity, but continues to exist not only in the Christian terms *agape* and *caritas*, but also in our art, music, poetry and literature. Ambiguity is not only inescapable, but philosophically very significant since it reflects the human condition.

In this volume, we have also attempted to retrieve the elements of sensuality and eroticism from the disciplines and topics in our contributor's essays. For, the retrieval of *eros* is vital, since it is a love that both points us to ourselves and to our need for transcendence.

WHENCE OUR CONFESSIONS OF LOVE?

Although our interest in this work began with our fascination with love itself, it was in fact Benedict XVI's use of the term *eros* in his first encyclical that intrigued us and moved us to pursue our present volume. Despite the philosopher Friedrich Nietszche's pronouncement, that "Christianity had killed *eros*," the pontiff has decided to resurrect it from its intellectual slumber. Perhaps, the reason for Benedict's interest in *eros* was to bridge the West to the East again and to reconnect the Latin and the Greek traditions in our experience of love and in our endless aspirations for God.

Our use of the term "confessions" in our discussion of love in this volume was inspired by St. Augustine, who rightly recognized that all confession is, indeed, a confession of love *and* that love is always a confession. For Augustine, the act of confessing (*confiteor*) is a profound profession of one's interior desire for the truth; it is an act that unites the mind and the heart of the lover with the Beloved. Thus, one's confession of praise to God, the confession of one's sin before God and others, and ultimately one's confession of faith is always a confession of one's love for God. Likewise, love itself is also a confession in its desire for the other and in its longing for the truth. As such, Augustinian confession is always a disclosure of personhood and one's true self as standing in the Divine presence. In confession, the individual discovers him or herself, as a creature, for God: he and she says, "I confess." Thus, the confession reveals our humanity, our finitude and ultimately our longing for transcendent solicitude.

In this volume, all of the scholars have focused their attention on the topic of love and its ambiguities with regard to their respective historical and literary texts. Most of the essays deal with either the use of Greek *eros* or Latin *caritas* in our pursuit of these two profound "confessions" of love that have dominated Western philosophy and literature throughout the ages.

THE SIGNIFICANCE OF THE CHRISTIAN CONFESSION OF LOVE

Indeed, our volume suggests that there are many "confessions" of love; in fact, perhaps there are as many confessions as there are individuals in love. Historically speaking, however, the Western world seems to be focused upon the apparent conflict between Greek *eros* and Latin *caritas*, and their respective traditions. Despite the fact that *eros* is employed by some in the Greek patristic tradition of the Church, the fact remains that it is not used by the New Testament writers in their reference to God as love. Nevertheless, many scholars like Roland Teske, have suggested that *eros* was used in the development of the Latin term *caritas*, transforming its ordinary antique Roman usage into its Christian formulation. The experience of *eros* was merged, so to speak, with *agape*, which perhaps seemed more acceptable to the Early Christian Church. Thus, perhaps, we can say that *eros* was not lost in the West, but absorbed by *caritas*, the Christian Latin translation of *agape*. Truly, what would Christian *agape* and *caritas* be like without *eros*? While the term *eros* does not appear in the New Testament for God's love, it exists within (and perhaps, beneath) the Christian use of *agape*. In this sense, then, the experience of *eros* permeates the *Gospels*. It is the love that moved Mary to clean the feet of Jesus with the precious, perfumed oil and wipe his feet with her long hair. It is the love that moved the beloved disciple, John, to rest his head upon the chest of Jesus. It is also the love that was felt by the many lepers, the blind and all of the sick who were healed by Jesus's hands and words. Indeed, *eros* is present in *agape*; and it reveals itself in all of the tears, sighs, touches and kisses that appear in the *Gospels*, revealing the flesh and blood of Jesus. What love could better express the profound Christian mystery of the incarnation than *eros*?

Notes

[1] Benedict XVI, Encyclical Letter, *Deus Caritas Est* (Vatican: Libreria Editrice Vaticana, 2006.)

[2] *Deus Caritas Est*, 9, where the pontiff cites Ps. Dionysius the Areopagite in his treatise *The Divine Names* (IV, 12-14; PG 3, 709-713), in calling God both *eros* and *agape*. Also, cf. *Deus Cartias Est*, 10.1.

[3] Anders Nygren, *Agape and Eros: A Study of the Christian Idea of Love*, Part I, trans. A. G. Herbert. (London: SPCK, 1932, 23-27.)

[4] Fergus Ferr, OP, "Charity as Friendship," in *Language Meaning and God: Essays in Honour of Herbert McCabe, OP*, ed. Brian Davies, OP. (London: Chapman, 1987) 7.

[5] Boris Pasternak, *Dr. Zhivago*, Pantheon Books, Inc., New York, 1958. p. 501.

[6] *Dr. Zhivago*, p. 395.

[7] *The Godfather*, (Putnam Edition, New York, 1969) 334.

The Ambiguity of Love in Augustine of Hippo

Roland Teske, S.J.
Marquette University

Almost a century has passed since the publication of Anders Nygren's classic work, *Agape and Eros*, and despite criticism of various sorts, the contrast between the Greek view of love as *eros* and the Christian view of love as *agape* retains much of its validity, especially with regard to the thought of Augustine of Hippo.[1] Since Augustine's conversion in 386–387 took place at least partially under the influence of the *libri Platonicorum* and was to a large extent made possible by his coming to the ability to conceive of God and the soul as incorporeal beings, it should hardly be surprising that much of what he says about love falls under the guise of a Platonic love as *eros*. And although Augustine's early enthusiasm for Neoplatonic philosophy was immense, he soon came to temper that enthusiasm as he came to a better grasp of the demands of the Christian faith; he, nonetheless, remained throughout his life deeply committed to aspects of Neoplatonism. For example, his early interest in a Platonic doctrine of the immortality of the soul was soon transferred to the Christian belief in the resurrection of the body.[2] So too, his earliest understanding of love of neighbor as oneself, which he early on understood as loving the neighbor was what one is oneself, namely, a soul, soon became a love for the neighbor as an embodied human being, whose temporal and bodily relationships to others make a real difference.[3]

In the present paper I want to examine some strands of what Augustine says on love as *eros* as well as his incorporation of an understanding of Christian love as *agape* and his attempt to combine them both in the view of love as *caritas*. I will first present Nygren's view of *eros* love and *agape* love as distinct and basically incompatible sorts of love. Secondly, I will look at examples of love as *eros* in Augustine, and thirdly, I will examine a particularly puzzling claim that Augustine makes about love and attempt to make sense of it. Finally, I will suggest that Augustine's puzzling claim goes a long way toward resolving the tension between love as *eros* and love as *agape* in Augustine. Augustine, of course, did not use the terms *eros* and *agape*, but rather used *amor, dilectio*, and *caritas*. Hence, some ambiguity perhaps arose from the different terminology.

EROS VERSUS AGAPE IN NYGREN

Nygren compares *eros* and *agape* as two "fundamental motifs" or different attitudes toward life, not simply as two different words, namely, ἔρος and ἀγάπη, nor as two different historical conceptions of love.[4] He bases his account of *eros* to a large extent on Plato's *Symposium* and *Phaedrus* and spells out the content of the idea in three points: 1) *Eros* is the love of desire or acquisitive love, 2) *Eros* is man's way to the Divine, and 3) *Eros* is ego-centric love.[5] He summarizes the content of the Christian idea of *agape* under four characteristics: *Agape* is 1) spontaneous and unmotivated, 2) is indifferent to value, 3) is creative, and 4) is God's way to man. Such love has "no motive outside of itself, in the personal worth of men."[6] Jesus came to save not the just, but sinners. Unlike human love, divine love is unmotivated. The second characteristic really does nothing more than spell out further the unmotivated character of God's love for human beings. Divine love as *agape* is rather creative of goodness and value through the forgiveness of sin and bestowal of justice. As God's way to man, *agape* is the initiator of our fellowship with God.[7] Given that God's love is such *agape*, Nygren interprets the command to love God and neighbor in terms of such love. "The Agape that is required here has its prototype in the Agape manifested by God, and there-

fore must be spontaneous and unmotivated, uncalculating, un-
limited, and unconditional."[8]

Clearly the two love motifs as Nygren sketches them are op-
posed in every respect so that, if *agape* is Christian love, it would
seem that *eros* cannot be Christian love. Furthermore, it would
seem that any attempt to combine the two can only be doomed to
failure. And yet, in Augustine who came to Catholic Christianity
through Neoplatonism, the worlds of Helenistic *eros* and primitive
Christian *agape* really meet and form a spiritual unity, although
Nygren claims that Augustine's "view contains not only strong
tensions, but real inner contradictions."[9] Nygren admits that Augustinian *caritas* is in some sense a synthesis of Hellenistic *eros* and
Christian *agape*, but he claims that "the strange thing is that
Augustine never sees that Christian Agape is the direct opposite
of Neoplatonic Eros, and these two motifs agree no better than fire
and water."[10]

LOVE IN THE EROS MOTIF IN AUGUSTINE

There are clearly aspects of what Augustine says about love
that square with the *eros* motif, as Nygren has described it. I shall
select three examples for the purposes of this paper: the desire for
happiness, the steps toward vision of the truth in *De quantiate animae*, and the ascents to vision in the *Confessiones*.

THE DESIRE FOR HAPPINESS

From the time of his earliest extant piece of writing, *De beata
vita*, Augustine was convinced that we all want to be happy. He
had read in Cicero's *Hortensius*, an exhortation to the life of philosophy, that "we all want to be happy," and the quest for happiness remained a constant in his writings from that time on.[11] In *De
beata vita*, an account of Augustine's birthday in 386—the first rec-
ord of a birthday party in literature—Augustine rapidly got the
agreement of his interlocutors on this basic point. He went on to
argue that no one is happy if he does not have what he wants, and
under Monica's guidance, Augustine, his son, and friends agree
that this is true only if one want something good. He goes on to

argue that one who has what he wants can only be happy if he has what he wants, if what he wants is something good, and if it cannot be lost against his will. Hence, he sees that the good that the happy person has must be something eternal, which can only be God.

Clearly such a desire for a happiness that can only be attained by possession of the eternal good, which is God, is an acquisitive sort of love, a path by which a human being moves toward God, a desire of which God is the object, an upward bound love, a love whose goal is union with God.

STEPS TOWARD THE VISION OF THE TRUTH

In *De quantitate animae* 32, 69, Augustine begins to explain the greatness of the soul, not in terms of space and time, but in terms of its power and capacity. In the following chapters he speaks of seven steps or levels in the soul's power in what Dom C. Butler has described as "the nearest approach to a formulation of mystical theology" in all of Augustine's writings.[12] The first step is the soul's activity in the body by which it unifies the organism and preserves it from disintegration. The second step is the soul's activity in the sensory powers of the soul. The third step, which is exclusively human, is the soul's memory of arts and skills, literature and music, history and everything that contributes to life in society—all of which are common to the learned and the unlearned and to good and bad people. At the fourth step the soul "ventures to place itself above not merely its own body ... but also the whole body of the universe and to regard such goods not as its own and distinguish and look down upon them compared to its own power and beauty."[13] At this step the soul turns to itself and strives to purify itself and strengthen itself against whatever might move it from its purpose. At this step the soul gradually overcomes its fear of death and grows stronger in the faith that everything is governed by the providence and justice of God and that his goodness helps it in the process of purification.

At the fifth step the soul has completed this purification and is free from all fear and anxiety. "On this step [the soul] conceives how great it is in every respect, and when it has grasped that, it

then advances toward God with unbounded and wondrous confi-
dence, that is, toward the very contemplation of the truth and toward that loftiest and most hidden reward for the sake of which it
labored so hard."[14] While at the fifth step the soul advances toward God (*pergit in Deum*), the sixth step consists in the highest
gaze (*aspectus*) of the soul, "than which it does not have any more
perfect, better, and more correct." This gaze is "the desire to understand those things that exist truly and supremely."[15] Augustine
distinguishes in his *Soliloquia* between having eyes to see, their
gaze or looking, and their actually seeing.[16] Here he explains that
the gaze, which is not yet seeing, is a desire or longing to understand what exists truly and supremely. That which exists truly
and supremely is, of course, God. For the conclusion of the ascent
to God in book two of *De libero arbitrio* terminated in God, who
truly exists, and for Augustine that truly exists which is eternal
and immutable.[17] Augustine here distinguishes between 1) "the
eye of the soul being cleansed so that it does not look in vain and
rashly and see what is evil," 2) "guarding and strengthening its
health," and 3) "directing its pure and correct gaze upon that
which is to be seen."[18]

Finally, the seventh step is found "in the very vision and contemplation of the truth, but is now not a step, but a certain abode
at which one arrives by those steps."[19] At this point Augustine ex-
claims, "What shall I say are the joys, what the enjoyment of the
highest and true good, what serenity and eternity of its breath."[20]

Clearly Augustine is describing an ascent of the human soul to
the point at which it sees God, the truth, that which truly exists,
and clearly it is desire (*appetitio*) that moves the soul from the sixth
to the seventh step, which is the soul's stopping point or abode.
This is the movement of *eros* toward God, and there is scarcely a
sign that this ascent to the contemplation the truth is helped by
God. In fact, Augustine immediately adds, "Certain great and
peerless souls have spoken these things to the extent that they
judged that they should be spoke, and we believe that they also
saw and see them."[21] Augustine does not here identify these great
and peerless souls, but in book twelve of *De Genesi ad litteram*, he
tells us that Moses saw God in the very substance of God, as did
Saint Paul when he was rapt to the third heaven.[22] However, it is

very likely that Augustine included among those who attained such a vision of God the great Platonists, such as Plotinus.[23] The present tense would seem to allow for the inclusion of some Platonists contemporary to Augustine, such as Theodorus, to whom Augustine dedicated *De beata vita* and who he thought was already enjoying the happy life.[24]

THE ASCENTS TO GOD IN THE CONFESSIONS

In *Confessiones* 7, 10, 6 and 7, 17, 23, Augustine describes two ascents to a vision of God, which have been described vain Plotinian attempts to ascend to a vision of God. Of the first he says,

> Being thus admonished to return to myself, under your leadership I entered into my inmost being. This I could do, for you became my helper. I entered there, and by my soul's eye, such as it was, I saw above that same eye of the soul, above my mind, an unchangeable light. It was not this common light, plain to all flesh, nor a greater light, as it were, of the same kind, as though that light would shine many, many times more bright, and by its great power fill the whole universe. Not such was that light, but different, far different from all other lights. Nor was it above my mind, as oil is above water, or sky above earth. It was above my mind, because it made me and I was beneath it, because I was made by it. He who knows the truth, knows that light, and he who knows it knows eternity. Love knows it, O eternal truth, and true love, and beloved eternity! You are my God, and I sigh for you day and night![25]

Certainly Augustine is here describing an ascent of his soul to a vision of the truth, a light above his mind, by which he has been made, a light that love (*caritas*) knows. This ascent to an immutable light and, therefore, to a non-bodily and non-temporal light is surely inspired by his reading of the books of the Platonists, which he mentions in the previous chapter and whose influence on him he is describing. He is, however, insistent upon the role of God's help, which he repeatedly mentions. He says, "By inner goads you roused me, so that I did not rest until you stood plain before my inner sight. By the secret hand of your Physician my swelling wound subsided, and day by day my mind's afflicted and darkened eyes grew sounder under the healing salve of sorrow."[26] He thanks God for first showing him the way of humility before procuring for him "certain books of the Platonists that had been translated out of Greek into Latin."[27] The love in this passage has many elements of the *eros* love that Nygren described, but also departs from such *eros* in many respects.

Whatever one might hold about the ascents in book seven of the Confessions, the vision at Ostia in book nine is, I think, undeniably a mystical experience of the divine that is upward bound, deeply influenced by Neoplatonism, and at the same time thoroughly Christian. Shortly before Monica's death, Augustine says of himself and Monica:

> We were alone conversing together most tenderly, *forgetting those things that are behind, and stretching forth to those that are before* (Phil 3:13). We inquired of one another *in the present truth* (2 Pt 1:12), which truth you are, as to what the eternal life of the saints would be like, *which eye has not seen, nor ear heard, nor has it entered into the heart of a man* (1 Cor 2:9). But we were straining out with the heart's mouth for those supernal streams flowing from your fountain, *the fountain of life*, which is *with you* (Ps 35:10), so that, being sprinkled with it according to our capacity, we might in some measure think upon so great a subject.[28]

The passage is clearly indebted to scripture, but the following paragraphs show an equally clear debt to the *Enneads*. For instance, Augustine and Monica say:

> If for any man the tumult of the flesh fell silent, silent the images of the earth, and of the waters, and of the air; silent the heavens; silent for him the very soul itself, and he should pass beyond himself not by thinking upon himself; silent his dreams and all imagined appearances, and every tongue, and every sign; and if all things that come to be through change should become wholly silent to him—for if any man can hear, then all these things say to him, *We did not make ourselves, but he who endures forever made us* (Ps 79, 3.5)—if when they have said these words, they then become silent, for they have raised up his ear to him who made them, then God alone would speak ... so that we hear his Word. ... If this could be prolonged, and other visions of a far inferior kind could be withdrawn! Then this one alone would ravish, and absorb, and hide away its be-

> holder within its deepest joys. ... Is not this: *Enter into the joy of your Lord* (Mt 25:21).[29]

Here we have Augustine's incorporation of *Ennead* 5, 1, 2, 14ff. into this most Christian moment in which he and his mother share a foretaste of the joys of eternal life. But although the *eros* theme of ascending love is certainly in play, there is no indication that this ascent is due to mere human effort and not to the fact that God has first loved us.

THE AMBIGUITY OF LOVE IN AUGUSTINE'S INVERSION OF JOHN

In the First Letter of John, the apostle twice said, *God is love* (1 Jn 4:8 and 16)—a statement that is quite astounding in its own rite. But in his *In Joannis epistulam* and elsewhere, Augustine was so bold as to say, *Love is God*, not once, but several times.[30] It is interesting to note that only one of the three English translations of Augustine's work follow his inversion, and in the NPNF translation the editors note that Augustine simply made a mistake, unaware that the Greek does not permit such a inversion.[31] Hence, they corrected him.

On the other hand, Augustine clearly knew what he was doing in saying, *Love is God*, and there is no reason for translating, "*Dilectio Deus est*," as if he had written, "*Deus dilectio est*." That Augustine knew what he was saying is clear from his early work, *De fide et symbolo*, a sermon in which Augustine, while still a priest, addressed the bishops of Africa in 393. Using 1 Jn 4:16 to argue for the divinity of the Holy Spirit, Augustine said that John "does not say, 'Love is God,' but, *God is love* so that the deity itself is understood as love."[32] But by the time of *In Joannis epistulam*, written in 407, he clearly inverts the word order and even attributes the inverted order to John:

> How did he previously say, *Love is from God*, and now say, *Love is God*? For God is the Father and the Son and the Holy Spirit. The Son is God from God; the Holy Spirit is God from God; and these three are one God, not three gods. If the Son is God and the Holy Spirit is God, and it is he in whom the Holy Spirit dwells who loves; therefore, love is God, but love is God be-

> cause it is from God. You have both in the Letter: both, *Love is from God*, and, *Love is God*.[33]

What on earth can that mean? Van Bavel says that the love of which Augustine is speaking here is "authentic human love."[34] It is "unselfish love (*benevolentia*). God is that benevolence, and thus He becomes the ideal model of all human love."[35] But even if God is the ideal model of human love, that hardly means that such ideal human love is God.

Later in the same homily Augustine uttered a similarly puzzling directive, "Love, and do what you will."[36] The immediate context of this directive, which follows only two paragraphs after the one in which he said that love is God, shows that he is speaking of the intention and will with which a human being acts and not of the action that a human being does. He points out that the Father handed over his only Son for all of us, that Christ handed himself over for us, and that Judas handed over Christ to the Jews, where the same Latin verb (*tradidit*) describes the action of handing over in each case.[37]

> But what is it that distinguishes the Father's handing over the Son, the Son's handing over himself, and Judas the disciple's handing over his master? The Father and the Son did this in charity, but Judas did this in betrayal. You see that one should consider not what a man does, but with what mind and will he does it. We find God the Father in the same action in which we find Judas; we bless the Father; we detest Judas. Why do we bless the Father and detest Judas? We bless love; we detest iniquity.[38]

The thoughts and the intentions of God and of Judas were different. "God thought of our salvation by which we were redeemed; Judas thought of the price for which he sold the Lord. ... A different intention made the actions different."[39] It is in this context then that Augustine said, "And so, once and for all, you are given a short commandment: Love, and do what you will. ... The root of love is within; only good can come from this root."[40]

Clearly it is the human act motivated by love that Augustine tells us comes from God and is God. In order to see why he calls such love God, we need to examine other passages in which he makes his daring inversion of the Johannine statement.

In *Sermo* 156, 5, Augustine tells his congregation that "faith can work in a good way only through love." Following James 2:19, he distinguishes the faith of believers from the faith of demons. The faith of believers

> is, therefore, praiseworthy faith; it is the true *faith* of grace *that works through love* (Gal 5:6). But we cannot, can we, give it to ourselves that we have love and can work in a good way because of it? For it is written, *The love of God has been poured out in our hearts through the Holy Spirit who has been given to us* (Rom 5:5). Love is the gift of God to the point that it is called God, for John the apostle says, *God is love, and he who remains in love remains in God, and God in him* (1 Jn 4:16).[41]

Here the Latin version has "*caritas*" instead of "*dilectio*," and Augustine seems to use the two nouns without any difference in meaning, although, to the best of my knowledge, he never does use "*amor*" in this context.

In another text from *In Joannis epistulam* 9, 2, Augustine also uses "*caritas*" in the inversion, although without explicit reference to the wording of the Letter of John. There he argues that, "if love is God, and God neither increases nor decreases, love is said so to increase in you because you yourself increase in it."[42] Because the love that is God is identical with God, it can neither increase nor decrease, but we can increase and decrease in it. Here it would seem that a metaphysics of participation lies behind Augustine's argument. In good Plotinian fashion a Platonic form is integrally present wherever it is present, and yet things participate in the form in different degrees.

In his *In Psalmum 98 enarratio*, possibly preached at Carthage in 411, Augustine again identifies "*caritas*" with God. Augustine is commenting on verse 4 of the psalm: "The Lord is great in Sion and on high over all peoples." He explains:

> It is, nonetheless, evident that Sion is the city of God. And what is the city of God but the holy Church? For human beings loving one another and loving their God, who dwells in them, make up a city for God. But a city is held together by a law, and their law is love, and love itself is God.[43] For it is clearly written, *God is love* (1 Jn 4:8). A person, therefore, who is full of love is full of God, and many persons full of love make up a city for God. This city is Sion; therefore, the Church is Sion.

> God is great in it; be in it, and God will not be apart from you.[44]

Here the expression "love itself: *ipsa caritas*" connotes, I suspect, subsistent love, the love by participation in which we love God and one another.

Before turning to any further attempt to determine of what Augustine means by the identification of love with God, let us look at still another text in which the daring inversion is found. In *In Psalmum 99 enarratio*, Augustine is speaking about verse 2: "Shout with joy, all the earth: *jubilate omnis terra*." He is explaining to the congregation how one can praise in jubilation what one cannot express in words. Stressing God's integral omnipresence, he says:

> And so God is present everywhere, whole everywhere. His wisdom *stretches from end to end with might, and arranges all things with gentleness* (Wis 8:1). But what God the Father is, that his Word and wisdom is, light from light, God from God. What then do you want to see? What you want to see is not far from you. The apostle of course says that he is not far from each of us, *for in him we live and move and have our being* (Acts 17:28). What a great misery it is to be far from him who is everywhere![45]

We are, of course, as sinners, far from him not in distance, but in unlikeness. In *De trinitate* 7, 6, 12, Augustine explains, "For it is not by intervals of place, but by likeness that one draws near to God, and one withdraws from him by unlikeness."[46] Twice in the *Confessions* Augustine borrows Plotinus' imagery and language from *Ennead* 1, 6, 8, 16–27 to speak about our distance from God, who is whole everywhere:

> I was far from your face in a darksome love. For it is not by feet or by distance of place that one departs from you or returns to you. But that younger son of yours did not look for chariots or ships, nor did he fly off on a visible wing or journey on foot in order to live prodigally and dissipate in a distant land what you had given him as he departed.[47]

Similarly, in the famous garden scene of his conversion, Augustine again borrows the same imagery from Plotinus to speak of his inability to return to God, to enter into covenant with God: "And one did not go there by ships or chariots or on feet, not even so far as I had gone to this place where we were sitting. For not only to go, but also to arrive there was nothing other than to will to go, but to will strongly and wholeheartedly."[48] So too, in book seven, where Augustine recounts the effect of his reading the books of the Platonists, he speaks of his distance from God in language that is both Christian and Plotinian:

> And when I first knew you, you took me up so that I saw that what I saw existed and that I who saw it did not yet exist. And you beat back the weakness of my gaze, sending your strong rays upon me, and I trembled with love and horror, and I found that I was far from you in a region of unlikeness.[49]

The phrase "in a region of unlikeness" comes from *Ennead* 1, 8, 13, 16–17: "ἐν τῷ τῆς ἀνομοιότητος τόπῳ." And the region of unlikeness also recalls the Prodigal's departing *in regionem longinquam* (Lk 15:13).[50] In *De civitate Dei* 9, 17, Augustine chides certain learned men who still speak of bodily contact when discussing the happy life. He quotes from Plotinus, when he asks:

> What has happened to that saying of Plotinus where he says: "We must therefore flee to the fatherland, and there the father is, and there is everything. What," he asks, "will be our ship or what our flight? Becoming like God." If then one becomes nearer to God the more one is like God, there is no other distance from him than unlikeness to him.[51]

Thus, in order to overcome the misery of their spiritual separation from God, Augustine teaches his congregation:

> Be therefore like him in piety and loving in thought, because his *invisible reality is seen, having been understood through the things that have been created* (Rom 1:20). Gaze upon the things that have been created. Wonder at them; seek their author. If you are unlike him, you will be rebuffed; if you are like him, you will exult. And when, like him, you begin to draw near and to be deeply aware of God, as that love grows in you—for love is also God—you will certainly become aware of what you said, but did not say. For before you were aware, you thought you spoke of God. You begin to be aware, and you are aware that what you are aware of cannot be said.[52]

Thus, unable to speak of the ineffable God, we shout in jubilation, by which Augustine means: in non-verbal sounds of joy. "What is jubilation? To be unable to express joy in words and yet to bear witness vocally to that which is grasped within and cannot be explained in words—that is jubilation."[53]

Van Bavel says that the inversion occurs at least ten times in the works of Augustine.[54] It is interesting that the inversion and its ascription to scripture is also found in Ambrose's *Expositio in Psalmum 118*, 20 and 39 and in his *Commentarius in Cantica Conticorum* 2, 28.[55] It is also found in Ambrosiaster, *In epistolam beati Paul ad Corinthios primam* 13, vv. 4–8.[56] and in the *Hypomnesticon* 5, 3, 5.[57] Hence, it is certainly not simply a mistake on the part of Augustine. It is also found three times in Caesarius of Arles, once in Leo the Great, and occasionally in various later writers.[58]

But what can Augustine have meant by his daring inversion of the text of John? Van Bavel says that at first glance "it is tempting to think that" Augustine said that love is God "under the influence of Neoplatonism," because "according to Neoplatonism the eternal ideas like truth, goodness, and so on, are substances."[59] He finds the difference between Neoplatonism and Saint John to lie in the fact that "in John, love is not conceived as an abstract substance as in Neoplatonism, but as the personal God."[60] On the other hand, Augustine's use of "*ipsa caritas*: love itself," does sound as though he is speaking of a subsisting love. Furthermore, Augustine was insistent that divine simplicity meant that "God is what he has"—except, of course, for the relations between the persons, for the Father has a Son, but is not the Son.[61] That is, when we say that God is good, or wise, or just, we are not predicating qualities that are added to his substance; rather, we have to understand that God is goodness, wisdom, and justice so that the propositions are convertible. Goodness itself, wisdom itself, justice itself—and love itself—are God.

Such a move, however, holds only if we are speaking of the absolute divine attributes, that is, of what is said of God nonrelatively, not of what the three persons are said to be in relation to one another nor of what God is said to be in relation to creatures.[62] Augustine, however, seems clearly to say that our love, the love of human beings for one another and for their God, is God. Such love is, of course, not merely ours since it is a gift of God, just as Augustine insists over and over again during the controversy with the Pelagians that we are righteous, not with a righteousness of our own, but with the righteousness of God.[63] So too, the love of God poured out in our hearts is a gift of God, but it "is a gift," as Augustine says, "to the point that it is called God" (*Charitas usque adeo est donum Dei, ut Deus vocetur*).[64]

There are two more texts from books eight and fifteen book of *On the Trinity* (*De trinitate*) in which Augustine says that love—indeed brotherly love—is God and which throw further light on the question. In book eight Augustine is arguing for the inseparability of the commandments to love God and one's neighbor and again clearly claims that brotherly love is God.

> Let us note how much John the apostle commends brotherly love. He says: *One who loves his brother remains in the light, and there is no scandal in him* (1 Jn 2:10). It is clear that he puts the perfection of righteousness in love of one's brother. For one in whom there is no scandal is surely perfect. And yet he seems to have been silent about the love of God, something he would never do save because he wanted God to be understood in brotherly love. For in the same letter he says quite openly a little later: *Beloved, let us love one another because love is from God, and everyone who loves is born of God and knows God. One who does not love has not known God because God is love* (1 Jn 4:7). This context shows quite clearly how this same brotherly love—for it is brotherly love by which we love one another—is proclaimed with such great authority not only to be from God, but to be God. When, therefore, we love our brother out of love, we love him out of God, and it is impossible that we do not especially love the love by which we love our brother. Hence, we infer that those two commandments cannot exist apart from each other.[65]

Augustine returns to the identification of love with God in the final book of *On the Trinity* where he argues that the Holy Spirit is properly referred to as love. He argues that, although the Father and the Son are said to be love, the Holy Spirit is to be properly named by the term "love." He says:

> if we carefully examine the words of John the apostle, we find where the Holy Spirit is said to be love. When he said, *Beloved, let us love one another, because love is from God,* he went on to say, *And everyone who loves is born of God; one who does not love, has not known God, because God is love.*

> Here he showed that he called that love God, which he said was from God. Love, therefore, is God from God. But because the Son too is from God the Father, and the Holy Spirit proceeds from God the Father, it is rightly asked of which of them we ought here to understand that it was said that love is God.[66]

In the following Augustine says,

> when [John] mentioned the love of God, not by which we love him, but by which he loved us and sent his Son as propitiation for our sins, he exhorted us by this that we might also love one another and that God might remain in us, for he had certainly said that love is God. Immediately wanting to say something clearer on this matter, he said: *In this we know that we remain in him and he in us, because he has given to us of his Spirit* (1 Jn 4:13). The Holy Spirit, therefore, of which he has given us, makes us remain in God and him in us. But this is what love does. He, therefore, is God Love.[67]

The final short sentence has presented a challenge to translators. The BA version says, "C'est donc le Saint-Esprit qui est le Dieu amour." The NBA version has, "dunque lo Spirito Santo il Dio amore." The WSA version says, "He then who is the gift of God is love," while the older McKenna translation says, "He, therefore, is the God who is love (*Deus dilectio*)."

Although, as we have seen, Augustine clearly has said at least ten times that love, that is, the love by which we love God and by which we love one another, is God, he was also absolutely clear that we are not God, as our mutability clearly proves. What then can he have meant by his daring inversion of Saint John?

SOME CONCLUDING REFLECTIONS

I have already suggested that a metaphysics of participation may well lie behind the inversion. For Augustine learned from Plotinus's twin treatises on omnipresence, *Ennead* VI, 4–5 to think of God as integrally present wherever he is, and he is of course present everywhere, but dwells only in the faithful.[68] Hence, if our love is a participation in the love that is God, we do not have a part of God, since he has no parts. Rather, if *the love of God is poured out in our hearts by the Holy Spirit*, as Saint Paul teaches in

Rom 5:5, that love is going be God. It is often said that the theme of our divinization plays a relatively minor role in Augustine's thought compared to the Fathers of the Eastern Church, and yet in his early correspondence with Nebridius Augustine could speak of his and his friend's desire to become divine or god-like in leisure, where the verb *"deificari"* may have a stronger sense than one initially suspects.[69] And in his *In Joannis epistulam* Augustine also spoke of our becoming gods. He urges his hearers to "hold onto the love of God in order that, as God is eternal, so you may remain eternally." And then he adds a general principle that one becomes what one loves:

> For each person is such as his love is. Do you love the earth? You will be earth. Do you love God? What shall I say: that you will be God? I do not dare to say so of myself. Let us listen to the scriptures: "I said: *You are all gods and children of the most high*" (Ps 81:6).[70]

If one loves God, one becomes God, not an alien god, and not a part of God, but God.

However, such love by which we love God is not simply something of our doing for it is a gift of God poured out in our hearts by the Holy Spirit and is the result of God's dwelling in us. If such love is God as Augustine has said at least ten times, it certainly shatters Nygren's dichotomy between *eros* and *agape*, between an ascending and a descending love, for it is the gift of God, the love poured out in our hearts by the Holy Spirit through the redeeming work of Christ, by which we rise up to the God, whose vision we desire as our abode.

Notes

[1] For a solid critique of many of Nygren's points, see John Burnaby, *Amor Dei: A Study of the Religion of St. Augustine*. The Hulsean Lectures for 1938 (London: Hodder and Stoughton, 1938, especially the introductory chapter. For a more contemporary assessment, see R. Canning, *The Unity of Love for God and Neighbor in St. Augustine*. (Heverlee-Leuven: Augustinian Historical Institute, 1993).

[2] On this point see John Mourrant, *Augustine on Immortality*. The Saint Augustine Lecture 1968 (Villanova: Villanova University Press, 1969).

[3] On this point see my "Love of Neighbor in St. Augustine," *Studia Ephemeridis "Augustinianum"* 26. Congresso Internazionale su S. Agostino nel XVI Centenario della Conversione. Roma, 15-20 settembre 1986. Atti III, pp. 81-102

[4] *Agape and Eros*, pp. 32–34.

[5] Nygren, p. 176.

[6] Nygen, p. 76.

[7] See Nygren, pp. 76–80.

[8] Nygren, p. 91. The sentence is italicized in Nygren's text.

[9] Nygren, p. 451.

[10] Nygren, pp. 471–472.

[11] See *De beata vita* 2, 10, PL 32: 964; *Confessiones* 10, 20, PL 32: 792; and *De trinitate* 13, 4, 7, PL 42: 1019.

[12] Cuthburt Butler, *Western Mysticism: The Teaching of Augustine, Gregory, and Bernard on Contemplation and the Contemplative Life*, 2nd. ed, with Afterthoughts (New York: Harper and Row, 1966), p. 48.

[13] *De quantitate animae* 33, 73, PL 32: 1075.

[14] Ibid. 33, 74, PL 32: 1076: "*In hoc gradu omnifariam concipit quanta sit: quod cum conceperit, tunc vero ingenti quadam et incredibili fiducia pergit in Deum, id est, in ipsam contemplationem veritatis, et illud, propter quod tantum laboratum est, altissimum et secretissimum praemium*".

[15] Ibid.: "*appetitio intelligendi ea quae vere summeque sunt. ...*"

[16] See *Soliloquia* 1, 6, 12, PL 32: 875: "*Non enim hoc est habere oculos quod aspicere; aut item hoc est aspicere quod videre. Ergo animae tribus quibusdam rebus opus est ut oculos habeat quibus jam bene uti possit, ut aspiciat, ut videat.*"

[17] See my "The Aim of Augustine's Proof that God Truly Is," *International Philosophical Quarterly* 26 (1986), 253-268.

[18] *De quantitate animae* 33, 75; PL 32: 1076: "*aliud est enim mundari oculum ipsum animae, ne frustra et temere aspiciat, et prave videat; aliud ipsam custodire atque firmare sanitatem; aliud jam serenum atque rectum aspectum in id quod videndum est, dirigere.*"

[19] Ibid, 33, 76, PL 32:1076: "*in ipsa visione atque contemplatione veritatis, qui septimus atque ultimus animae gradus est; neque jam gradus, sed quaedam mansio, quo illis gradibus pervenitur. ...*"

[20] Ibid.: "*quae sint gaudia, quae perfructio summi et veri boni, cujus serenitatis atque aeternitatis afflatus, quid ego dicam?*"

[21] Ibid.: "*Dixerunt haec quantum dicenda esse judicaverunt, magnae quaedam et incomparabiles animae, quas etiam vidisse ac videre ista credimus.*"

[22] *De Genesi ad litteram* 12, 27, 55–28, 56, CSEL 28: 420–423, where Augustine is writing about 2 Cor 12:2–5. Also see my "St. Augustine and the Vision of God," in *Augustine: Mystic and Mystagogue*, ed. F. Van Fleteren, J. Schnaubelt, and J. Reino (New York: Peter Lang, 1994), pp. 287–308.

[23] In his *Vita Plotini* 23, Porphyry "attests that [Plotinus] enjoyed mystical contemplation in the highest degree, and ... himself gives indications of ecstacy (*Enn.* 1. 6. 7; 6. 7. 34" (Joseph Colleran, *St. Augustine: The Greatness of the Soul* and *The*

Teacher. Ancient Christian Writers 9 [Westminster, MD: The Newman Press, 1964], p. 214, note 101).

24 See *De beata vita* 1.5 and my *"Función de la segunda mitad de Confesiones 10," Augustinus* (Madrid) 49 (2004): 377–388, in which I argued that the role of the second half of book ten of the *Confessions* was a retraction of Augustine's earlier excessive optimism about the possibility of souls attaining a perfect happiness in this life by the power of their own will.

25 *Confessiones* 7, 10, 16, PL 32: 742 *"Et inde admonitus redire ad memetipsum, intravi in intima mea, duce te; et potui, quoniam factus es adjutor meus. Intravi, et vidi qualicumque oculo animae meae, supra eumdem oculum animae meae, supra mentem meam, lucem incommutabilem; non hanc vulgarem et conspicuam omni carni: nec quasi ex eodem genere grandior erat, tanquam si ista multo multoque clarius claresceret, totuque occuparet magnitudine. Non hoc illa erat; sed aliud, aliud valde ab istis omnibus. Nec ita erat supra mentem meam sicut oleum super aquam, nec sicut coelum super terram; sed superior, quia ipsa fecit me, et ego inferior, quia factus sum ab ea. Qui novit veritatem, novit eam; et qui novit eam, novit aeternitatem. Charitas novit eam. O aeterna veritas, et vera charitas, et chara aeternitas! tu es Deus meus; tibi suspiro die ac nocte."*

26 *Confessiones* 7, 8, 12, PL 32: 740: *"et stimulis internis agitabas me, ut impatiens essem, donec mihi per interiorem aspectum certus esses. Et residebat tumor meus ex occulta manu medicinae tuae, aciesque conturbata et contenebrata mentis meae, acri collyrio salubrium dolorum de die in diem sanabatur."*

27 Ibid. 7, 9, 13, PL 32: 740: *"quosdam Platonicorum libros ex graeca lingua in latinam versos. ..."*

28 *Confessiones* 9, 10, 23, PL 32: 774: "colloquebamur ergo soli valde dulciter; et praeterita obliviscentes, in ea quae ante sunt extenti (Phil 3:13), quaerebamus inter nos apud praesentem Veritatem, quod tu es, qualis futura esset vita aeterna sanctorum, quam nec oculus vidit, nec auris audivit, nec in cor hominis ascendit (1 Cor 2:9). Sed inhiabamus ore cordis in superna fluenta fontis tui, fontis vitae qui est apud te (Ps 35:10), ut inde pro captu nostro aspersi, quoque modo rem tantam cogitaremus."

29 *Confessiones* 9, 10, 26, PL 32: 774–775 "Si cui sileat tumultus carnis, sileant phantasiae terrae et aquarum et aeris, sileant et poli, et ipsa sibi anima sileat, et transeat se non se cogitando, sileant somnia et imaginariae revelationes, omnis lingua et omne signum, et quidquid transeundo fit, si cui sileat omnino; quoniam si quis audiat, dicunt haec omnia, Non ipsa nos fecimus, sed fecit nos qui manet in aeternum (Ps 49:3.5): his dictis si jam taceant quoniam erexerunt aurem in eum qui fecit ea, et loquatur ipse solus ... ut audiamus verbum ejus. .... si continuetur hoc, et subtrahantur aliae visiones longe imparis generis, et haec una rapiat et absorbeat et recondat in interiora gaudia spectatorem suum ... nonne hoc est, Intra in gaudium Domini tui? (Mt 25:21)

30 I have borrowed the phrase "daring inversion" from Johannes van Bavel, O.S.A., "The Double Face of Love," *Louvain Studies* 12 (1987): 116–130. Although the Vulgate has *"caritas,"* Augustine's version at times uses *"dilectio."*

[31] "If now and then he seems to mistake in interpretation (as in Homily VII.), not considering that in the Greek such propositions as 'God is love,' are not convertible, the subject ὁ θεός being marked by the article, and the predicate indicated by not having the article, let it be remembered that some exegetical canons of the kind were unknown in his time" (NPNF 7, tr. by H. Browne with additional notes by J. H. Myers, p. 594). See also "Ten Homilies on the First Epistle of St. John," *Augustine: Later Works*, ed. John Burnaby (Philadelphia: Westminster Press, 1995). *Tractates on the First Epistle of John*, tr. John W. Rettig. Fathers of the Church 92 (Washington, DC: The Catholic University of America Press, 1995), follows the inversion as does the Italian translation by G. Madurini in *Nuova biblioteca agostiniana* Pt. 3, vol. 24 (Rome: Citt⊛ nuova, 1968), which correctly translates the inversion: "L'Epistola ha le due espressioni: L'amore proviene da Dio e l'amore ⊛ Dio."

[32] *De fide et symbolo* 9, 19, PL 40:194 "Etiam hic enim non ait, Dilectio Deus est; sed, Deus dilectio est; ut ipsa deitas dilectio intelligatur."

[33] *In Joannis epistulam* 7, 6, PL 35: 2031–2032: "Quomodo ergo jamdudum, Dilectio ex Deo est; et modo, Dilectio Deus est? Est enim Deus Pater et Filius et Spiritus sanctus: Filius, Deus ex Deo; Spiritus sanctus, Deus ex Deo; et hi tres unus Deus, non tres dii. Si Filius Deus, et Spiritus sanctus Deus, et ille diligit in quo habitat Spiritus sanctus: ergo dilectio Deus est; sed Deus quia ex Deo. Utrumque enim habes in Epistola; et, Dilectio ex Deo est, et, Dilectio Deus est."

[34] Van Bavel, "The Two Faces of Love," p. 120.

[35] Ibid., p. 124.

[36] *In Joannis epistulam* 7, 8, PL 35: 2033: "Dilige, et quod vis fac."

[37] Ibid. 7, 7, PL 35: 2032, where he cites Rom 8:32 and Gal 2:20. See also Mt 26:25 for Judas.

[38] Ibid., PL 35: 2032–2033: " sed quae res discernit Patrem tradentem Filium, seipsum Filium tradentem, et Judam discipulum tradentem magistrum suum? Quia hoc fecit Pater et Filius in charitate; fecit autem hoc Judas in proditione. Videtis quia non quid faciat homo, considerandum est; sed quo animo et voluntate faciat. In eodem facto invenimus Deum Patrem, in quo invenimus Judam; Patrem benedicimus, Judam detestamur. Quare Patrem benedicimus, Judam detestamur? Benedicimus charitatem, detestamur iniquitatem."

[39] Ibid., PL 35: 2033: "Deus cogitavit salutem nostram qua redempti sumus; Judas cogitavit pretium quo vendidit Dominum. ... Diversa ergo intentio diversa facta fecit."

[40] Ibid. 7, 8, PL 35: 2033: "Semel ergo breve praeceptum tibi praecipitur, Dilige, et quod vis fac. ... radix sit intus dilectionis, non potest de ista radice nisi bonum existere."

[41] *Sermo* 156, 5, 5, PL 38:852–853: "Quia fides bene operari non potest, nisi per dilectionem. Ipsa est enim fidelium fides. ... Illa est ergo laudabilis fides, ipsa est vera gratiae fides, quae per dilectionem operatur (Gal 5:6). Ut autem habeamus dilectionem, et ex ea possimus habere bonam operationem, numquid eam nobis dare non possumus, cum scriptum sit, Charitas Dei diffusa est in cordibus nostris

per Spiritum sanctum qui datus est nobis (Rom 5:5). Charitas usque adeo est donum Dei, ut Deus vocetur, apostolo Joanne dicente, Deus charitas est, et qui
manet in charitate, in Deo manet, et Deus in eo (1 Jn 4:16)."
42 *In Joannis epistulam* 9, 2, PL 35, 2045: "Nam si charitas Deus est, nec proficit nec
deficit Deus: sic dicitur proficere in te charitas, quia tu in ea proficis."
43 In WSA 2/18, Sr. Maria Boulding translates *"lex ipsa eorum, charitas est; et ipsa
charitas, Deus est"* as "And the law of this city is charity. But God himself is charity." That misses Augustine's daring inversion and undermines the conclusion
that one who is full of love is full of God.
44 *In Psalmum 98 enarratio* 4, PL 37: 1261: "Quia tamen manifestum est Sion civitatem Dei esse; quae est civitas Dei, nisi sancta Ecclesia? Homines enim amantes
se invicem, et amantes Deum suum qui in illis habitat, faciunt civitatem Deo.
Quia lege quadam civitas continetur; lex ipsa eorum, charitas est; et ipsa charitas,
Deus est: aperte enim scriptum est, Deus charitas est (1 Jn 4:8). Qui ergo plenus
est charitate, plenus est Deo; et multi pleni charitate, civitatem faciunt Deo. Ista
civitas Dei vocatur Sion: ergo Ecclesia est Sion. In illa est magnus Deus. In illa
esto, et non erit praeter te Deus."
45 *In Psalmum 99 enarratio*, 5, PL 37: 1274: "Sic et Deus ubique praesens est, ubique
totus. Sapientia ejus attingit a fine usque ad finem fortiter et disponit omnia
suaviter (Wis 8:1). Quod autem Deus Pater, hoc Verbum ejus et Sapientia ejus,
lux de luce, Deus de Deo. Quid ergo optas videre? Non est a te longe quod vis
videre. Apostolus dicit equidem non longe positum ab unoquoque nostrum: in
ipso enim vivimus et movemur et sumus (Acts 17:28). Quanta ergo miseria est;
longe esse ab eo qui ubique est?"
46 *De trinitate* 7, 6, 12, PL 42: 946: "Non enim locorum intervallis, sed similitudine
acceditur ad Deum, et dissimilitudine receditur ab eo."
47 *Confessiones* 1, 18, 28, PL 32: 674: "Nam longe a vultu tuo, in affectu tenebroso.
Non enim pedibus aut spatiis locorum itur abs te, aut reditur ad te. Aut vero filius ille tuus minor equos, aut currus, vel naves quaesivit, aut avolavit penna
visibili, aut moto poplite iter egit, ut in longinqua regione vivens prodige dissi-
paret quod dederas proficiscenti."
48 Ibid. 8, 8, 19, PL 32: 758: "et non illuc ibatur navibus aut quadrigis, aut pedibus,
quantum saltem de domo in eum locum ieram, ubi sedebamus. Nam non solum
ire, verum etiam pervenire illuc, nihil erat aliud quam velle ire, sed velle fortiter
et integre. ...."
49 Ibid. 7, 10, 16, PL 32: 742: "Et cum te primum cognovi, tu assumpsisti me, ut
viderem esse quod viderem, et nondum me esse qui viderem. Et reverberasti in-
firmitatem aspectus mei, radians in me vehementer, et contremui amore et hor-
rore; et inveni longe me esse a te in regione dissimilitudinis. ...."
50 See James J. O'Donnell, *Augustine's Confessions*. 3 vols. (Oxford: Clarendon
Press, 1992, here vol. 3, pp. 443–444.
51 *De civitate Dei* 9, 17, PL 41: 271: "Ubi est illud Plotini, ubi ait, 'Fugiendum est
igitur ad charissimam patriam, et ibi pater, et ibi omnia? Quae igitur, inquit, clas-

sis aut fuga? Similem deo fieri.' Si ergo deo quanto similior, tanto fit quisque propinquior; nulla est ab illo alia longinquitas quam ejus dissimilitudo."

[52] *In Psalmum 99 enarratio*, 6, PL 37: 1275: "Esto ergo similis pietate, et diligens cogitatione: quoniam invisibilia ejus per ea quae facta sunt intellecta conspiciuntur (Rom 1:20); ea quae facta sunt intuere, mirare, quaere auctorem. Si dissimilis sis, repelleris; si similis, exsultabis. Et cum accedere coeperis similis, et persentiscere Deum, quantum in te charitas crescit, quia et charitas Deus est, senties quiddam quod dicebas, et non dicebas. Ante enim quam sentires, dicere te putabas Deum: incipis sentire, et ibi sentis dici non posse quod sentis."

[53] *In Psalmum 94 enarratio 94*, 3, PL 37: 1218: "*Quid est jubilare? Gaudium verbis non posse explicare, et tamen voce testari quod intus conceptum est et verbis explicari non potest: hoc est jubilare.*"

[54] I find the reading "*dilectio deus est*" five times in *In Joannis epistulam 7*—only four times in the version in PL, but five times in the version that the late William Mountain was preparing for CCL and that is found on CETEDOC. I discount the reading in *De fide et symbolo*. I find the reading "*caritas deus est*" once in *In Joannis epistulam* and twice in the *Enarrationes in Psalmos*. With the passage in *Sermo 156*, 5, 5 that makes nine occurrences of the inversion. There are two passages in *De trinitate* 8 and 15 where love is said to be God. The inversion also occurs in two sermons that PL and other sources list as being of an uncertain author or inauthentic, namely, *Sermones* 133 and 269.

[55] See Ambrose, *Expositio in Psalmum 118*, 20, CSEL 62: 92: "*caritas deus est, ut legimus*," and 29, CSEL 62:351: "*caritas deus est, caritas dei verbum est*," and *Commentarius in Cantica Conticorum* 2, 28; PL 15:1878,

[56] See Amrosiaster, *In epistolam beati Paul ad Corinthios primam* 13, 4–8, PL 17: 252.

[57] Uncertain author, *Hypomnesticon* 5, 3, 5, PL 45: 1651.

[58] Caesarius Arelatensis, *Sermo* 23, 4: CCL 103: 106–107, *Regula ad monachos* 1, 13: PL 67: 1100, and *Exhortatio ad tenendam vel custodiendam charitatem* PL 67: 1154. See Leo the Great, *Tractatus septem et nonaginta*, tr. 38, 4, CCL 138: 208 and *Sermones* 98, 3, PL 53: 299 and 38, 4, PL 54: 262. Whether some of these references in PL are authentic or not is unimportant for my point here, namely, that the inversion is not found only in Augustine, although he may have been the source of some of them.

[59] Van Bavel, "The Double Face of Love," p. 124.

[60] Ibid., p. 125.

[61] *De civitate Dei* 11, 10, 1, PL 41: 325: "sed ideo simplex dicitur, quoniam quod habet, hoc est, excepto quod relative quaeque persona ad alteram dicitur. Nam utique Pater habet Filium, nec tamen ipse est Filius; et Filius habet Patrem, nec tamen ipse est Pater. In quo ergo ad se ipsum dicitur, non ad alterum, hoc est quod habet: sicut ad se ipsum dicitur vivens, habendo utique vitam, et eadem vita ipse est."

[62] See Augustine, *De trinitate* 5, 16, 17, PL 42: 924. See my "Properties of God and the Predicaments in *De Trinitate* V," *The Modern Schoolman* LIX (1981), 1–19.

[63] See, for example, *De gratia novi testamenti* 30, 73, PL 33: 570: "Ut nos simus justitia Dei in ipso (2 Cor. 5:20.21): id est, in ejus corpore quod est Ecclesia, cui caput est, nos simus justitia Dei; quam ignorantes illi, et suam volentes constituere, id est tanquam de suis operibus gloriantes, justitiae Dei non sunt subjecti."

[64] *Sermo* 156, 5, 5, quoted above in note 51.

[65] *De trinitate* 8, 8, 12, PL 42: 958: "Dilectionem autem fraternam quantum commendet Joannes apostolus, attendamus: Qui diligit, inquit, fratrem suum, in lumine manet, et scandalum in eo non est (1 Jn 2:10). Manifestum est quod justitiae perfectionem in fratris dilectione posuerit: nam in quo scandalum non est, utique perfectus est. Et tamen videtur dilectionem Dei tacuisse: quod nunquam faceret, nisi quia in ipsa fraterna dilectione vult intelligi Deum. Apertissime enim in eadem Epistola paulo post ita dicit: Dilectissimi, diligamus invicem, quia dilectio ex Deo est; et omnis qui diligit, ex Deo natus est, et cognoscit Deum. Qui non diligit, non cognovit Deum; quia Deus dilectio est (1 Jn 4:7). Ista contextio satis aperteque declarat, eamdem ipsam fraternam dilectionem (nam fraterna dilectio est, qua diligimus invicem) non solum ex Deo, sed etiam Deum esse tanta auctoritate praedicari. Cum ergo de dilectione diligimus fratrem, de Deo diligimus fratrem: nec fieri potest ut eamdem dilectionem non praecipue diligamus, qua fratrem diligimus. Unde colligitur, duo illa praecepta non posse esse sine invicem."

[66] *De trinitate* 15, 17, 31, PL 42: 1082: "Spiritus autem sanctus ubi sit dictus charitas invenimus, si diligenter Joannis apostoli scrutemur eloquium; qui cum dixisset, Dilectissimi, diligamus invicem, quia dilectio ex Deo est; secutus adjunxit, Et omnis qui diligit, ex Deo natus est: qui non diligit, non cognovit Deum, quia Deus dilectio est. Hic manifestavit eam se dixisse dilectionem Deum, quam dixit ex Deo. Deus ergo ex Deo est dilectio. Sed quia et Filius ex Deo Patre natus est, et Spiritus sanctus ex Deo Patre procedit, quem potius eorum hic debeamus accipere dictum esse dilectionem Deum, merito quaeritur."

[67] Ibid.: "cum Dei dilectionem commemorasset, non qua nos eum, sed qua Ipse dilexit nos, et misit Filium suum litatorem pro peccatis nostris; et hinc exhortatus esset ut et nos invicem diligamus, atque ita Deus in nobis maneat, quia utique dilectionem Deum dixerat, statim volens de hac re apertius aliquid eloqui, In hoc, inquit, cognoscimus quia in ipso manemus, et ipse in nobis, quia de Spiritu suo dedit nobis. Spiritus itaque sanctus de quo dedit nobis, facit nos in Deo manere, et ipsum in nobis: hoc autem facit dilectio. Ipse est igitur Deus dilectio."

[68] On the doctrine of integral omnipresence in Augustine and Plotinus, see Robert J. O'Connell, *St. Augustine's Early Theory of Man, A.D. 386–391* (Cambridge, MA: Belknap Press, 1968), pp. 33 and 39–40.

[69] See Augustine, *Epistula* 10, 2, PL 33: 74, where Augustine says to his friend, "*deificari enim utrisque in otio licebat.*" See my "St. Augustine's Epistula X: Another Look at 'Deificari in otio,'" *Augustinianum* 32 (1992), 289-299.

[70] Augustine, *In Joannis epistulam* 2, 14, PL 35: 1997: "Tenete potius dilectionem Dei, ut quomodo Deus est aeternus, sic et vos maneatis in aeternum: quia talis est quisque, qualis ejus dilectio est. Terram diligis? terra eris. Deum diligis? quid di-

cam? deus eris? Non audeo dicere ex me, Scripturas audiamus: Ego dixi, Dii estis, et filii Altissimi omnes (Ps 81:6)."

Love and Tears: Augustine's Project of Loving Without Losing

Phillip Cary
Eastern University

G RIEF AS MORAL IMPERFECTION

Why does Augustine not want to weep when his mother dies? The first thing he narrates after her death in the ninth book of the *Confessions* is how he closed her eyes and kept his own eyes dry despite his grief: "I pressed her eyes [shut]," he writes, "and a huge sorrow flowed together into my chest and flowed over into tears, and at the same time by a violent command of my mind my eyes sucked back their fountain even to the point of dryness."[1] In some ways it is the most shocking event in the *Confessions*. A modern audience can condone fornication and heresy, but suppressing his feelings—that's truly offensive! And more seriously, even for those of us who think there are such things as wicked feelings that need to be suppressed, this does not seem to be one of them. Do the lessons in holiness he has been learning over the course of the narrative really lead to this: that he has become such an enemy of human love that he is ashamed of grieving for his mother?

My answer to this question will be a qualified yes. Yes, the author of the *Confessions* really does think there was something morally wrong with his grief for his mother, but he's about to change his mind concerning the underlying ethics that leads to this conclusion.[2] For in later writings Augustine becomes an eloquent defender of the natural, human need of grief. "How could the death of someone whose life is sweet not be bitter to us?" he writes in the *City of God*. "Hence the mourning of a heart that is not inhuman is like a kind of wound or sore...."[3] In one sense of course we would prefer not to be wounded, but the cost of such invulnerability is inhumanity. As he puts it in one sermon, "It *is* possible for a human heart not to grieve when one who is most dear to it dies; but it is better for the human heart to be healed when it grieves, than to become inhuman by not grieving."[4] When Augustine talks like this, he speaks in terms we can readily understand. But in *Confessions* 9 he speaks in a way that is not so easy to understand--or accept. What is going on in this disturbing text? Why does he try not to weep?

Let me begin by saying a bit more about the narrative in *Confessions* 9. First of all, it is important to be clear that Augustine does not deny his grief, in the sense of denying he feels it. He knows all too well what he feels. But he does hide it from other people, and in particular he holds back his tears, which are the external expression of the grief in the heart. Partly he seems ashamed of behaving childishly like his own son Adeodatus, whose loud lamentations are forcibly silenced "by all of us," he says.[5] This external, social coercion is paralleled by Augustine's inward efforts to get control of his own grief. "And in Your ears," he writes to God, "where none of them heard, I scolded my feelings as softness and restrained the flood of sorrow."[6] But what is there to be ashamed of in this softness or weakness (*mollitiam*) of his feelings for his mother? At first glance this looks like some ancient Roman type of macho—and there does seem to be some of that in the air, but there is much more as well. Augustine is quite explicit about why he fights his grief: "It intensely displeased me that these human things had so much power over me [more literally, "could do so much in me"], which necessarily happen by due order and the lot of our condition."[7] The human condition is mortal and it belongs to our lot, in the due order of things, to die. That is what his feelings, in their weakness, cannot accept. It is the same underlying problem that produced the torture of grief back in book four, when his best friend dies: "He was dead, whom I had loved as if he would not die....I had poured my soul out on the sand, loving one who would die as if he would not die."[8] This is love out of touch with reality and disordered, Augustine thinks, and duly punished by the torment provided by mortality itself. That he has the same problem in book 9, after his conversion and baptism, exasperates him. It is as if to say: haven't I learned *anything* yet?

And it really is a matter of a long process of learning. As Augustine, the narrator comments, speaking again to God, "I believe You were reminding me, by a kind of object lesson, that the chain of every habit is against the mind, even a mind that no longer feeds on deceptive words."[9] The newly bereaved Augustine is torn, exasperated and ashamed because he knows better, yet he still cannot help himself. He knows that he has not really lost his mother, who is safe with God, yet he still misses her presence as if he were a motherless child. The force of carnal habit (*consuetudo*), the great enemy of the moral life from whose chains he was freed in book 8, is still not entirely vanquished. It seems what he needs to learn, according to the reflections of Augustine the narrator some ten years later, is not how to overcome all grief but how to live with his own moral imperfection. The day when no carnal habit causes us to be pained by the loss of temporal things is the day when our loves are no longer morally disordered, and that day does not come in this life. So Augustine the narrator puts the shame and exasperation of Augustine the character in proper perspective: yes, this paroxysm of grief may indeed be due to moral imperfection, to "carnal feelings" as he puts it,[10] but no, it is not an imperfection one can simply eliminate so long as one is still on the road of this mortal life—though all of us should be working to overcome it as we progress along the road which leads us to life eternal, where nothing is lost.

Hence Augustine the narrator defends the weakness of Augustine the character, who finally does let himself weep when he is all alone. The narrator rebukes any reader who would "proudly interpret my crying"[11] as something to deride. But this same narrator, we should notice, never expresses grief of his own when describing the death of loved ones. The grief portrayed in the *Confessions* is always the character's, not the narrator's. For while the main character of the *Confessions* has a lot to learn and is often presented as an example of how not to do things, the narrator of the *Confessions*, at least up through book 9, is presented implicitly as a spiritual model for us to follow. By "narrator" I do not mean the historical Augustine, the author of the *Confessions*, whose thoughts and feelings we must guess at by a process of historical inference. [12] (Who knows how he *really* felt about his mother's death at the time he was writing the *Confessions*? I don't.) I am referring rather to the narrative voice or literary persona to whom we are listening when we read the *Confessions* aloud. That's the one from whom we are to learn by imitation, and he expresses no grief for temporal losses. So when we make the necessary distinction between the narrator and the character in *Confessions* 9, we still have the same problem, though more complexly posed: the narrator does defend the character's grief, but also treats it as a weakness to be excused rather than a strength to be imitated.

Why? That's my question. Why are tears shed at the death of one's mother a sign of moral imperfection rather than an appropriate model to follow? To answer this question, I think, is to uncover something fundamental about the development of Augustine's ethics of love, and also to come upon one of the strangest and most beautiful features of the narrative structure of the *Confessions*.

THE DEVELOPMENT OF AUGUSTINE'S ETHICS OF LOVE

Let's start with the fundamental point about Augustine's ethics of love. The first of Augustine's extant writings to be completed is a little treatise on happiness, *On the Happy Life*, which argues that the goal of human life is achieved only when we have what we can't lose. For the goal is true happiness, which is not merely what we want but what we *ought* to want above all things. So what we must learn to do if we are to be happy is not to want what we can lose. This key thesis of Augustine's early ethics should be mapped against the background of classical philosophy, for there is certainly nothing specifically Christian about it. The thesis is essentially Stoic: true happiness is to have a good you cannot lose against your will, because you have it precisely by willing it.[13] But Augustine immediately points out that this Stoic ethics needs a Platonist ontology at its foundation, for "whatever is mortal and can fall, is something we cannot have whenever we will it and as long as we will it."[14] The only thing we can have without fear of loss is something that can never perish, which really means, Augustine proceeds to argue, something immutable and divine. Hence what we need to have, in order to be happy, is nothing less than God—not the very physical god of the Stoics, which is a divine fire (rather like the Manichaean worship of physical light which Augustine condemns so frequently in the *Confessions*) but a God who is incorporeal and immutable, transcending the times and changes of the physical world.

In the early years of Augustine's career as a Christian writer, he develops this Platonist ontology as the foundation of an ethical project of loving what can't be lost.[15] At the conclusion of the first book of his treatise *On Free Choice* (a book written about a year after *On the Happy Life*) he presents an account of the eternal law which commands us "to turn our love away from temporal things...and toward eternal things."[16] For it is only eternal things that we can have simply by willing them.[17] Since only God is eternal and immutable by nature this means, quite simply, that we should love nothing but God—a conclusion he draws explicitly in the treatise *On the Morals of the Catholic Church*, written at about the same time.[18] At this point Augustine has really dug himself into a hole: for if it is wrong to love anything but God then Jesus must be commanding us to sin when he tells us to love our neighbors. This is only one example of the way in which ancient philosophy, and especially Platonism, is much more spiritual than Christianity—and certainly more spiritual than Christ. Augustine has a lot of work to do to adjust his ethics to Christianity. If your project is to love what you cannot lose, then how it is legitimate to love your friends and neighbors, not to mention your enemies, becomes a major point of inquiry.

The basic tack Augustine will take to solve this problem emerges already in the treatise *On the Morals of the Catholic Church*, where he proceeds to contrast loving God with merely using temporal things: "God alone is to be loved, and all this world, i.e., all things of the senses, should be despised—but should be used for the needs of this life."[19] In this treatise using is contrasted with loving, but in the solution Augustine develops a decade later, in the first book of *On Christian Doctrine*, using is classified as one kind of loving. This yields the famous Augustinian ethics of use and enjoyment, *uti* and *frui*, both of which are forms of love.[20] So now Augustine can say we should love temporal things, for precisely in using them the right way we are loving them as we should, not despising them. But we are loving them without any permanent attachment, which means we will not be grieved by losing them. For use is related to enjoyment as means to end, so that the right way to use temporal things is temporarily, as a means of arriving at lasting enjoyment of eternal things. (Incidentally, the plural should not mislead us: "eternal things" means nothing but God, who alone is immutable, being eternal Truth and Goodness and Beauty and Righteousness and Wisdom and so on. Thus the eternal things we are to love are Platonic Ideas in the mind of God, as Augustine makes clear in his little essay "On Ideas.")[21]

Now comes the really tricky question. We are of course to love our neighbors, just as Christ says—but does that mean using them or enjoying them? After introducing the *uti/frui* distinction Augustine is actually willing, for the first and only time in his career, to argue for the startling conclusion that the proper way to relate to our neighbors is to use them.[22] For human beings are not eternal and therefore not to be enjoyed. Even God does not enjoy human beings but uses them—for their own good, Augustine immediately explains, since God, being perfect goodness, needs nothing from his creatures but gives them all the good they need.[23] The explanation is convoluted and not very convincing, and indeed it does not appear to have convinced Augustine himself, because he never repeats it. [24] In later writings Augustine abandons the thesis that the proper way to love our neighbors is to use them, adopting instead a suggestion made at the end of the discussion of love in *On Christian Doctrine* 1, to the effect that "all of us who enjoy God may be said to enjoy one another in Him."[25] This means that what we are really enjoying when we take delight in our Christian friends, with whom we seek to enjoy God, is God Himself, not our friends.[26]

THE STRANGE AND BEAUTIFUL ASSURANCE

Something like this concept of enjoying our friends in God must be what Augustine has in mind when he speaks of loving our friends "in God" in the *Confessions*, which was written about the same time as *On Christian Doctrine*. Notice this is the reverse of the common modern phrase, "to love God in our friends," which is more explicit about making sure that we do not allow anything human to be the object of the verb "to love." (This business of being more spiritual than Christ has a long history in the Christian tradition, which cannot be pinned on Augustine or even on ancient philosophy). Augustine's phrasing at least allows him to raise the question: what about the problem that the human beings we love are mortal, temporal creatures and therefore can be lost? If Christ is right that we are to love them and not God alone, then it does appear that we will get attached to them, and therefore that we cannot but grieve when we lose them. Here comes the really striking claim, which I described earlier as both strange and beautiful. After explaining what was wrong about his desperate grief for his best friend in *Confessions* 4, Augustine tells us how things go right if we love our friends in God: "Happy is he who loves You, and his friend in You, and his enemy because of You. For he alone loses nothing dear to him, to whom all are dear in Him who is never lost."[27]

If you love your friends in God, you cannot lose them. How wonderful, if only it were true! I still do not understand how Augustine thinks he can get away with making this claim. It is not one he defends or even repeats in other works. And his defense of it here lies not so much in the arguments he makes as in the narrative structure of the *Confessions* itself. The *Confessions* is the story of a character who starts out miserable because of his attachment to temporal things—for in Augustine's thinking love is a kind of spiritual glue which unites your soul with what you love,[28] and when you love things that perish the inevitable result is that your soul is torn apart when they are taken from you. That rending pain of loss is both the sign of our disordered loves and the goad which drives young Augustine away from his carnal love for transitory things to find that Beauty which is eternal, both ever ancient and ever new, and not found among external things.[29] But to love this Beauty is also to love all those who love it with you, to be united with them in the inward fellowship of love, which Augustine later calls the City of God. This fellowship too you cannot lose, except in the most superficial and transitory sense. The Christian friends whom you love in God can die, but you have not really lost them. You have lost only their mortal bodies, and that only temporarily. You cannot lose their souls. And that is a strange, bold, questionable claim. To see why, we need to look beyond the usual consolations of Christian Platonism, which are still very much with us.

It is easy enough to say we will see our Christian friends by and by, and Augustine in fact makes much of this traditional claim in later works, such as his sermons on grief. Pious hearts are permitted to grieve for a while, he says, with a pain willing to be healed and tears willing to be consoled, for the Christian faith tells us that our losses are only temporary. We do not mourn as those who have no hope, as Paul says.[30] Likewise when Augustine holds back his tears for his mother, it is because he is convinced he must not grieve over her as if she had died in misery or even as if she were fully dead.[31] Once again, it is as if to say: why haven't I learned this yet? What he needs to learn, to put it in Platonist terms, is that he has lost only her body, not her soul. The narrator of the *Confessions* reinforces this Platonist interpretation of Christian consolation by emphasizing Monica's own freedom from concern about her body. She once was anxious to be buried next to her husband in Africa, but as she lies dying in Italy she no longer cares where they lay her corpse. The physical proximity of bodies is not what matters to her any more.[32] Her attitude, as our narrator portrays it, resembles Socrates' unconcern about his corpse in Plato's *Phaedo*[33] more than the attitude of the women going to tomb at Easter, for whom the physical location of Jesus' body is everything. Once again, this Platonist lesson is far more spiritual than the Christian Gospel. And this Platonist lesson is the one which young Augustine, the grief-stricken character in *Confessions* 9, has not yet fully learned—he has learned it with his head, we might say, but not with his heart. His tears are a sign of carnal feelings because they are evoked by the loss of his mother's body, her physical presence, not her soul.

So far we have the traditional motifs of Christian Platonism, where life after death is interpreted not just in terms of the resurrection of the body, as in the Gospels, but also in terms of the immortality of the soul, as in the *Phaedo*.[34] The problem is that in Christianity there is such a thing as the death of the soul, its eternal death in punishment and separation from God,[35] and the fear of *that* loss is a central concern of the narrative in *Confessions*. The reason Augustine the narrator is consoled rather than grief-stricken at the death of his best friend so long ago is that his friend was thereby saved from efforts by young Augustine the Manichaean to lead him into heresy and therefore (in the judgment of the mature Augustine, the bishop) into eternal death. But that didn't happen, because Augustine's friend died a Catholic, abjuring Augustine's heresy—a great grief for Augustine the character, but a great consolation for Augustine the narrator: "He was snatched away from my madness, to be kept safe with You for my consolation."[36]

The obvious problem here is that not everyone you love gets saved in the end. Or so it would seem—unless loving your friends in God is some kind of guarantee against the eternal damnation of their souls. The strange and beautiful thing about the narrative in the *Confessions* is that it presents a world with just such a guarantee. For the great test of the claim that we cannot lose what we rightly love is of course the story of Augustine himself, as the object of his mother's love. Indeed, everything that is puzzling about his grief for his mother becomes clear in the light of her grief for him. In the early books of the *Confessions* she is always weeping for him, because he is a heretic in danger of the eternal destruction of his soul. Hence "she wept for me before You...more than mothers weep for bodily deaths."[37] There is no hint of moral disapproval of *these* tears, though they have to be sharply distinguished from the more carnal tears she weeps when she misses her son's bodily presence.[38] There is no hint of macho in Augustine's attitude toward this kind of tears—he will never disapprove of weeping for the soul, one's own or another's.[39] Quite the contrary: these tears are signs of deep spiritual power.

For if Augustine's project of never loving what you can lose is to make sense of human love, then the inward prayer of the heart for the soul of one's beloved, of which such tears are the outward expression, cannot be rejected.

This stunning claim is the explanation Augustine gives for why he was safe even from bodily death as long as he was a heretic. Despite a life-threatening illness, he could not die as a heretic and thus suffer the eternal death of his soul. That would break his mother's heart and therefore God cannot allow it.

> If *that* wound had struck my mother's heart, it would never have healed...I can't see how she could be healed if such a death had pierced clear through the bowels of her love....[And then he asks God:] Could You despise the tears by which she prayed not for gold or silver, nor any mutable and transitory good, but for the salvation of her son's soul, and push her away from Your help—You, by whose gift she was like that? No, Lord, not at all.[40]

God *cannot* refuse the prayer of love for another soul. Strong words! But we have heard this same message earlier in the *Confessions*, in the famous words with which a Catholic priest comforted Monica, saying, "It *cannot* be that the son of these tears should perish."[41] Augustine, I think, means us to take this word of comfort quite literally: God *cannot* refuse the prayers expressed by such tears, for God *cannot* break the heart of such a mother, who *is* such a mother, full of such prayers and tears, by God's own gift of grace. And so the passage in book 6 continues:

> But rather You were present and You heard and You did all things in the order that You had *predestined* them to be done. Far be it from You to deceive her in her visions and Your replies to her.[42]

Augustine alludes here to visions Monica had assuring her that she would see her son a Catholic before she died.[43] But he is also interested in a yet deeper assurance. The reason the son of Monica's tears cannot perish is because of the character of the grief her tears express, which is the effect of her love for his soul, not his body, a love which is hers by virtue of a divine gift of grace which was predestined from all eternity. So behind Monica's tears is her grief, behind her grief is her rightly ordered love, behind this love is divine grace, and behind divine grace is God's own predestination. That is the surest possible foundation for the conviction that we cannot lose what we love in God. For what God *cannot* do is violate his own predestined plan—because he is immutable, not someone whose mind changes with circumstances. And if he predestines you to love someone with Monica's kind of love, then you cannot lose what you love. At least that is the message of the *Confessions*—without which the whole story falls apart.

Monica's visions, as our narrator uses them, serve to confirm the general principle of the narrative: that "he alone loses nothing that is dear to him, to whom all are dear in God." Monica is exceptional only in that she has direct assurance of the deep truth so often hidden from us: that when you love other human beings with a rightly ordered love, you cannot lose what you love. This truth is the backbone of the narrative of the *Confessions*, essential for its happy ending and also for the explanation of what is so wrong about the main character's experience of carnal love and tormented grief. For this is a providential narrative, and essential to the concept of providence built into it is the conviction that it would be contrary to God's predestined plan for a heart like Monica's to be broken.

AN APPARENT CHANGE OF MIND

It would be wonderful if it were true, wouldn't it? If you love someone the right way, you can't lose them. But Augustine cannot really give us an argument for thinking this is true as a matter of general principle. His mature theology of predestination in fact clearly rules out any such principle, for the simple common-sense reason that nobody knows the future well enough to predict who will remain a faithful Christian until the end of their lives. None of us knows, even in our own case, whether we will receive the divine gift of perseverance in the faith—much less in the case of our friends.[44] Augustine is not a Calvinist, thinking that believers can know they are among the elect (that is Calvin's radical innovation in the doctrine of predestination.[45]) Unlike most Protestants, therefore, Augustine is in no position to assume that once converted we are sure to be saved. On the contrary, Christians in this mortal life are saved in hope (*in spe*) but not in reality (*in re*), which means precisely that they are "not yet saved" (*nondum salvos*).[46] So the conversion narrative of the *Confessions* cannot be read as if it were a Protestant story about how Augustine got saved.

This means that even the narrative of the *Confessions* fails, in the end, to substantiate Augustine's claim that those who love their beloved in God, as Monica does, cannot lose what they love. For Augustine is in no position to narrate the ultimate happy ending of his life, his eternal salvation. As book 10 of the *Confessions* makes quite clear, the dangers and temptations ahead of him on the road of this mortal life are real, and he has no ironclad guarantee that he will overcome them. That is why the *Confessions* must conclude by leaving Augustine's individual life behind and expounding the Scriptures, which indicate the ultimate happiness of the human soul by describing its blessed beginning. Books 11-13 of the *Confessions*, with their astounding exegesis of the opening chapters of Genesis, provide the only possible happy ending of Augustine's story. He is not certain of his own individual destiny, and therefore does not really know whether the son of Monica's tears will be saved or perish in the end. If his mother remains attached to him even in heaven, then it is still within the realm of possibility that God might break her heart.

In light of this failure to sustain such a key thesis, it is not surprising that (so far as I have been able to see) the *Confessions* is the last time Augustine makes a serious effort to work out his ethical project of not loving what you can lose. For in fact, the project doesn't work—not if we are to love our neighbor. In the long run Augustine cannot avoid the conclusion that it is possible to love as we should, and yet lose what we love. So after the *Confessions*, Augustine's writings contain no more scoldings for those who grieve. This opens up a deep human sympathy for human losses, including even the loss of beloved souls. The defense of grief in the *City of God*, which I quoted at the beginning, belongs to an extended meditation on the grief suffered in this life even by the saints—including how even the best friendships, which involve the love of two kindred Christian souls, can go sour.[47]

Along with deeper sympathy for human grief comes less hostility toward temporal loves. In the last book of the *City of God*, written near the end of Augustine's life, he devotes chapters not only to the misery of the afflictions of this mortal life but also to the blessing of its consolations, temporary though they be.[48] The contrast with *Confessions* has always struck me. In the discussion of temptation in the second half of *Confessions* 10, grief is always taken as the sign that we have attached ourselves too much to some temporal good. For Augustine at this point in his career even the light of day is a temptation, as shown by the fact that we miss it if it is absent too long. It goes near to breaking my heart that a man who obviously loved the light so much should come up with the wonderful epithet "queen of colors" to describe the physical light—in the course of explaining why it was an enticement and a temptation to him.[49] I don't suppose he ever gives up the notion that any temporal good is something to which we can become too attached. But at least at the end of his life, in the last book of the *City of God*, he can speak of "the abundance of light and its wonderful beauty"[50] and it is simply a word of praise and thanksgiving, accompanied by no moral warning. Though there is much to say about the development of Augustine's thought from the *Confessions* to the end of the *City of God*, some three decades later, one crucial change that explains a great deal, I think, is that he no longer talks as if there is something wrong with loving what you can lose.

Notes

[1] *premebam oculos eius, et confluebat in praecordia mea maestitudo ingens et transfluebat in lacrimas, ibidemque oculi mei violento animi imperio resorbebant fontem suum usque ad siccitatem.* Confessiones 9:12.29. All translations are mine.

[2] In my "yes" answer I follow the philosophical interpretation of the *Confessions* by Nicholas Wolterstorff, "Suffering Love" in T.V. Morris (ed.) *Philosophy and the Christian Faith* (Notre Dame: University of Notre Dame Press, 1988). The developmental analysis, however, is my addition. Also, though I join Wolterstorff in regretting the ethics I find underlying *Confessions* 9, I do not draw from this regret the same theological conclusion, viz. that God is by nature capable of suffering. It seems to me better to embrace the patristic trinitarian view, affirming

deipassionism (God suffered because Christ, who in his human nature was crucified, is God) but denying *patripassionism* (the Father did not suffer because he
was not crucified and the divine nature remains impassible).

[3] *hoc quo pacto futurum est, ut eius nobis amara mors non sit, cuius dulcis est vita?
Hinc enim est et luctus quoddam non inhumani cordis quasi vulnus aut ulcus.... De
civitate Dei* 19:8.

[4] *Potest non dolere cor humanum defuncto charissimo; melius tamen cum dolet sanatur
cor humanum quam non dolendo fit inhumanum.* sermo 173.2.

[5] *puer Adeodatus exclamavit in planctu atque ab omnibus nobis cohercitus tacuit.
Confessiones* 9:12.29.

[6] *at ego in auribus tuis, ubi eorum nullus audiebat, increpabam mollitiam affectus mei et
constringebam fluxum maeroris. Confessiones* 9:12.31.

[7] *mihi vehementer displicebat tantum in me posse haec humana, quae ordine debito et
sorte conditionis nostrae accidere necesse est. ibid.*

[8] *ille, quem quasi non moriturum dilexeram, mortuus erat.... fuderam in harenam
animam meam diligendo moriturum acsi non moriturum. Confessiones* 4:6.11 and
4:8.13.

[9] *credo commendans memoriae meae vel hoc uno documento omnis consuetudinis
vinculum etiam adversus mentem, quae iam non fallaci verbo pascitur. Confessiones*
9:12.32.

[10] *carnalis affectus, Confessiones* 9.13.34.

[11] *hominis superbe interpretantis ploratum meum, Confessiones* 9:12.33.

[12] The literary distinction between the author and the narrator, obvious once it is
stated, has usually been overlooked in Augustine scholarship, including my
own. I have learned its value for reading the *Confessions* from Robert McMahon,
"Book Thirteen: The Creation of the Church as the Paradigm for the *Confessions*"
in K. Paffenroth and R.P. Kennedy (eds.) *A Reader's Companion to the Augustine's
Confessions* (Louisville: Westminster John Knox Press, 2003).

[13] *ei comparandum est, quod cum vult habet. De beata vita* 2.11. The Stoic conviction
that true happiness is immune from the vicissitudes of fotune is central to
Cicero's *Tusculan Disputations* 5, a book which, if it stood alone, would aptly bear
the title *De beata vita* and stands as the immediate precursor to Augustine's
treatise by that name.   The idea that this Stoic conviction has a Platonic
foundation is already broached by Cicero, *Tusculan Disputations* 5:34-36.

[14] *Nam quidiquid mortale et caducum est, non potest a nobis, quando volumus et
quamdiu volumus, haberi. De beata vita* 2.11.

[15] In addition to *De libero arbitrio*, book 1, and *De moribus ecclesiae catholicae* (see
especially paragraphs 5 and 10), the philosophical foundation for this ethics of
not loving what can be lost is developed in *De vera religione* 86-89 and perhaps
most illuminatingly in *De diversis quaestionibus 83*, 33-36, built around an analysis
of fear and love that becomes fundamental for Augustine's later treatment of the
Pauline theology of grace in *ibid.* 66, *Expositio quarundam propositionum ex epistula
apostoli ad Romanos* 44-52, and *De spiritu et littera* 8.13.

[16] *Jubet igitur aeterna lex avertere amorem a temporalibus et eum mundatum ad aeterna convertere. De libero arbitrio 1:15.32.*

[17] *dum vult habet...velle solum opus est, ut habeatur. De libero arbitrio* 1:12.26. Cf. the Stoic philosopher Seneca, epistula 80:4: *Quid sibi opus est ut bonus sis? Velle!*

[18] *De moribus ecclesiae catholicae* 20.37. See quotation below.

[19] *amandum igitur solus Deus est; omnis vero iste mundus, id est omnia sensibilia contemnenda; utendum autem his ad huius vitae necessitatem. ibid.*

[20] The *uti/frui* contrast is introduced in *De doctrina christiana* 1:10.10, but *uti* is not explicitly classified as a form of love until Augustine asks the question, in what sense we are to love our neighbor, *ibid.* 1:22.20. Evidently Augustine classifies *uti* as a form of love only in order to explain how loving something besides God can be legitimate.

[21] *De diversis quaestionibus 83,* 46.

[22] *De doctrina christiana* 1:22.20-21.

[23] *De doctrina christiana* 1:31.34-32.35.

[24] As Oliver O'Donovan argues in his fundamental study of the development of Augustine's language of use and enjoyment, this attempt to classify human beings among the things to be used is "quite simply a mistake, with which Augustine cannot live." O'Donovan, "*Usus* and *Fruitio* in Augustine, *De doctrina christiana* 1" in *Journal of Theogical Studies*, n.s., 33/2, Oct. 1982, p 390.

[25] *omnes, qui eo fruimur, nobis etiam invicem in ipso perfruamur. De doctrina christiana* 1:32.35.

[26] *quum autem homine in Deo frueris, Deo potius quam homine frueris. De doctrina christiana* 1:33.37.

[27] *beatus qui amat te et amicum in te et inimicum propter te. solus enim nullum carum amittit cui omnes in illo cari sunt qui non amittuntur. Confessiones* 4:9.14.

[28] The soul is joined to whatever it loves by "the glue of love" (*glutine amore*) in *Confessiones* 4:10.15. The metaphor of love as glue is common in Augustine, though not always rendered in the translations; cf. e.g. *De libero arbitrio* 1:33, *De Trinitate* 10:7, *Enarrationes in Psalmos* 62:17, as well as the study by Lienhard, "'The Glue Itself is Charity': Ps 62:9 in Augustine's Thought" in *Augustine: Presbyter Factus Sum* (New York: Peter Lang, 1993) pp. 375-384. That love is a kind of unitive force is a key feature of Augustine's psychology, well-explained by Burnaby, *Amor Dei* (London: Hodder and Stoughton, 1938) pp. 100-103. It is also fundamental to Augustine's account of the relations of self and other; see Cary, "Augustine's Social Ontology" in *Augustine and Politics* (Lexington, 2004).

[29] *sero te amavi, pulchritudo tam antiqu et tam nova, sero te amavi. Et ecce intus eras et ego foris, et ibi te querebam. Confessiones* 10: 27.38.

[30] 1 Thess. 4.12 See Augustine's sermon 172 on grief, which has this passage as its text.

[31] *at illa nec misere moriebatur nec omnino moriebatur. Confessiones* 9:12.29.

[32] *Confessiones* 9:11.27-28.

[33] Plato, *Phaedo* 115c-e.

[34] Compare the description of Monica's death as the release of the soul from the body in *Confessiones* 9:11.28 (*anima...corpore soluta est*) with Plato's definition of death as the separation of soul from body in *Phaedo* 64c. The fact that Augustine (almost certainly) learned this language from the Christian tradition rather than by reading it directly in Plato does not change the fact of its ultimately Platonic origin; it simply means that much of Augustine's Christian Platonism is not original with him.

[35] Augustine is an eloquent exponent of this concept, *De civitate Dei* 13:2 and 20:6.

[36] *ille abreptus dementiae meae, ut apud te servaretur consolationi meae. Confessiones* 4:4.8.

[37] *pro me fleret ad te mea mater, fidelis tua, amplius quam flent matres corporea funera. Confessiones* 3:11.19.

[38] See esp. *Confessiones* 5:8.15.

[39] Hence in *Confessiones* 9:13.34 Augustine the narrator wholly approves of the "far different sort of tears" (*longe aliud lacrimarum genus*) that he currently weeps when he prays for his mother's soul. Likewise there is no hint of shame or embarrassment when the narrator tells us about the tears of repentance copiously shed in *Confessiones* 8.

[40] *quo vulnere si feriretur cor matris, numquam sanaretur.... non itaque video quomodo sanaretur, si mea talis illa mors transverberasset viscera dilectionis eius....huiusne tu lacrimas, quibus non a te aurum et argentum petebat, nec aliquod mutabile aut volubile bonum, sed salutem animae filii sui, tu, cuius munere talis erat, contemneres et repelleres ab auxilio tuo? nequaquam, domine. Confessiones* 5:9.16-17.

[41] *fieri non potest, ut filius istarum lacrimarum pereat Confessiones* 3:12.21.

[42] *immo vero aderas et exaudiebas et faciebas ordine quo praedestinaveras esse faciendum. absit ut tu falleres eam in illis visionibus et responsis tuis. Confessiones* 5:9.17.

[43] *Confessiones* 3:11.19-20.

[44] See esp. *De correptione et gratia* 9.20-25.

[45] See my "Why Luther is not Quite Protestant: The Logic of Faith in a Sacramental Promise" in *Pro Ecclesia*, forthcoming.

[46] *De civitate Dei* 19:4.

[47] *De civitate Dei* 19:5-9.

[48] *De civitate Dei* 22:22-24.

[49] *Confessiones* 10:34.51.

[50] *in ipsius lucis tanta copia tamque mirabili specie! De civitate Dei* 23:24.

Love Lost and Found: The Ambiguities of *Amor, Caritas* and *Concupiscentia* in St. Thomas Aquinas' *Summa Theologiae*

Patrick A. Messina
Gwynedd Mercy College

I dare say that some Thomists may cringe tightly when they hear the word ambiguity associated in any way with the Angelic Doctor. Moreover, I am certain that this apoplectic response derives from the noblest of philosophical motives, working as an early warning signal against an imminent misreading or misrepresentation of his thought. After all, the undeniable fame of Aquinas' great theological patrimony lay in its highly systemized, logically impregnable methodology. But those who appreciate the monumental scope of Aquinas' synthetic task will have to admit that at least some ambiguity is unavoidable, perhaps even necessary in tackling the overwhelming complexities of the human condition. Hence, I will appeal to those for whom ambiguity presents no real or perceived methodological threat when I highlight some examples of its presence specifically within Aquinas' treatment of love (*amor*) and its relationship to concupiscence (*concupiscentia*) and charity (*caritas*) as developed in the *Summa Theologiae*.[1] For, when the reader pays close attention to the relationship between these three psychological movements, there emerge some interesting conceptual fissures, dialectical moments of ambiguity that leave the reader with an uncanny sense that when defining and analyzing these phenomena there is more than meets the argument, so to speak.

For me, the ambiguities at issue center upon (but are not restricted to) four questions where Aquinas' dialectic ventures into some unusual and even unsuspected areas: the question concerning God's love (I, 20); the question of love as the principle passion (I-II, 26); the question of concupiscence (I-II, 30); and the question of charity itself (II-II, 23). Of these four questions, the one concerning God's love first ignited my curiosity; for it is there in his reply to the third objection of article two Aquinas admits that God (*caritas ipsa*) can actually love with concupiscence. To quote his precise words:

> God does not love irrational creatures with the love of friendship; but as it were with the love of desire [*amore quasi concupiscentiae*]; in so far as He orders them to rational creatures and even Himself.[2]

The first thing that struck me was obviously the presence of concupiscence, a strange word to use concerning God's love. While I was aware that Aquinas' view of concupiscence had always had its optimistic side (unlike Augustine),[3] it was nonetheless shocking to find the term applied in any way to God or His actions. Even the presence of the qualifying term *"quasi"* could not ease my bewilderment when I first fell upon the passage. Yes, it's true that the metaphysics of analogy can provide great elasticity to divine predication, but concupiscence carries with it such a problematic connotation, associated as it were with the sensitive appetite and Original sin, that I would have thought it anathema to use in a divine context.[4] Nor was I satisfied to relegate this application of divine concupiscence to some methodological constraint necessitated by the Augustinian-Aristotelian synthesis.[5] This explanation seemed too easy given Aquinas' genius for circumspection. Moreover, when I began to look at Aquinas' treatment of human love, an interesting connection seemed to coalesce between the strange bedfellows of concupiscence and charity. Thus, I realized that this brief moment of ambiguity arising from an assertion of divine concupiscence was just the beginning, a sumptuous by scant intellectual appetizer leaving me with a sincere craving for more.

Driven by this craving, I dove headlong into I-II, 26 only to find that the real linchpin between concupiscence and charity lay in Aquinas' treatment of friendship in the same section on the passions. It is here in question four that he divides love into the love of concupiscence (*amor concupiscentiae*) and the love of friendship (*amor amicitiae*). However, as Aquinas develops this division, the lines of demarcation become somewhat obscure, allowing for an equivocal, more interdependent relationship between concupiscence and friendship, and thus by implication between the sensual and spiritual. Once convinced of this interdependence, I was naturally led to the question of charity where Aquinas defines it as friendship with God. The improbable pot of gold at the end of this dialectical rainbow, as it were, would be to find out that if God can love with concupiscence and concupiscence could be allied with friendship and friendship with charity, could one further conclude according to the order of reciprocity that the human being can love God with concupiscence. This would be an interesting conflation of the ideas of sensual and spiritual love, a conflation somewhat unexpected of Aquinas and surely out of sync with the predominant Augustinian tradition of his day; a tradition that had always placed concupiscence against charity (*cupiditas/caritas*)[6] and had always seen the will as the genuine source of our rightly ordered love of God. Hence, for my present purpose, I would like to follow this dialectic of love through the appearances of these fissures of ambiguity, tracing the path from divine concupiscence through human love and friendship to the virtue of charity, exploring the possibility of a more amenable relationship (if there is one) between the seemingly disparate notions of concupiscence and charity; or, to understand why Aquinas would choose such a problematic word to distinguish to kinds of love inherent in friendship.

AMBIGUITY OF SOUL AND APPETITION

The ambiguities of love do not spring forth from the text spontaneously *ex nihilo* but are rooted deeply in Aquinas' theory of the soul. One can begin to see profound ambiguity in the relationship between the soul's essence and its powers, wherein Aquinas takes great pains to preserve their distinctiveness. His motive in doing so is obvious: if the soul's essence is its power, then the human being possesses the same simplicity as God. This heretical notion forces Aquinas to offer an equivocal solution; one that seems to focus on the soul's reflexive quality: the essence of the soul is both provider and receiver of its own powers; provider insofar as the substantial form is prior in being to its accidents and receiver insofar as the subject is actualized by its accidents. And so Aquinas situates the soul's structural complexity within the following metaphysical principle:

> So the subject forasmuch as it is in potentiality, is receptive of the accidental form; but forasmuch as it is in act, it produces it.[7]

According to the above explanation, when considering the soul as a substantial form, it is the cause and principle of its own powers, which are its proper accidents; but considering the soul as a subject in potentiality to further perfection, it is the recipient of its powers.[8] While the hylomorphic logic appears unassailable here, it's difficult to deny that there remains a modicum of the *causa sui* in Aquinas' psychology. This paradoxical circumstance of the soul's relation to its powers can be seen as a foundational ambiguity that sets the tone for similar, relevant occurrences in Aquinas' further treatment of the soul's powers and operations.

Of all the powers distinguished in Aquinas' psychology, appetition may be the most impalpable.[9] Unlike the structure of apprehension, which is based upon the more approachable idea of its specific powers resting in a simulacrum, the appetitive powers desire the fullness of their objects; unsatisfied by a mere intention, they rest only in the obtainment of natures as they exist in themselves. As Aquinas puts it:

> The soul has, through its appetitive power, an order to things as they are in themselves . . . on the other hand the apprehensive power is not drawn to a thing, as it is in itself; but knows it by reason of an "intention" of the thing.[10]

And herein lays the fundamental distinction between the appre-
hensive and appetitive powers, as well as the problem of grasping
the mystery of appetition. A plethora of ancient and perennial
questions ensue: how can one conceive of the soul possessing the
fullness of any autonomous being outside itself? How is this kind
of immanence or ontological unity possible? What is the true nature of the relationship between the appetite and its object? In the
final analysis, what is appetite? We know the human being longs,
strives and even moans and sighs for something other than itself,
something it lacks, something it knows it lacks (or suspects any-
way), something that once possessed can ironically fulfill it. In
western philosophy we can go back as far as Plato to see this psychic power assigned its proper place in the make up of the soul.[11]
But what is it really? Is it anything else but love? Can one ade-
quately distinguish the soul's appetite from its love?[12] Or is the
line between the two illusory, reducing the experience of love to
an insurmountable abstraction?[13] Of course, Aquinas will make an
ingenious attempt to clarify the difference between the two.

AMBIGUITY OF LOVE AND APPETITE

The indistinguishable unity between appetite and love finds
some support in the choice of terms used to designate them both.
For Aquinas, appetite (*appetitus*) is essentially an inclination (*inclinatio*) towards the good that follows upon an apprehension.[14]
However, the term *inclinatio* is not only used to denote appetite
itself but also appetitive movement in general and love specifically;[15] in fact, Aquinas defines the passion of concupiscence as an
appetite (*appetitus*) for the pleasant.[16] Furthermore, *inclinatio* is
also used in tandem with *aptitudo* to connote natural tendency and
fittingness;[17] and in turn, *aptitudo* is used along with *coaptatio* to
define love (*amor*) in Aquinas' treatment of the passions, both
terms sounding very much like *appetitus* in their capacity to in-
cline a power to what is suitable.[18] To add yet more equivocation,
the term *habitudo* is employed by Aquinas in arguing for the existence of divine will, using the term to outline the hierarchy of appetites.[19] Moreover, both *habitudo* and *aptitudo* are used to
articulate the nature of virtue and how it provides the proper

measure between powers and their acts. Punctuating this dizzy-
ing array of terminology is Aquinas' interchangeable use of *amor*
and *appetitus* in his treatise on the angels: "But it is common to
every nature to have some inclination; and this is its natural appetite or love."[20] In this passage Aquinas asserts that every power
of the soul inasmuch as it's a form has its own natural appetite
that provides it with an initial inclination or proportion to its
proper end.[21] This claim is problematic when applied to the appetitive faculty itself; for one is forced to conclude that the appetitive power has its own natural appetite guaranteeing its proper
orientation towards the good, as if being an appetite were not
enough to ensure its own inclination. The presence of such ambiguity in the relationship between appetite and love in no way de-
ters or diminishes Aquinas' attempt to distinguish them. But it
does cause the reader to reflect on the wisdom of dissecting what
might be better left whole; for the problem of the appetite aside,
the treatment of love and the passions will have its own heavy
cargo of ambiguity to be unpacked.

THE AMBIGUITIES OF LOVE AND PASSION

Our look at the problems of appetition has thus far given only
a scant, general preview of the problems of love in Aquinas. However, these problems dovetail into the more specific ambiguities
that result from Aquinas' discussion on the passions. Predictably,
the problem of passion, like that of appetition, begins with the
terminology. Oddly enough, however, one of the best passages
foreshadowing this problem is contained in the question of God's
love where Aquinas writes, "Therefore acts of the sensitive appetite, inasmuch as they have annexed to them some bodily change,
are called passions."[22] Hence we begin with the discomfortingly
ambiguous principle that acts are in fact passions, perhaps reflec-
tive of the ambiguity I mentioned earlier regarding the relationship between the soul and its powers (i.e., soul-producer and soul-
receiver).[23] This would be more palatable if Aquinas were talking
about the will; since the will is clearly the principle of our actions.
But one is harder pressed to conceive of how we commit specific
acts by sensuality; or is the word "act" used analogically to con-

note *inclinatio*?[24] In the end, however, love is the principle act (i.e. passion), underlying all others in every power of the soul.

Adding further to the ambiguity is the many faces (or names) of love employed by Aquinas when he admits,[25] "We find four words referring in a way to the same thing: *viz.*, love, dilection, charity and friendship."[26] Conspicuously missing from this list are the passions classically understood as forms or species of love, i.e., desire, joy, fear and sorrow. However, for Aquinas, these passions are not forms of love, despite what Augustine says on the matter.[27] They are generically different movements of the sensitive appetite, related to love as an effect to the principle cause. And that is exactly what love (*amor*) is for Aquinas: the first, principle movement of the sensitive appetite, a kind of initial awakening of the power that results from sensation. It is more universal than the other movements which are related to the good under various aspects; for example, desire (*concupiscentia* or *desiderium*) is the good not yet possessed; while joy (*delectatio* or *gaudium*) is the good possessed.[28] Despite Aquinas' assertion that the classical passions are not essentially related to love, it is nonetheless hard to imagine that love is not the very essence of desire (love-moving) and joy (love-possessing). That love is causal in the way of motion, like the way one moving object imparts its motion to another, seems an untenable, abstract reduction.[29]

There are still more substantive ambiguities to be identified with love than the ones resulting from nomenclature. Although Aquinas says that love (along with all the passions) belongs principally to the sensitive appetite, he admits that love – in the form of natural love – resides in every power of the soul, each representing a different kind of love.[30] Not to mention, there are certain corresponding loves that belong to the intellectual appetite, and by virtue of which are not properly called passions. For Aquinas, love is only properly so called when it resides in the sensitive appetite; when it is found in the will, it is called love by "extension (*extenso*)."[31] His insistence upon sensation being the literal or true basis of love seems discordant with his related view of "true" friendship (*vera amicitia*), which is denigrated by its proximity to the sensual:

> Friendship of the useful or pleasant, insofar as it is connected with the
> love of concupiscence, loses the character of true friendship.[32]

Hence, by analogy, since the authenticity of friendship is determined by its greater distance from the sensual (either literal or
metaphoric), then the same logic should apply to love, friendship's primary force. It's important to remember, the above passage is found in the section on the passions in the article dealing
with the division of love into love of concupiscence and love of
friendship, the key passage that brings us back to divine concupiscence. For, God loves the things He wants for us by concupiscence and loves us by friendship (charity).

LOVE OF CONCUPISCENCE AND LOVE OF FRIENDSHIP

In I-II, 26, 4, Aquinas divides love according to what he calls
love of concupiscence (*amor concupiscentiae*) and love of friendship
(*amor amicitiae*):

> Accordingly, man has love of concupiscence towards the good that he
> wishes to another, and love of friendship, towards him to whom he
> wishes good.[33]

In other words, the friend loves the other with the love of friendship while any particular good he wishes for the friend he loves
with concupiscence. This relation clearly harkens back to divine
concupiscence which implies a similar dynamic; however, there
are some troubling questions that present themselves in the human treatment of these loves that did not emerge in the divine
consideration. For one thing, in I-II, 28, 2, Aquinas seems to lose
his footing a bit while again attempting to clarify the relation between love and appetite, contradicting his previous distinction of
loves:

> As the appetitive power, the object loved is said to be in the lover, in-
> asmuch as it is in his affections, by a kind of complacency, causing him
> either to take pleasure in it, or in its good, when present; or, in the ab-
> sence of the object loved, by his longing, to tend towards it with the love

of concupiscence, or towards the good that he wills to the beloved, with the love of friendship.[34]

Unfortunately, the formulation here is subject to some serious ambiguity, as Aquinas seems to be confusing the love of friendship with the love of concupiscence. Continuing on in the same article, Aquinas asserts that with regard to the beloved, concupiscence has a more serious goal than friendship, explaining that unlike friendship concupiscence is "not satisfied with any external or superficial possession or enjoyment of the beloved."[35] But what does this say about the ranking of the two generic loves? Must one conclude that due to the greater profundity and extension of concupiscence that "in a certain sense" the love of concupiscence out-ranks the love of friendship?

If however, we chose to interpret these ambiguities of concupiscence and friendship somehow differently (whatever that may be), disregarding the difficult conclusion about ranking, we could perhaps appreciate the old scholastic adage at work here: one distinguishes in order to unite. For inasmuch as Aquinas establishes the difference between the two loves, he implies the necessity of both in the act of friendship. This could be a splendid integration of two orders of inclination converging upon a unity of love towards another person. However, what strikes so peculiar about this double presence of loves is the juxtaposition of the sensual and the spiritual. Spiritual goods are accessible through the will (as in the case with God), not through the sensitive appetite;[36] and friendship is largely held to be spiritual for Aquinas, at least in its true or virtuous form.[37] More to this, when friendship is given a definitive context in charity, there doesn't seem to be a conceptual place set aside at all for sensuality, unless we use the term by *extenso* to connote a vigorous and intense desire. Or contrary to my initial instinct, does the answer to these strange appropriations of concupiscence in divine love and friendship boil down to the simple, inherent distinction between the goods we love and the persons for whom we wish them?[38]

Actually, this bifurcation of love is not too troublesome until one considers the possibility of desiring a spiritual good for another, as in the case when one wishes virtue for his friend; or even more perplexing, when one wishes friendship itself for his friend.

In the latter case, one would desire friendship with the love of concupiscence while desiring the other with the love of friendship; as problematic as this may sound, there is a logical integrity to this proposition. In his article "The Problem of Love," Robert Johann explains that the love of concupiscence, when conjoined with the love of friendship, is not drawn to the subsistence of its object, but only desires it in an "abstractive" and "functional" way, which is to say, only insofar as the good desired can be of use to the beloved friend in his own subjective perfection.[39] This explanation, however, does little to persuade the reader as to the relevance or necessity of the distinction when applied to self-love or the alter-egoism of friendship. In the case of self-love, must I require two modes of love (one for the object and one for me) when I unite with the object of my love, producing in me an authentic fulfillment, a true state of perfection?[40] By this logic (as was the case above with desiring friendship for my friend), I would need to love virtue with the love of concupiscence, and love myself with the love of friendship; even though when I embrace virtue, in a certain sense, I become one with virtue, albeit as an accident becomes one with its subject. In the case of friendship as alter-ego, when I consider, as Johann does, that my love of a spiritual good serves a higher "synthesis," i.e. the perfection of my friend, do I not love the same way when I love it for myself? When I desire something for my friend's perfection that I would also desire for my own, then why must I require different modes of loving to accomplish this unity or solicitude? Isn't easier to say that I love my virtue as I love myself as I love my friend – all with the same love? Again, it's not that these distinctions suffer contradiction; it's that the distinctions are woefully equivocal, somewhat confusing, and clearly abstractive in a reductionist sort of way. To punctuate this confusion we can consider the distinction Aquinas makes between love of concupiscence and love of friendship in the opening article on the question of Charity. In II-II, 23, 1, he says:

> If, however, we do not wish good to what we love, but wish its good for ourselves, it is love not of friendship, but of a kind of concupiscence.[41]

In this alternative formulation, the preferred distinction between the two loves rests upon the difference between self-love and benevolence, not between the object loved and the person for whom we love it.⁴² Now, we can directly conclude from the above passage that desiring the good for another is the love of friendship. But the previous distinction forces us to accept the notion that any good loved for the sake of another is loved with concupiscence, not friendship; the latter is reserved only for the person as the proper terminus of our love. Hence, according to the logic of this new distinction, I can love an object (not the friend) with both concupiscence and friendship, so long as I love it for another instead of myself. I'm not suggesting that Aquinas intended this interpretation, but the difference between the distinctions of love made here on his treatment of charity and previously in his treatment of the passions, leads us finally by way of ambiguity to explore any possible connections made between love, concupiscence and charity.

THE AMBIGUITY OF CHARITY

A good way to begin this exploration of charity would be to pose a question similar to the ones just asked: by which form of love do I love God when I desire Him for myself and my friend?

Do I love Him by concupiscence? Do I love Him by friendship? Or, do I love Him by both? As I have shown thus far, Aquinas seems to have allowed the possibility of both; however, when addressing the subject of charity in II-II, 24, 1, he replies with an unequivocal opposition to the proposed objection that charity is found in both the concupiscible and intellectual appetites:

> The concupiscible is a part of the sensitive, not of the intellective appetite, as proved in the First Part (Q. 81, A. 2): wherefore the love which is in the concupiscible is the love of sensible good: nor can the concupiscible reach to the Divine good which is an intelligible good; the will alone can. Consequently the concupiscible cannot be the subject of charity.⁴³

This would have been an opportune moment for Aquinas to relate the ambiguous nature of the term *concupiscentia*, since this argument brings to mind the divisions of *amor concupiscentiae* and *amor amicitiae*, as well as summoning the specter of divine concupiscence introduced in I, 20. For example, he could have argued that in a certain sense, we love God by concupiscence when we desire Him for our friend. Further, we can love God with concupiscence when we desire to help accomplish his providential plan for us, for in the divine economy, God is identical with His Providence.[44] But there is no mention of the ambiguity anywhere in the article. The desire born of the sensitive appetite simply cannot reach God! And thus concupiscence too is summarily disqualified, since it is, by definition, the second movement of the concupiscible appetite.[45] It is also defined as both the ordinate and inordinate desires of the concupiscible appetite, and even Original sin itself.[46] Therefore, it would seem grossly inappropriate to suggest, even by analogy, any role at all for concupiscence in the love of God, as I have remarked previously.

The detractor might argue that the passage cited above in no wise precludes the analogical use of concupiscence in the case of *amor concupiscentiae*, or divine concupiscence. Further, the only thing it does preclude is that the human being can ever love God by the concupiscence of the sensitive appetite; thus, to prevent confusion, it makes sense to avoid the term altogether in defining the essence of charity. Yet, when speaking of the mystery of love, especially when it denotes the union between the divine and the human, it is difficult to speak in such exclusionary terms. In fact, when one considers the question of charity's object, the confident exclusion of concupiscence becomes somewhat dubious, as Aquinas' logic, nonetheless, implicates its presence. Take for instance, what he says in II-II, 25, 2:

> Charity is love. Now love, by reason of the nature of the power whose act it is, is capable of reflecting on itself; for since the object of the will is the universal good, whatever has the aspect of good, can be the object of an act of the will; and since to will is itself good, man can will himself to will . . . Love, however, even by reason of its own species, is capable of reflecting on itself, because it is a spontaneous movement of the lover towards the beloved, wherefore from the moment a man loves, he loves himself to love. Yet, charity is not love simply, but has the nature of friendship . . . Now by friendship a thing is loved in two ways: first, as the friend for whom we have friendship, and to whom we wish good things: secondly, as the good which we wish to a friend. It is in the latter and not in the former way that charity is loved out of charity, because

charity is the good which we desire for all those whom we love out of charity.[47]

In this powerful and complex passage, the concepts of love, concupiscence and charity form an interesting union, the clearly defined boundaries between them, charted by numerous, ingenious distinctions, almost disappearing under the weight of love's ambiguity. Here Aquinas, in typical Augustinian style, gives us a glimpse into the *Imago Dei* in our will and its love; and by emphasizing its reflexive capacity (*seipsum reflecti*), shows us how tightly and intricately woven our own complex of love really is.[48] As God is the object of His Own love, our own will and its action can be the object of our love and desire. Hence, not only can the human being will its own willing, but it can love its own loving.[49] Now, the text here in II-II, 25, 2 calls to mind what Aquinas says in I, 20, 1 and II-II, 23, 1: first, in II-II, 25, 2 charity is love (*caritas amor quidam est*); and in I, 20, 1 God is charity (*Deus caritas est*); finally, in II-II, 23, 1, charity is friendship (*Ergo caritas est amicitia*).[50] With these three passages we can see love, charity and friendship conflate in the divine essence.[51] However, since charity is friendship, the love of friendship (*amor amicitiae*) must refer back to charity; thus, Aquinas reminds us of its twofold aspect: we love the friend and we love the good for our friend's sake. But the latter aspect is understood to be the love of concupiscence (*amor concupiscentiae*). Furthermore, Aquinas claims that loving the good for one's friend is the way we love charity by charity. Therefore, in its reflexive mode, the love of charity becomes the love of concupiscence; for when we desire charity (God) for the sake of our friend, we are loving charity by concupiscence. The conclusion is unavoidable when we hear the following from Aquinas:

> Nevertheless we can love irrational creatures out of charity, if we regard them as the good things that we desire for others, in so far, to wit, as we wish for their preservation, to God's honor and man's use; thus too does God love them out of charity.[52]

There is no doubt that Aquinas is talking here about *amor concupiscentiae*; the question is why hasn't he referred to it as such? The answer might be found in what he says later concerning the order of charity: "That a man wishes to enjoy God pertains to that love of God which is love of concupiscence (*amor concupiscentiae*)."[53] With this statement, Aquinas has come very close to bringing down the potential boundaries between a metaphoric concupiscence that loves rationally (*benevolentia*), and one that loves with sensuality, a more self-centered love (*concupiscentia*). Again, it appears that Aquinas wanted to avoid the term concupiscence in defining the *useful* aspect of charity; since he doesn't mention it directly anywhere else in his treatment of charity (i.e., as *amor concupiscentiae*); and yet, he declares in a brief reply to article three of question twenty-six, that man enjoys God by concupiscence. Perhaps he wanted to avoid any confusion that might have come from using the term *amor concupiscentia* in relation to charity; however, whatever equity was gained by avoiding it had been lost by pointing out that man enjoys God by the *amor concupiscentiae*.

Although Aquinas seems to derive the two distinct loves from Aristotle – which could explain the inherent ambiguities when applied to charity – there are some like Anthony Keating who suggest that these distinctions are better understood in relation to Augustine's *uti/frui* dichotomy.[54] Accordingly, *uti*, whereby we love things only as useful to our general well being, would correspond to the love of concupiscence; while *frui*, whereby we love things *per se* (like God), would correspond to the love of friendship. The problem with this correspondence is that for Augustine, if our love is rightly ordered, it can only be directed to God *per se*.[55] In Book IV of the *Confessions*, Augustine admits that the love of his friend for his own sake was more an expression of concupiscence than true friendship.[56] In light of this insight, the *uti/frui-amor concupiscentiae/amor amicitiae* analogy really cannot hold. Applying this logic to the reflexive law of charity, when we love charity for the sake of our friend, we would be relegating charity itself to use, making the friend absolute and God relative.[57]

CONCLUSION

In tracing Aquinas' dialectic of love from the divine to the human, what is it that I have really found? If there is an interpretive connection between God's love, human love, concupiscence, friendship and charity, what is the philosophical windfall? There are at least three possible conclusions to take from this inquiry: 1. Aquinas' logic can, despite (or in virtue of) its meticulousness, be taken to problematic conclusions; 2. his system can, at times, suffer from an over-conceptualized treatment of God, allowing for the strange concept of divine concupiscence; and 3. there is an unwitting or subconscious appropriation (or preservation) of sensuality in our perfected love of God (*caritas*) and even in God himself (divine concupiscence). That is to say, the use of the term *concupiscentia* in describing God's love is not a simple analogy or just a methodological necessity or a theological word-play or even an attempt at poetics.[58] It may be that for Aquinas there is a more intimate or even commensurate relationship between natural and divine love in the human being (one might find a good analogy by imagining a friendly relationship between Augustine's *concupiscentia* and *caritas*). And despite the natural enmity placed between them by St. Paul and St. Augustine, concupiscence remains tied to charity, the latter retaining the sensual quality of the former while elevating the human will to perfection, converting natural, fallen love in a way that recalls Plato's love of beauty in the *Symposium*, where sensuality is not destroyed in love's ascent to the ideal, but remains rooted in its erotic origins, pursuing God's beauty reflected throughout all of His creation. Perhaps Aquinas' dialectic of love provides concupiscence with a rehabilitative chance; rather than seeing charity purge concupiscence from the soul (as Augustine did); the former simply re-forms the latter, re-ordering a disordered natural love.

Notes

[1] All Latin citations are taken from the Leonine edition, *Sancti Thomae Aquinatis Opera omnia iussu impensaque Leonis XIII P. M. edita, t. 4-12: (Ex Typographia Polyglotta S. C. de Propaganda Fide, Romae, 1888-1906)*.

[2] ST I, 20, 2, ad. 3. All of the English translations are from *St. Thomas Aquinas Summa Theologica*, trans. Fathers of the English Dominican Province (Westminster, MD: Christian Classics, 1981).

[3] It may be countered that Augustine did recognize a good concupiscence; however, in *De civitate dei* IV, 7, he opts for a preponderance of the negative connotation over the positive. Cf. Gerald Bonner's article *"Concupiscentia"* in *Augustinus Lexikon*, ed. Cornelius Mayer (Basel: Schwabe & Co. AG, 1994) cols.

1113-1114 and his article "*Libido* and *Concupiscentia* in St. Augustine," in *Studia Patristica* VI, ed. F.L. Cross (Berlin: *Akademie Verlag*, 1962), 303-314.

[4] Even if Aquinas recognized a synonymity between *concupiscentia* and the neutral term *epithumia*, by the middle ages, the former had already been well established as a Christian technical term culled from the Latin Scriptures and as such carried a distinctly derogative connotation. Cf. Gerald Bonner's "*Concupiscentia*" in *Augustinus Lexikon*, col. 1114.

[5] This was an explanation offered by my esteemed colleague at Gwynedd-Mercy College, Dr. Edward Miller, Professor of Religious Studies, when I asked him about this passage.

[6] *Enchiridion ad laurentium sive de fide, spe et caritate* CXXI.

[7] ST I, 77, 6.

[8] Cf. Romanus Cessario, *The Moral Virtues and Theological Ethics* (Notre Dame: University of Notre Dame Press, 1991) pp. 57-58 where he admits and tries to answer the critics who "complain that such a conception of the soul, known since the eighteenth century as 'faculty psychology,' results in a fragmented impression of the human person." I admit that I am partially sympathetic to this critique and find Cessario's solution inadequate.

[9] For an admirable attempt at clarifying the obscurity of appetition, see Benedict Endres, *The Contact of Man with God: How Charity Loves God Immediately* (River Forest: The Aquinas Library, 1959), pp. 8-11.

[10] ST I-II, 22, 2.

[11] Plato, *Republic*, 440e.

[12] I admit that this is undoubtedly an Augustinian question. At times, Augustine saw little or no real distinction between the will and its love. He says as much in *De trinitate* IX, 12, identifying the principle of self love as the will's (or mind's) own lovable-ness. He also implies their identity in *De civitate dei* XIV, 7. Cf. Marianne Djuth's article "Will" in *Augustine Through the Ages: An Encyclopedia*, ed. Allan D. Fitzgerald, O.S.A. (Grand Rapids: William B. Eerdmans Publishing Company, 1999), pp. 883-884. Also cf. Gilson, *The Christian Philosophy of Saint Augustine*, trans. L.E.M. Lynch (New York: Random House, 1960), p. 162 where he says that for Augustine, "will is essentially love."

[13] Cf. Gilson, *The Christian Philosophy of St. Thomas Aquinas*, trans. L.K. Shook (Notre Dame: University of Notre Dame, 1956), p. 272: "The inadequacy of language to express the complexity of the real is nowhere more noticeable than in the analysis of the life of the soul."

[14] ST I, 80, 1.

[15] ST I-II, 35, 1. ST I-II, 25, 2, ad. 2.

[16] ST I-II, 30, 1.

[17] ST I, 76, 1, ad. 6.

[18] ST I-II, 26, 1.

[19] ST I, 19, 1.

[20] ST I, 60, 1. *Appetitus naturalis vel amor.*

[21] ST I, 80, 1, ad. 3.

22 ST I, 20, 1.

23 To be fair, the idea of an appetite as a moved-mover seems to necessitate such ambiguity. For a recent analysis of the passions that appreciates their ambiguous structure, see Elisabeth Uffenheimer-Lippens' article "Rationalized Passion and Passionate Rationality: Thomas Aquinas on the Relation Between Reason and the Passions," in *The Review of Metaphysics*, vol. 56, no. 3 (March, 2003): pp. 525-558.

24 Cf. *The Catholic Encyclopedia: An International Work of Reference on the Constitution, Doctrine, Discipline and History of the Catholic Church*, ed. Charles G. Herbermann (New York: The Encyclopedia Press, 1913), p. 656: "In the natural and the sensitive appetites there is no freedom."

25 Cf. Gilson, *The Christian Philosophy of St. Thomas Aquinas*, p. 272.

26 ST I-II, 26, 3. We can also include the terms Aquinas uses to define love, for example, *inclinatio, aptitudo, coaptatio, complacentia,* to name a few. For a more comprehensive list, cf. D.M. Gallagher, "Person and Ethics in Thomas Aquinas," *Acta Philosophica* 4, no. 1 (1995): 51-71.

27 *De civitate dei* XIV, 7: "Therefore a love which strains after the possession of the loved object is desire; and the love which possesses and enjoys that object is joy. The love that shuns what opposes it is fear, while the love that feels that opposition when it happens is grief." English translation by Henry Bettenson, *St. Augustine City of God* (London: Penguin Books, 1972), p. 557

28 In ST I-II, 31, 4 we find yet another ambiguity when Aquinas claims that joy (*gaudium*) belongs to the will, not the sensitive appetite. Yet, in I-II, 25, 4 he lists joy (*gaudium*) as one of the four principle passions.

29 Cf. Christopher J. Malloy in his article "Thomas on the Order of Love and Desire: A Development of Doctrine," *The Thomist*, vol. 71 (2007): p. 82 where he recognizes an interesting ambiguity between love and desire in Aquinas' early thought.

30 This ambiguity is linked to that which exists between *appetitus naturalis* and *amor naturalis*, which I mentioned earlier.

31 ST I-II, 26, 2.

32 ST I-II, 26, 4, ad. 3.

33 ST I-II, 26, 4.

34 Because of this potential confusion, I have included the complete Latin text here: "*Sed quantum ad vim appetitivam, amatum dicitur esse in amante, prout est per quandam complacentiam in eius affectu, ut vel delectetur in eo, aut in bonis eius, apud praesentiam; vel in absentia, per desiderium tendat in ipsum amatum per amorem concupiscentiae; vel in bona quae vult amato, per amorem amicitiae.*"

35 ST I-II, 28, 2.

36 Cf. ST II-II, 24, 1, ad. 1.

37 ST I-II, 26, 4, ad. 3.

38 David M. Gallagher seems to think so in his article "Person and Ethics in Thomas Aquinas, *Acta Philosophica*, vol. 4, no. 1 (1995): 51-71 where he argues that these two loves are really one act of the will (*dilectio*) exercised on two objects. Therefore, since love of concupiscence is an act of the rational appetite,

the term concupiscence must be employed analogously in this context. Furthermore, in the case of spiritual goods (e.g. virtue), Gallagher thinks that the love of concupiscence refers to those "qualities" that we desire for our friends, reducing the division to a metaphysical distinction between substance and quality, subject and accident.

[39] Robert O. Johann, "The Problem of Love," *The Review of Metaphysics* vol. 8, no. 2 (December, 1954): pp. 235-236. This distinction is consistent with one of Aquinas' own concerning the love of concupiscence and the love of friendship; for he calls the former "relative" love and latter "simple" love. Cf. ST I-II, 26, 4.

[40] Again, Gallagher seems to think so in "Person and Ethics in Thomas Aquinas," p. 57: "Hence, when a person loves what is not a person with a love of concupiscence, he must have a corresponding love of friendship, either for himself or for another person."

[41] Cf. ST I-II, 28, 2.

[42] Cf. Anthony W. Keaty, "Thomas' Authority for Identifying Charity with Friendship: Aristotle or John 15," *The Thomist*, vol. 62 (1998): 587-588: "It is true that Thomas's manner of distinguishing love of friendship and love of concupiscence in this first article on charity implies that disinterestedness provides the principle for the distinction: benevolence involves wishing good to another, and concupiscence involves wishing the good for ourselves. However, Thomas's discussion of friendship and concupiscence in his treatise on the passions (ST I-II, 26, 4) suggests that these two loves are not distinguished principally according to the disinterest of the love but rather in terms of their ordered relationship."

[43] ST II-II, 24, 1, ad. 1.

[44] Cf. Paul J. Wadell, *The Primacy of Love: An Introduction to the Ethics of Thomas Aquinas* (New York: Paulist Press, 1992), pp. 66-68 where he refers to this desire to help God as "Benevolence for God." Not only does he believe such a thing possible but in a way necessary by the law of reciprocity in friendship. Cf. also Christopher J. Malloy in his article "Thomas on the Order of Love and Desire: A Development of Doctrine," n. 6.

[45] Love (*amor*) is the first.

[46] ST I-II, 82, 3.

[47] "*Quod caritas amor quidam est. Amor autem ex natura potentiae cuius est actus habet quod possit supra seipsum reflecti. Quia enim voluntatis obiectum est bonum universale, quidquid sub ratione boni continetur potest cadere sub actu voluntatis; et quia ipsum velle est quoddam bonum, potest velle se velle, sicut etiam intellectus, cuius obiectum est verum, intelligit se intelligere, quia hoc etiam est quoddam verum. Sed amor etiam ex ratione propriae speciei habet quod supra se reflectatur, quia est spontaneus motus amantis in amatum; unde ex hoc ipso quod amat aliquis, amat se amare. Sed caritas non est simplex amor, sed habet rationem amicitiae, ut supra dictum est. Per amicitiam autem amatur aliquid dupliciter. Uno modo, sicut ipse amicus ad quem amicitiam habemus et cui bona volumus. Alio modo, sicut bonum quod amico volumus. Et hoc modo caritas per*

caritatem amatur, et non primo, quia caritas est illud bonum quod optamus omnibus quos ex caritate diligimus. Et eadem ratio est de beatitudine et de aliis virtutibus."
[48] ST II-II, 25, 2.
[49] *De trinitate* IX, 5.
[50] This might be the most important and fundamental statement of the three. Cf. William McDonough, "*Caritas* as the *Prae-Ambulum* of All Virtue: Eberhard Schockenhoff on the Theological-Anthropological Significance and the Contemporary Interreligious Relevance of Thomas Aquinas's Teaching on the *Virtutes Morales Infusae, Journal of the Society of Christian Ethics*, vol. 27, no. 2 (2007): p. 113.
[51] Friendship exists between the divine persons. Cf. Anthony W. Keaty, "Thomas' Authority for Identifying Charity with Friendship: Aristotle or John 15," p. 583.
[52] ST II-II, 25, 3.
[53] ST II-II, 26, 3, ad. 3.
[54] Anthony W. Keating, "Thomas' Authority for Identifying Charity with Friendship: Aristotle or John 15," 590-592.
[55] Cf. Thomas Williams, "Biblical Interpretation," *The Cambridge Companion to Augustine*, ed. Eleonore Stump and Norman Kretzmann (Cambridge: Cambridge University Press, 2001) p. 67: "Even human beings, including ourselves, should be 'used' in this sense – which does not mean exploited. But Augustine cannot quite bring himself to talk consistently of 'using' ourselves and our fellow human beings." Cf. also Hannah Arendt, *Love and Saint Augustine*, ed. Joanna Vecchiarelli Scott and Judith Chelius Stark (Chicago: The University of Chicago Press, 1996) p. 13 where she concludes that "fearless possession can be achieved only under the conditions of timelessness, equated by both Augustine and Plotinus with eternity. Thus, Augustine proceeds to strip the world and all temporal things of their value and to make them relative."
[56] *Confessiones* IV, 8.
[57] Cf. Declan Lawell, "Thomas Aquinas, Jean-Luc Marion, and an Alleged Category Mistake Involving God and Being," *American Catholic Philosophical Quarterly*, vol. 83, no. 1 (2009): pp. 35-36. Lawell seems to unwittingly admit that the division of love into *amor concupiscentiae* and *amor amicitiae* can lead to what he calls "an attitude of *techné* which manipulates the goods of the world not so much in a will to power as a will to give." Of course, Lawell accuses Marion's phenomenology of this "foul;" however, it's difficult to see how Aquinas' logic of love avoids a similar pitfall, or what one might call "an attitude of *uti*."
[58] In his article "A Postmodern Aquinas: The *Oeuvre* of Olivier-Thomas Venard, O.P.," *American Catholic Philosophical Quarterly*, vol. 83, no. 3 (2009): p. 334, David Burrell identifies in Aquinas' writing (*via* Venard) the inextricable connection between analogy, metaphor, and poetic language in expressing the impalpable nature of God.

Marsilio Ficino's Neoplatonic Ascent of the Soul in Relation to His Augustinian Notion of Friendship

Catherine Conroy de Paulo
Pennsylvania State University

Marsilio Ficino (1433-1499) has been described as one of the "most illustrious philosophers" of the Italian *quattrocento*;[1] and his influence was far reaching. According to Paul Kristeller, "all of educated Florence in the second half of the fifteenth century came under the intellectual influence of Ficino's Academy."[2] In fact, his doctrine of spiritual love, for instance, greatly influenced Bembo, Castiglione, Giordano Bruno and the like.[3] More importantly, perhaps, was his neoplatonic notion of the immortality of the soul, which was a central issue during the Fifth Lateran Council (1512-17) and substantially contributed to Council's articulation of the doctrine.[4]

In his corpus, Ficino examines the ascent of the soul to God while explaining the complex relationship of the soul and the intellect and the substantial role of Christian love in the soul's journey back to God. He explains that the soul, perpetually searching for completion, is, in fact, searching for love; and thus, seeks the Eternal through images or manifestations in the world. In this chapter, I intend to explore Marsilio Ficino's treatment of the soul with regard to the Christian neoplatonic notion of its ascent to God.

FICINO ON THE SOUL

First, I will discuss Ficino's notion of the soul with regard to its relationship to the intellect, to the will and to the body. I will discuss the duality of the soul as a major cause of restlessness, which naturally leads the soul to seek the Divine. Third, following Professor Lauster's thesis, I will consider Ficino's notion of the soul in the context of the ascent as a function of withdrawal (*purgatio*) and deification (*deificatio*),[5] emphasizing the role of contemplation and love in the ascent while exploring the connections between Ficino and Augustine on love and friendship.

As an Italian Renaissance thinker, Marsilio Ficino was focused on the importance of the individual and believed, in theory, that it is possible for man to achieve a divine-like quality on earth at least for some brief moments. However, Ficino is intimately aware that full participation, and what we might term "authentic union," with the Divine occurs only after death when the soul is finally released from the limitations of the body and the infection of the corporeal world.[6] Prior to death, man must prepare himself for his re-union with the Divine. He must begin a process rooted in contemplation and love that will permit him to ascend from the depths of temporality and vice to gaze and accept the light of the divine ray.

For Ficino, man certainly has a soul with an intellect, a will and, of course, a body. These four things relate and, in a sense, "combine" imperfectly[7] to produce a man who experiences the effects of the imperfect relations, which, in turn affects the soul's ability to ascend to the divine Will.[8] For example, Ficino believed that the soul experiences a type of blindness infected by the "contagion" of the body, it becomes distracted by the various functions required of it while it inhabits the body.[9] He states, the soul "has become many because it has fallen into the body, is distributed into various operations and pays attention to the infinite multiplicity of corporeal things. As a result, its higher parts are almost asleep; the lower parts dominate the others."[10] To rectify this, Ficino determines that the intellect (as a function of the soul) must separate from the body: "The mind will be most perfect when it has soared completely beyond this body."[11]

Ficino also determines that there must be something within the body that unites it, that moves the body but is not dependent on the body.[12] Of course, the unitive force or principle, for Ficino, is the soul. Ficino further emphasizes the importance of the soul when he proposed the placement of it in the center of his hierarchy of being; above the soul are angels and God, below it—body and quality. Due to this central position, the soul, Ficino writes, "appears to be the link that holds all nature together—it controls qualities and bodies while it joins itself with angel and with God."[13]

In addition to being the unitive principle in the body, the soul gives life to the body, as well as motion.[14] Even though the soul has a significant role in the function of the body, it was neither created exclusively for the body, nor was it created at the same time as the body, but its creation precedes the body.[15] As a good commentator of Plato, Ficino articulates the relationship between the body and the soul: "For the body is the shadow of the soul; the form of the body, as best it can, represents the form of the soul."[16]

The soul, for Ficino, also suffers from a complex duality. It is that element which can (and does) participate in both Eternity (since the soul was created by God whose end is a return to God) and in time (as being housed in the body).[17] The soul is substance, yet not corporeal.[18] It does not admit death, yet exists in a dying body.[19] It is unchanging by virtue of its relationship to the "unchangeable God," yet it desires change, namely, rid itself of its temporal multiplicity to be wholly restored to eternity.[20] Finally, the soul is rational, but "is not reason itself."[21]

As I mentioned earlier, the intellect is a faculty of the soul and enables the soul in its power of understanding.[22] In Ficino's notion of the soul we can also hear the influence of the Christian tradition, and especially St. Augustine and St. Thomas Aquinas, when he writes, that "the soul's most outstanding parts are the intellect and the will."[23] What is peculiar to Ficino's schema, however, is the way in which the intellect, body and soul act— the intelligence in Eternity, the body entirely in the temporal and the soul in both.[24] Because of this, the soul is continually defining it-self between Eternity and time and experiences a type of uneasi-ness or restlessness.[25]

This ambiguous position floating between the temporal and eternal, in part, is what motivates the soul to obtain that which would alleviate the ailment, namely reunion with the Eternal.[26] Before re-unification can occur, Ficino's neoplatonic soul must first concentrate on severing itself from the body, which is the very thing that is embittering it in the temporal.[27] To do this, the soul, while still inhabiting the body, must use the intellect to con-template the Divine and must rely on the Divine to help its as-cent.[28] With insights from Plato and Augustine, Ficino insists that the soul must turn away from the lesser distractions of the corpo-real and focus completely on the image of the Divine through contemplation, and it must use love (*eros*) to help find its own per-fection, its own unity.[29] Ficino further observes that this break with the body may be more difficult for some due to the intimate connection that the soul perceives with the body.[30] In light of this, he advises his readers, "Seek yourself beyond the world and look back on it."[31]

FICINO'S ASCENT - *PURGATIO* AND *DEIFICATIO*

In Jörg Lauster's analysis of Ficino's views on the ascent of the soul, he notes that "Ficino characterizes the ascent as *purgatio* and as *deificatio*," that is, purging "the soul from the sensible and mate-rial sphere" and deifying it "through the intelligibility and the Spirit of God."[32] This purgation is realized through the act of withdraw from the corporeal world and increasing the purifying action of contemplation, thus allowing man to concentrate upon himself, and upon knowing himself in order to attain a more per-fect knowledge of the Divine and of himself.[33] Deification occurs when the soul seeks and participates in those aspects of God mir-rored in the corporeal world, for example, love and beauty.[34]

PURGATIO

As stated earlier, Ficino contends that true happiness only can occur after the separation of the soul from the body.[35] In the *Meditations*, he reminds his dear friend, Giovanni Cavalcanti, "Every soul should withdraw from the encumbrance of the body and become centered in the mind."[36] This occurs most perfectly in the death of the body, but the soul should also begin the process of separation while still inhabiting the body through focusing on the intellect. For Ficino writes, The ray of divine truth "purges intelligences and soul with heat, separating them from lower things; it illuminates them with light."[37] Ficino cannot seem to stress enough the importance of the intellect in the soul's ascent. He states, "In feeding the mind we ought to imitate gluttons and the covetous, who always fix their attention on what is still left."[38] He firmly believes that the intellect is intimately connected with the divine intellect and that the "divine ray" moves, or perhaps more properly, guides the intellect back to the Divine.[39]

DEIFICATIO

Lauster asserts, "The cognition of God is a kind of deification."[40] Yet, it is Ficino who instructs his readers that to attempt to understand God is to limit Him within the finiteness of the human intellect. Deification, according to Ficino, occurs in the act of loving God, since Love transcends finitude. For Ficino plainly states, "What restores us to heaven is not knowledge of God but love,"[41] and "The soul becomes divine, not by considering God but by loving Him."[42] In writing to Lorenzo de' Medici, Ficino further clarifies his position: "We find more merit with God in this life by loving Him than by searching for Him ... no one in this life truly knows God. But a man truly loves God, no matter how he understands Him."[43]

Therefore, while the cognition of God is important in the fuller context of perfecting the soul, it neither allows man to begin nor to sustain the process of deification.[44] That sustenance is rooted most deeply in love and in the act of loving. Through the process of loving, say another as friend, the lover loves that which is eternal in the friend. The body, the vice, at times overcoming and moving the body, are mere shadows that attempt to detract from the love-as-ascent and beckon the soul, in a sense, to continue to participate in the corporeal world.[45] But the lover only truly loves the eternal within the friend - that is, beauty, virtue and those things that most intimately emulate or participate in the Divine.[46] This type of love, which begins, is sustained and ends in the Divine, seems to be the true mode of *deificatio*.

Like the soul inhabiting the body, human love desires completion; it desires unity and wholeness, which can only be found in the Divine.[47] Through loving and especially loving the Divine, the soul begins to find that unity with which it so deeply desires.[48] To explain this, Ficino quotes St. Augustine: "Only he never loses any beloved one, for whom all are beloved in that one who is never lost."[49] And again, "Blessed is a man once he loves with all his might that form which alone can never be truly loved enough."[50] However, because human love is incomplete or lacking perfection, it attempts to find *its* perfection in lesser temporal things, whether it be in the body (which Ficino warns as not ideal), or in the manifestations of the Divine found in the corporeal realm, as in human virtue or beauty, or another man who embodies virtue, beauty of the soul, etc.[51] When a man loves another man (that is, those aspects which mirror the Divine) with the love of God, friendship is produced. Further, when a man participates in friendship, he is finding some rest or some type of quasi-completion to the "feelings" of imperfection. This rest is due to the fact that, for Ficino, friendship is the reunification of two bodies that share the same will.[52]

Ficino, according to Kristeller, "links" his theory of Platonic love with that of friendship and *caritas*;[53] what may have begun as utilitarian, ends in loving the other "solely for the sake of God."[54] As friendship produces the light of love, the soul is attracted to the light of God as seen through this light of love, it impels him upwards, "his soul loves the light which illuminates and sets him afire."[55]

FRIENDSHIP AND *DEIFICATIO*

Contemplation is, undeniably, a central theme in Ficino's thoughts on the nature of the ascent, but as was shown, contemplation seems to only comprise one part of the ascent, namely *purgatio*. The process of *deificatio*, or deifying the soul, is rooted in and based on love—the love of God and the love of neighbor. Man is an imperfect being whose body is subject to the forces of time and resultant corruption produced by time. Ficino, in his total view of the ascent, must have realized that the attempt or process of purging the soul from the body can not be completed or even possibly begun without being situated in the larger context of love. Ficino plainly states, "Nothing is dearer to God than love. There is no surer sign of madness or of future misery than cruelty."[56] For contemplation without love—the love of God, the love of self and soul—would seem to be an empty exercise aimed at a vacant end or no end at all.[57]

Ficino describes the generation of friendship, through an analogy of friendship being a child of Faith and Love. He writes, "Grace moves Love, Love begets Faith. Faith embraces her father Love, and through the heat of this embrace, by Love gives birth to Friendship. Then Faith feeds this infant Friendship, allowing her to grow daily, and completely protecting her from destruction."[58] As such, the production of friendship is divinely sanctioned and divinely protected. Ficino writes, God "is the unbreakable bond of friendship, and our constant guardian."[59] Further he writes to his dear friend, Giovanni Cavalcanti, that it was through the "decree of God" that they were united in friendship.[60]

Ficino believes that friendship is "a kind of union" of two bodies that share the same will—a will directed towards loving God.[61] Ficino writes, "And so friendship, as it endeavors through the single aim of two men to cultivate the soul through virtue, is clearly nothing but the supreme harmony of two souls in the cultivation of God."[62] And for Ficino, these two men will enjoy a "heavenly life on earth and in heaven a life that is beyond the heavens."[63]

AUGUSTINE AND FICINO ON FRIENDSHIP

The influence of St. Augustine on Marsilio Ficino's work is unquestionable. As Paul Kristeller states, "When Ficino announces his intention of interpreting Plato's philosophy primarily in terms of the soul and of God, he is clearly following the lead of St. Augustine."[64] Yet the influence of Augustine does not end there, for early in his career, Ficino used Augustine's interpretations of Plato for his study.[65] He also, in his time, relied on the authority of Augustine in his attempts to reconcile pagan and Christian philosophy.[66] It also seems that Ficino was influenced by St. Augustine in developing his notion of friendship and love.[67] For example, Ficino in writing to Cavalcanti about friendship states, "I am filled with joy in exclaiming, with our guide St. Augustine, as I often do both secretly and openly: 'Only he never loses anyone beloved, for whom all are beloved in that which is never lost.'"[68]

One may question why it would be primarily St. Augustine and not, say, Cicero, Pythagoras or Horace that influence Ficino on his views of friendship.[69] I believe the key lies in the difference between pagan and Christian philosophy.[70] Cicero, Pythagoras and Horace all lack what Augustine discusses extensively, that is, his treatment of *caritas* especially in Christian relations. Ficino does use the ideas from pagan philosophers but, like Augustine, he places his views firmly on the foundation of the love of God and the love of neighbor.

Both Ficino and Augustine agree that friendship is divinely sanctioned, meaning given by God, maintained by God, and protected by God.[71] As such, true friendship, being of divine origin, cannot be coerced into being.[72] Further, both would concur that it is only through the grace of God that friendship exceeds the boundaries of human limitations and human vice.[73] In the case of Augustine, as Eoin Cassidy maintains, various friendships played an integral role in his conversion.[74] Likewise, Ficino believed that his friendship with Giovanni Cavalcanti would assist them "in discovering the divine."[75]

There is a common theme of a return to the Divine in Ficino and Augustine when they consider friendship.[76] As the grace of

God pours onto the union of the friends, they are naturally directed to the origin of their friendship. The friends are drawn to the source of the love, to the source of beauty found in friendship. In fact, it is necessary, according to Augustine, that a friend must love the source to be able to truly love the object.[77] Likewise, Ficino asserts, "if we love bodies, souls or angels, we shall not really be loving these things, but God in them."[78] Again, Augustine writes, "you ought not either to love yourself for your own sakes, but for the sake of the one to whom your love is most rightly directed as its end,"[79] that is, God. Hannah Arendt, the renowned Augustine scholar and phenomenologist, best summarizes Augustine's views when she states, "The lover reaches beyond the beloved to God in whom alone both his existence and his love have meaning."[80] Further, she writes, "Every beloved is only an occasion to love God." [81] Ficino, as stated earlier, most certainly agrees with this.

With respect to the unity of souls produced by friendship, that is, unifying two bodies with the same soul, Ficino writes to Cavalcanti, "the same spirit or a very similar one guides us both. God has ordained... that we should live on earth with a single will."[82] Similarly, Augustine writes, "Yet even of friends you could say they may seem to be separated in body, but they cannot be so in spirit insofar as they are friends."[83]

CONCLUSION

Ficino understands the soul was created by God, inhabits a body and is *drawn* back to God through an experience of chronic restlessness. This restlessness is due to the distractions experienced by the soul when it inhabits the body and when it is focused on various operations in the corporeal. It is caused by disunion and multiplicity, and by a desire to be loved and to love. The soul is restless, too, due to the duality it experiences while inhabiting the body, namely its relationship between the eternal and the temporal. Ficino also believes that the soul, when functioning in the corporeal realm, can begin a process of ascent through contemplation and love to prepare itself via spiritual conditioning for full exposure to the divine ray.[84] This ascent takes on two processes, namely *purgatio* and *deificatio*.

The soul on earth must purge itself of the corporeal to begin its ascent by concentrating on the intellect and the life of the mind. Ficino repeatedly states that stability and peace found in the mind; contemplation allows the intellect to focus on the Divine. However, the soul still inhabits the body in the temporal, and as such acts with in the corporeal realm. Not to negate the process of *purgatio*, Ficino allows for a condition that permits the soul to function in the temporal but still actively pursue its ultimate goal, rest in the Eternal. This condition is friendship. Ficino states, "Wise men have always thought it necessary to have God as their guide, and a man as a companion for the safe and peaceful completion of the heavenly journey."[85]

Through friendship, man is allowed to prepare the soul for the love of God and to allow the soul to develop its own love of the Divine. It begins in the world to allow the friends to ascend together, to experience human love imitating divine love. It allows the friends to quell some of the restless pains they experience through the unity of their will.

Ficino and Augustine use the same language of friendship. They both agree that it is rooted in, sanctioned, maintained and protected by the Divine. This type of friendship can exceed the boundaries of human limitations and human vice... so much so, that it is a considerable factor in allowing the soul to break away from the corporeal and focus on the Divine.[86]

In the end, we see that Ficino, following in the footsteps of his teachers, believes that contemplation is a major factor for the ascent, but we also see that Ficino places contemplation onto the foundation of love.

Notes

[1] Paul Oskar Kristeller, *Marsilio Ficino and His Work After Five Hundred Years* (Florence: Leo S. Olschki, 1987), 2. (It should be noted that henceforward this work will be referenced as: *M.F. ... After Five Hundred Years*).

[2] Paul Oskar Kristeller, *The Philosophy of Marsilio Ficino*, translated by Virginia Conant (Glouster, MA: Peter Smith, 1964), 18-19. (Henceforward, this work will be referenced as *Philosophy of M.F.*).

[3] *M.F. ... After Five Hundred Years*, 11.

[4] Professor Raffini asserts, "Ficino was one of the first in the context of Christianity to emphasize belief in the immortality of the soul, a doctrine which, curiously, had been neglected during the Middle Ages" (Christine Raffini, *Marsilio Ficino, Pietro Bembo, Baldassare Castiglione: Philosophical, Aesthetic, and Political Approaches in Renaissance Neo-Platonism,* (New York: Peter Lang, 1998), 11).

[5] Cf. Jörg Lauster, "Marsilio Ficino as a Christian Thinker: Theological Aspects of his Platonism," in *Marsilio Ficino: His Theology, His Philosophy, His Legacy,* eds. Michael J. B. Allen, Valery Rees (Leiden: Brill, 2002), 45 - 69.

[6] Ficino writes plainly, "it is only after death of the body that his greatest happiness may be achieved" (*Theologica Platonica,* I.1.1). Elsewhere, Ficino states, "There is immeasurable space in the spirit, but in the body one could say infinite constriction" (Marsilio Ficino, *Meditations on the Soul, Selected Writings of Marsilio Ficino* (Rochester, VT: Inner Traditions International, 1996), 79). Finally, on a personal note, Ficino writes that in his search for the Divine, he found "neither much delight nor rest. Yet he who discovers what he is looking for, at once rejoices and is at rest" (Marsilio Ficino, *The Letters of Marsilio Ficino* (vol. I) (London: Shepheard-Walwyn, 1975), 78).

[7] Ficino makes the distinction that the elements are joined together but not "mixed with the body, connect to but not dispersed through it" (Marsilio Ficino, *Philebus Commentary,* translated by Michael J.B. Allen (Berkeley: Uni. of California Press, 1975), 100). Furthermore, when considering the exact relationship between the body and soul, Ficino states, "When [the soul] enters a body, it is present in its entirety in the individual parts of the body. It is not divided up or separated into any parts in order to be present in the parts of the body that are distant from each other. For it is through undivided power... that it makes contact with the body" (*Theologica Platonica,* III.2.4).

[8] Collins states, "Man [Ficino] says, suffers from a chronic dissatisfaction with his life on this earth. Restless in soul, weak in body, frustrated by the poverty of all he sees, he continually yearns for something more fulfilling than anything he can find in his earthly environment" (Collins, 3).

[9] Cf. *De amore,* VI.16 and *Theologica Platonica,* VI.7 and 8, *et al.* In fact, for Ficino, "The entire structure of the world consists in multiplicity and unity, because it consists of many things which have been bound together by continuity, contiguity, similarity, equality, suitability" (*Philebus Commentary,* 88).

[10] *De amore,* VII.14. Further Ficino asks, "Since souls are divine, why do they live such unholy lives? Because they inhabit an unholy land. ... Others err through too great a love for the body" (*Meditations,* 138).

[11] *Theologia Platonica,* IX.2.3.

[12] Ficino writes, "So the soul which in truth is the body's mover does not depend on the body, as if it were the body's lackey" (*Theologia Platonica,* VI.7.2). Also, cf. *Theologica Platonica,* I.3.9 and IX.1.1.

[13] *Theologia Platonica,* I.1.2. In his *Philebus Commentary,* Ficino further contemplates the position of the soul: "The soul in turn, since it is midway

between the spirits and bodies, is accordingly endowed with a triple power. One power is that by which it is joined to higher things. Another is that by which it is extended to lower thing. The middle power is that by which it retains its middle position and its proper energy. In the soul's highest part the ray received from the divine intelligence is call the light of the human intelligence, and it raises the soul upwards to the contemplation of higher things. The ray in the middle of the soul is the ability of the reason to make judgements; it teaches civic disciplines. The ray in the soul's lowest part... supplies the skills necessary for human livelihood" (*Philebus Commentary*, 240). Also cf. *Philebus Commentary*, 100.

[14] Ficino states, the rational soul "is life that of its owns nature gives life to bodies." (*Theologica Platonica*, III.2.9). Further, "For one part of the soul doesn't move while another part is moved, but the soul is moved by itself: that is, it runs to and from and brings to completion by means of time's intervals the works of nutrition, growth and reproduction, the products of reasoning and cogitation" (*Philebus Commentary*, 100). Also cf. *Philebus Commentary*, 102; *Theologica Platonica*, I.IV.1; *De amore*, IV.3 and *Meditations*, 40.

[15] Cf. *Meditations*, 40 and *Theologia Platonica*, IX.1.1 and III.2.3.

[16] *Meditations*, 4.

[17] *De amore*, VI.16. Likewise, Ficino states, "The intelligence stays the same in essence and operation; the body changes in operation. The intelligence is completely in eternity; the body is in time; the soul is in both" (*Philebus Commentary*, 100).

[18] *Letters* (vol. 1), 148.

[19] *Theologica Platonica* V.10.3, 4.

[20] Ficino states, the soul, "being related to unchangeable God through its own unchangeable essence, it remains unchanging" (*Theologica Platonica*, V.10.5).

[21] *Letters* (vol. 1), 148.

[22] Ficino writes, "Through the intelligence, the soul always possesses the ability to understand, just as through the soul the body can move itself" (*Philebus Commentary*, 98). Furthermore, he states, "The soul is always capable of understanding only by virtue of the intellect" (*De amore*, VI.15).

[23] *Theologia Platonica*, IX.2.2

[24] *Philebus Commentary*, 100. Cf. *Letters* (vol. 3), 13. Ficino writes, "The reasonable soul is set on a horizon, that is the line dividing the eternal and temporal, because it has a nature midway between the two. Being in the middle, this nature is not only capable of rational power and action, which lead up to the eternal, but also of energies and activities that descend to the temporal. Since these divergent tendencies spring from opposing natures, we see the soul turning at one moment to the eternal and at another to the temporal and so we understand rightly that it partakes of the nature of both" (*Meditations*, 41).

[25] Cf. *De amore* VI.15. Ficino concludes, "The happiness of man therefore consists in God alone, from which it follows that nothing can rest except in its own cause. And since God alone is the real cause of the soul it rest in God alone" (*Meditations*, 128).

[26] Ficino writes: "As in nature motion is properly directed towards something, and as it stops once it has that something, it is therefore moving towards an end" (*Philebus Commentary*, 72). Also, Ficino asserts, "For if by nature the mind desires certain things, we should acquire them. And certainly, in acquiring them, the soul would at some time be fulfilled by them" (*Letters* (vol. 2), 79). Also see *Letters* (vol. 1), 166 - 167.

[27] Ficino writes, "When the soul despises corporeals and when the senses have been allayed and the clouds of phantasmata dissipated, and it perceives something on its own, then the intellect can discerns truly and is at its brightest" (*Theologia Platonica*, IX.2.2).

[28] Lauster defines this dependence on God for the ascent as *raptus*. (Lauster, 59). For example, Ficino states, "The conscious force in the brain does not equip us for divine actions" (*Meditations*, 27). And "God illuminates any intelligence directly and also one through another indirectly." (*Philebus Commentary*, 238).

[29] Ficino writes, "It is better to raise ourselves to higher things through love than to reduce them to our level by judgement" (*Meditations*, 41). Elsewhere, Ficino writes, "Happiness lies in action of will rather than the action of intellect" (*ibid.*, 125). Further, Ficino writes, "The soul cannot return to the One unless itself becomes one" (*De amore*, VII.14). Furthermore, Ficino writes, "Since it is impossible to approach the heavenly regions through the bodily strength, the soul, having acquired the power of mental discernment as guide by the gift of philosophy, transcends the nature of all things through contemplation" (*Meditations*, 81). Also, *cf. Theologica Platonica* IX.2.2 and XIV.7; *De amore* VI.9 and *Letters* (vol. 1), 162.

[30] Ficino warns, "Beauty and bodily strength often lead to deformity and weakness of the soul" (*Meditations*, 118).

[31] *Meditations*, 79.

[32] Lauster, 59.

[33] Ficino asserts, "Our body is attracted in a violent attack by the body of the world through the forces of fate... Every soul should retire from the pestilence of the body and withdraw into the mind" (As reported in Charles Trinkaus, "The Problem of Free Will in the Renaissance and Reformation," in *Renaissance Essays* edited by Paul Oskar Kristeller *et al.* (New York: Harper Torchbooks, 1968), 193). Further, Ficino states that once removed from the body, the mind will be able to observe much more and much more clearly (*Meditations*, 43-44).

[34] For example, *cf. De amore*, IV.6 and *Philebus Commentary*, 108.

[35] For example, Ficino writes, "Only after the death of the body can man become any happier" (*Theologica Platonica*, I.1.1). He also states, "Having relinquished the body, the soul directs every intention towards the intelligence" (*Philebus Commentary*, 354; see also *Philebus Commentary*, 372). And finally, "Happiness cannot be obtained without the right use of our gifts, and since knowledge reveals their proper use, we should leave all else aside and strive with full support of philosophy and religion to become as wise as possible. For thus our soul becomes most like God" (*Meditations*, 123).

[36] *Meditations*, 119.

[37] *Philebus Commentary*, 246.

[38] *Meditations*, 77. Also cf. *Theologica Platonica* XIV.8.

[39] Ficino writes, "If the human mind has such a capacity for rational ascent, though it is only a part of the universe and encumbered by the chains of the body, even more certainly the universe possesses within itself a far greater capacity for the same ascent, especially as the order of the lowest mind takes its origin from the order of the universe" (*Theologica Platonica*, I.3.11). And again, The light of God embodied as grace and beauty "also compels him to revere its splendor more than all else, as if it were a divine spirit, and, once his former nature has been cast aside [through contemplation], to strive for nothing else but to become this splendor" (*Letters*, (vol. 1), 84 - 85).

[40] Lauster, 60. Preceding this statement, Lauster asserts, "For Ficino, thinking - the activity of the human intellect - is the path via which the soul can reach God. The cognition of God is nothing else than the formation of the human intellect by the divine intellect caused through the mediation of the divine ray" (Lauster, 59). Cf. *Letters* (vol. 3), 12).

[41] *De amore*, IV.6.

[42] *Meditations*, 129.

[43] *Meditations*, 128. Ficino also notes to Lorenzo, "By cognizing God, we reduce His size to the capacity and understanding of our mind; but by loving Him we enlarge our mind to the immeasurable breadth of divine goodness" (*Meditations*, 130).

[44] Eventhough Ficino places great importance on the intellect, he also believes that unity of self and soul is important for the ascent to the Good. Ficino writes, "Now all things are preserved by unity, but perish from disunity. The good is present to everything; it preserves things because it unites them and makes them one and contains them in the one" (*Philebus Commentary*, 102). When considering the self, Ficino states, "For unless you have possession of yourself, through whom you may possess other things, you will have nothing at all." (*Letters* (vol. 3), 62). Ficino continues to state, "When man finds all things in [God], he also finds himself" (*ibid.*, 63). Finally, Ficino asserts that this unity is, in reality, a process of preparation for receiving the "grace of the divine light" (Cf. *Philebus Commentary*, 110).

[45] Since the ascent in Lauster's model contains two processes - *purgatio* and *deificatio* - participation in the corporeal, although not ideal in Ficino's view, is acceptable when considering the importance of deifying or conditioning the soul for (or even during) the ascent.

[46] Ficino asserts, "The single beauty of many bodies derives from some single incorporeal maker," that is, God (*De amore*, VI.18). In the same chapter, Ficino writes, "If we love bodies, souls or angels, we shall not really be loving these things, but God in them. In loving bodies we shall be really loving the shadow of God; in souls, the likeness of God; in angels, the image of God" (*ibid.*, VI.19). Ficino also writes, "Love... is the longing for beauty. The beauty of the body lies

not in the shadow of matter, but in the light and grace of form... We come to that light, that grace... only through thinking, seeing, and hearing" (*Meditations*, 173).

[47] *De amore*, I. 4 and *Letters* (vol. 1), 91. Ficino writes, love "is born from the Good and returns to the Good" (*ibid.*, II.2).

[48] Ficino writes, "The more ardently a man loves, the happier he becomes in that he approaches the very substance of happiness itself" (*Meditations*, 130).

[49] *Letters* (vol. 3), 53.

[50] *Letters* (vol. 2), 29.

[51] Ficino asserts, "if we love bodies, souls or angels, we shall not really be loving these things, but God in them. In loving bodies we shall be really loving the shadow of God; in souls, the likeness of God; in angels, the image of God" (*De amore*, VI.19).

[52] Ficino, speaking of his friendship with Giovanni Cavalcanti, writes, "and the same spirit or a very similar one guides us both. God has ordained... that we should live on earth with a single will" (*Letters* (vol. 1), 89).

[53] M.F. ... *After Five Hundred Years*, 10-11.

[54] *Eight Philosophers*, 47-8. Ficino asserts, "if we love bodies, souls or angels, we shall not really be loving these things, but God in them. In loving bodies we shall be really loving the shadow of God; in souls, the likeness of God; in angels, the image of God" (*De amore*, VI.19). Cf. M.F. ... *after Five Hundred Years*, 10 - 11 and *Philosophy of M.F.*, 268.

[55] Ficino writes, "the soul catches fire with burning love only when it has found some attractive image of a beautiful thing and is incited by that foretaste to full possession of that beauty" (*De amore*, VI.2).

[56] *Meditations*, 26.

[57] Ficino writes, "So the action of the intelligence is directed to some end. For in so far as it understands, its end is the truth; in so far as it will, its end is the good; in so far as it acts, its end is beautiful" (*Philebus Commentary*, 78). Furthermore, he writes, "...the intelligence enjoys by understanding and by loving" (*ibid.*, 112). And finally, "It is plain that the mind is eternal and not devoted to death, because its true food is eternal" (*Meditations*, 49).

[58] *Meditations*, 176.

[59] *Meditations*, 178. Ficino candidly states, "...God [is] the author of friendship" (*Letters* (vol. 3), 52). Ficino also writes, "For a true and abiding union of many cannot be accomplished except through the eternal unity itself" (*ibid.*, 67). And further, "Between religious people there is not true friendship except that which true religion has formed" (*Letters* (vol. 2), 36).

[60] *Letters* (vol. 2), 11. In the same letter, Ficino writes, "There cannot be the two friends on their own, but there must always be three, the two men and God" (*ibid.*).

[61] *Letters* (vol. 3), 65. Cf. *ibid.*, 66.

[62] *Meditations*, 178. Ficino also writes, Minds which are dedicated to God before all other things "are straightway drawn by ardour and sweetness of love beyond

telling, towards both God and each other, as they first freely give themselves back to Him, as to a father and then give themselves up in utter joy to each other, as to brothers" (*Letters* (vol. 3), 67).

[63] *Letters* (vol. 3), 67.

[64] See Paul Oskar Kristeller, *The Classics and Renaissance Thought*, (Cambridge, MA: Harvard University Press, 1955), 85.

[65] When discussing the influences on Ficino, Professor Levi asserts that Ficino "relied partly on the Plotinian interpretation of Plato in Augustine, and partly on Neoplatonist elements derived from elsewhere" (Anthony Levi, "Ficino, Augustine and the Pagans," in *Marsilio Ficino: his Theology, His Philosophy, His Legacy*, edited by Maichael J.B. Allen and Valery Rees (Leiden: Brill, 2002), 99). Furthermore, Professor Allen states, "For the path of the Renaissance Platonist was always to be Augustine's and Ficino had no interest in reviving ancient Platonism for is own sake… Augustine had used the Platonists but only as stepping stones" (Michael J.B. Allen, "Marsilio Ficino on Plato, the Neoplatonists and the Christian Doctrine of the Trinity" in *Plato's Third Eye: Studies in Marsilio Ficino's Metaphysics and its Sources*, edited by Michael J.B. Allen (Aldershot, Hampshire: Variorum, 1995), 582 - 583).

[66] Kristeller states, "Augustine's repeated assertion that Platonism is closer to Christian doctrine than any other pagan philosophy went a long way to justify later attempts to combine or reconcile them with each other" (*Classics and Ren. Thought*, 55). Further, Levi asserts, Ficino "eagerly sheltered under the unassailable authority of Augustine, particularly the early Augustine, and found ingenious ways of reaffirming a pre-Christian historical tradition which allowed him to envisage the authenticity of pagan virtue" (Levi, 113).

[67] It should be noted that for my investigation into Augustine's notion of friendship I heavily relied on Marie Aquinas McNamara's book, *Friends and Friendship for Saint Augustine* (Staten Island, NY: Alba House, 1964), especially pp. 213- 238; and Carolinne White's book, *Christian Friendship in the Fourth Century* (Cambridge: Cambridge University Press, 1992).

[68] *Letters* (vol. 2), 11. Cf. *Confessions* IV, cap. IX and *Letters* (vol. 2), 28.

[69] For a discussion of the Classical references in the thought of St. Augustine on friendship, see White, 18ff and 187ff.

[70] Kristeller asserts, "Augustine is Ficino's guide and model in his attempt to reconcile Platonism and Christianity. … His emphasis on the relation between the Soul and God is also due to Augustinian inspiration" (*Philosophy of M.F.*, 15). Further, Joseph Milne writes, "What is new with Ficino is his philosophical understanding of the nature of love as the active creative principle…" (Joseph Milne, "Ficino on the Nature of Love and the Beautiful" in *Friend to Mankind, Marsilio Ficino (1433 - 1499)*, edited by Michael Shepherd (London: Shepheard-Walwyn, 1999), 79).

[71] McNamara, 215. Cf. *Confessions* IV.4 and *Contra duas epis. Pelag.* I.1 (as reported in McNamara, 284). Also cf. *Meditations*, 178; *Letters* (vol. 2), 11; *Letters* (vol. 3), 52 and 67.

[72] Cf. *Epistles 155* (as reported in White, 199) and *Meditations*, 175.

[73] McNamara, 215-16.

[74] Eoin Cassidy, "The Recovery of the Classical Idea of Friendship in Augustine's portrayal of *Caritas*" in *The Relationship between Neoplatonism and Christianity*, edited by Thomas Finan and Vincent Twomey ((Kill Lane, Blackrock, Co., Dublin): Four Courts Press, 1992), 132.

[75] *Meditations*, 178.

[76] Cf. *Tractates on the Gospel of John* 77.4 and *Letters* (vol. 3), 67.

[77] Cf. Sermon 336.2.2 "He truly loves his friend if he loves God in his friend, either because God is in him or so that God may be in him" (as reported in White, 201-202).

[78] *De amore*, VI.19.

[79] *De doctrina christiana*, I.22.21. Cf. *Confessions*, X, 29 and *City of God*, XIX.8.

[80] Hannah Arendt, *Love and Saint Augustine* edited by Johanna Vecchiarelli Scott and Judith Chelius Stark, (Chicago: University of Chicago Press, 1996), 96.

[81] Hannah Arendt, *Love and Saint Augustine* edited by Johanna Vecchiarelli Scott and Judith Chelius Stark, (Chicago: University of Chicago Press, 1996), 96.

[82] *Letters*, (vol. 1), 89. Cf. *Meditations*, 174.

[83] *De trinitate*, IX.6.

[84] Ficino writes, Those that want to reach the truth "must prepare themselves especially by purity of soul for the flowing in of the divine splendour" *(Philebus Commentary*, 246-8).

[85] *Meditations*, 178.

[86] McNamara, 215-16.

Francisco Gómez de Quevedo y Villegas: How Laughter Replaces *Eros* in *"Apolo siguiendo a Dafne."*

Luis Gomez
La Salle University

The preponderance of literary criticism concerning the works of Quevedo has always considered him to be, at least, misanthropic. In addition, many have focused on his apparent misogynist streak. Therefore, it seems unusual to want to include him in a collection of essays dealing with the subject of love. At the same time, few would argue that Quevedo has to his credit perhaps the greatest love sonnet ever written in Spanish: *"Amor constante más allá de la muerte."* Roque Esteban Scarpa, in his *Antología poética: Francisco de Quevedo* writes: "Time has not been benevolent and just with don Francisco; his fame—that common 'murmur' of the world—has only gathered on to itself his titillating and less challenging youthful works, leaving in the shadows the deepest thoughts of his thinking."[1] Scarpa's observations are also echoed by Pablo Jauralde Pou: "His contemporaries did not know, in an effort to point out the scandalous nature of his writings, that Quevedo was a passionate love poet."[2] Consequently, at a dynamic level, Quevedo's literary output (particularly his poetry) is a lengthy manifestation of a shifting and ambiguous view of love. On the one hand, his love poems are intensely amorous, following a neoplatonic tradition. On the other hand, his satirical/burlesque poetry has no time for neoplatonic contemplations. However, it is essential to keep in mind that Quevedo, who considered himself a humanist and inheritor of the Greco-Roman traditions in literature, as practiced by Petrarch, Garcilaso de la Vega, Herrera, Marino, the Argensola brothers, etc., particularly in their use of mythology for love poems, does not hesitate to leave his *imprimatur* by inserting linguistic devices of his own creation and that are intrinsic to his so-called "conceit"style. This results in a different perspective concerning Ovid's myths and Virgilian pastoral and epic constructions.[3]

Additionally, the presence of neoplatonic coordinates in Quevedo's love poems is hardly debatable – notwithstanding Otis Green's insistence on courtly love as the principal source of referential poetics in Quevedo's love poetry.[4] José María Pozuelo Yvancos clearly demonstrates the all-permeating presence of neoplatonic coordinates in Quevedo's love poetry (1976, 548-568). Equally clear is Quevedo's inheritance from Baldesar Castiglione through his *Courtier* (translated and published in 1534 by the great Renaissance Spanish poet Juan Boscán and clearly well known by Quevedo), Pietro Bembo's *Prose e Rime*, León Hebreo's *Diálogos de amor*, and Ibn Hazm de Cordoba's *El collar de la paloma*. All of these highly influential poets/writers were practitioners/theorists of the neoplatonic conceptions of love. That is, neoplatonism devoid of any connection to the carnal.

It is appropriate, at this junction, to construct a working definition of the term "ambiguity" as it will be used in this study. To achieve that objective, it is also useful to reference the work by William Empson: *Seven Types of Ambiguity*. Since it is difficult to argue that Quevedo is, perhaps, the highest example of conceit language stylistics in Spanish letters, I will limit my analysis to a particular sonnet classified within Quevedo's "satirical/burlesque" poetry ("*A Apolo siguiendo a Dafne*"). In general, I will be dealing with the first, second and third types of ambiguities as defined by Empson. These types of ambiguities are delineated by Empson as follows: First Type Ambiguity: "[…] First type ambiguities arise when a detail is effective in several ways at once, e.g., by comparison with several points of likeness, antitheses with several points of difference, 'comparative' adjectives, subdue

metaphors, and extra meanings suggested by rhythm (1956, V)."
Second Type Ambiguity: "In second type ambiguities two or more
alternative meanings are fully resolved into one (1956, V)." Third
Type Ambiguity occurs when: "...two apparently unconnected
meanings are given simultaneously...and where there is a reference to more than one universe of discourse; allegory, mutual
comparison, and pastoral (1956, V)."

Clearly, all three types of ambiguities selected for study within
Quevedo's poem are related to linguistic/conceptual manipulation. When studying Quevedo, it is nearly impossible to ignore his
most salient attribute: his linguistic creativity. That creativity is
particularly evident in his satirical, burlesque and festive production, whether in prose or verse.

Ignacio Arrellano Ayuso, in examining the wittiness and
sharpness (i.e., his "*conceptismo*") of Quevedo's satirical/burlesque
poetry, is concerned with the comprehension issues that a modern
reader may encounter with texts written by Quevedo and, in particular, with those of a satirical/burlesque nature.[5] Thus, Arrellano-Ayuso provides ample text characteristics that such a reader
must take under consideration in his/her approach to Quevedo's
writings (1998, 9). In the first instance, claims Arrellano-Ayuso,
Quevedo's texts are intentionally difficult. Difficulty is an artistic
objective in Quevedo. Secondly, the intelligibility of the text is
highly dependent on the "sharpness" (linguistically and culturally) of the reader to avoid absurd or irrational interpretations or
conclusions (1998, 10).

In Quevedo's "A *Apolo siguiendo a Dafne*,"[6] we are able to
clearly experience many examples of the ambiguities which interest us:

> *Bermejazo Platero de las cumbres*
> *A cuya luz se espulga la canalla,*
> *La ninfa Dafne, que se afufa y calla,*
> *Si la quieres gozar, paga y no alumbres.*
>   *Si quieres ahorrar de pesadumbres,*
> *Ojo del cielo, trata de compralla:*
> *en confites gastó Marte la malla,*
> *y la espada en pasteles y en azumbres.*
>   *Volvióese en bolsa Júpiter severo;*
> *levantóse las faldas la doncella*
> *por recogerle en lluvia de dinero.*

Astucia fue de alguna dueña estrella,
Que de estrella sin dueña no lo infiero:
Febo, pues eres sol, sírvete de ella. (213)

The mythological allusion is to the story of "Daphne and Apollo" found in Ovid's *Metamorphoses*,[7] Book One. Ovid narrates how Daphne flees from Apollo's attempts to possess her (after Apollo had been wounded by Cupid's "sharp-tipped" arrow)[8] and, when finally caught, she asked her father to transform her into a laurel tree rather than to succumb to Apollo's sexual advances. In this mythological tale, Daphne is clearly a figure who rejects her suitor(s), as she has also been pierced by Cupid's "blunt tipped" arrow that causes the daughter of Peneus to flee from the very word "lover," and to pursue a life similar to Diana: in the woods and isolated from all men.[9] Thus, Ovid tells us: (referring to Daphne): "Many a suitor wooed her but, turning away from their entreaties, she roamed the pathless woods, knowing nothing of men, and caring nothing for them, heedless of what marriage or love or wedded life might be (1968, 41)."

Quevedo goes well beyond the Apollo-Daphne myth and includes in this sonnet similar mythological "illicit love" stories that he will demystify, or "degrade," so to speak. These stories are: 1) In the second stanza of the sonnet the illicit love presented deals with the story of Venus and Mars, as told by Leuconoe (one of Minyas' daughters and storytellers in Book IV) in the *Metamorphoses*.[10] It is the story of the clandestine affair of Venus and Mars. Vulcan, Venus' husband, upon learning of the affair (from Apollo), lays a trap by forging invisible bronze chains and snares and uses them to set a trap for the lovers. Consequently, Mars and Venus are "caught in the act," for the entire Pantheon to see and ridicule. 2) In the third stanza, Quevedo addresses one of the "illicit" love affairs of Jupiter. In this case, it is the story of how Jupiter turned into a "golden" shower to impregnate Danae and thus become the father of Perseus.

There is clearly a connection among all three myths presented in this sonnet.[11] That connection is the "illegitimacy" of the relationships selected. In the case of Venus and Mars it is adultery. In the case of Apollo and Jupiter, "attempted rape" and a form of "rape," respectively, and all three stories are driven by lust. Saint

Augustine had directly addressed sexual lust in his *De civitate Dei:* "Sexual lust is not the sin of beautiful and pleasant bodies but of souls wickedly loving bodily pleasures to the neglect of moderation, which makes us fit for things that are spiritually more beautiful and pleasant (2005, 356)." Augustine's view of lust reaches Quevedo through a long literary history as well. It was central to the work by Fernando de Rojas en *La Celestina,* at the very start of the Spanish Renaissance. Previously, it had also been addressed by Juan Ruiz, Archpriest of Hita, in his *Libro de buen amor.* Further, St. Thomas Aquinas had also addressed this subject in his *De malo:* "Sexual lust indeed chiefly signifies a disorder by reason of excess regarding desires for sexual pleasures (2003, q. XV, "On Sexual Lust"). In addition, St. Thomas Aquinas maintains in his *Summa Theologiae* that our patterns of behavior as persons, and thus our tendencies, do not take place in a vacuum. They are molded by *"habitus,"* the sum of all past and repeated experiences/behaviors. Thus, Aquinas defines "sin" as: "nothing else than to neglect eternal things, and to seek after temporal things (1981, 71)."[12]

In this sonnet, Quevedo completely degrades the classical image of these gods.[13] The degradation/demystification is achieved at various levels: (1) linguistically; (2) philosophically and (3) thematically. For the reader to understand, it is essential that he/she be acquainted with the specific mythological events referenced by the poem. The antithesis that is linguistically achieved, in contrast with the mythological tale, is sharp and immediate. Let us take the first verse: *"Bermejazo Platero de las cumbres."* The initial images to be kept in mind are classical Greco-Roman images: Apollo, the sun, brilliant, shining as his carriage goes across the firmament, blinding light, masculine beauty, the envy of other gods, the irresistible lover of women (mortal and immortal),[14] etc. The poem reduces, linguistically, all images having to do with the splendor and brilliance of Apollo to two words: *"Bermejazo Platero."* *Bermejazo* alludes to the color red. However, it is also the color of a drunk's face when he is inebriated or when drunkenness has become a *"habitus."* Further, as indicated by Arrellano Ayuso, in western tradition, the redhead is archetypical of evil as it is associated with Judas (2003, 427). These observations are further supported by J.E. Gillet (1925, 316-41) and F. González Ollé (1981,

153-163). On the other hand, *"platero de las cumbres"* also refers to the Sun that with its light turns the peaks of mountains golden. At the same time, *"platero"* is the artisan who, among other things, gold-plates lesser metals. As we will shortly see, Apollo will have to become Daphne's *"platero"* ("covering" her with gold) – if he has any hope of satisfying his sexual desires.

By using the augmentative[15] form of the adjective *"Bermejo (bermejazo),"* Quevedo further reinforces the image of a scarlet color drunk or evilness that is the antithesis of the classical description of Apollo: "Apollo was depicted as a god of extreme beauty and great stature, especially distinguished for his long curling, black hair with tinges of blue, like the petals of a viola (Grimal, 1996, 48)." The splendor of Apollo is then reduced to an adjective that has a very ambiguous semantic and semiotic nature. It is a form of red, but it is also part of the criminal underworld dialectology that connects this image of Apollo with the lowest social strata. Later we will see that the linguistic use of the criminal underworld dialectology is also used by Quevedo to deconstruct other gods in the poem. In essence, Quevedo achieves, in one adjective, ambiguities of the First and Second Types as delineated by Empson.

The use of color in Quevedo's poetry has been studied by José M. Pozuelo Yvancos. The critic concludes, generally, that there is a propensity in Quevedo for the use of black and red: "Next to the color black, red is the preferred color for Quevedo. D. Alonso reviewed colors and shades in several of Quevedo's poems and determined that indeed red was his preferred color."[16] Pozuelo Yvancos further found that while Quevedo's color range is limited, he utilizes many hues and variations of the color red (1980, 438). The use of *"Bermejazo"* is clearly and example of this variation in the use of red by Quevedo. Equally, Quevedo's insistence on word-parody is clear in this use of a variation of red. In his review of Quevedo's idiomatic parody, Emilio Alarcos García points out that it is intrinsic to Quevedo's technique for word-parody to substitute part of a word – that is correctly or incorrectly broken-down – by another word that imposes itself as a result of what it is being said or as a result of the situation that it is presented (2007, 1). Therefore, it becomes clear to the reader that *"Bermejazo"* (a corruption of a type of red, made more intense by the use of the augmentative ending) functions in a great variety of lexical universes with a multiplicity of purposes: (1) as a myth degradation; (2) as a word parody and (3) as a deconstructing[17] neologism adapted to the "theme" of the poem.

The second verse ("*A cuya luz se espulga la canalla,*") goes to further degrade the splendor of Apollo as signified by his role as the Sun. This Sun is neither the "giver of life" nor the "vanquisher of darkness," the traditional metaphoric usage. His purpose is to "light the day" so that the mob, the rabble, the riffraff may delouse each other.[18] Consequently, while Apollo is, indeed, the source of light as the Sun, there is more than one universe of discourse in play and a Third Type of Ambiguity is achieved by Quevedo.

The third verse: "*La ninfa Dafne, que se afufa y calla*" shifts the focus from Apollo to Daphne. From a mythological perspective, Daphne's behavior is reminiscent of "*la dame sans merci*" of courtly love. In Ovid's narration, Daphne is clearly a "victim," choosing to undergo metamorphosis (into a laurel tree) rather than submit to Apollo's sexual intentions – although both are not acting from the perspective of freewill but as a result of Cupid's volition and his arrows. At some level, the mythological Daphne has renounced "*amor ferino,*" lacking all interest in carnal matters. She values her freedom and solitude while roaming the woods – a condition that pre-dates Cupid's interference. In many ways, she is a heroic figure. However, Quevedo's verb selection in this verse eliminates all heroic and grandiose qualities from Daphne: "*Se afufa*" is the reflexive form of the verb: to run away noisily dragging skirts.[19] The choice of the verb "afufar" is extremely significant as it is also part of the criminal underworld dialectology, and at a linguistic level degrades the subject to whom it is directed. Arrellano Ayuso also comments on the double meaning of *ninfa* in his analysis of the third verse of the sonnet: "*ninfa: doble sentido, 'ser mitológico' y prostituta tributaria de un rufián...degradación del mito mediante el uso de la lengua de germanía* (2003, 428).[20] In other words, Daphne is degraded to the role of a prostitute miffed and hastily running away. However, while the mythological Daphne ran away from Apollo to preserve her virginal status and to affirm her desire to be left free of men, Quevedo's Daphne runs away miffed because there is no payment for sexual favors forthcoming from Apollo (other than "his light") and, in essence, she takes her business elsewhere. Naturally, Apollo's association with this degraded Daphne accords an equal degradation to him. It is noteworthy to point out that in Quevedo, even when deconstructing and degrading classical themes, the reader never feels any sense of sadness, depression, resentment or rejection in relation to the degraded icons. As Jauralde Pou has already observed, in Quevedo there is always a sole obsession in his festive and burlesque works; one that insists in an attitude perceived by the reader as lighthearted as a smile (2007, 11).

There is a significant departure in the fourth verse of the first stanza that resurfaces again in the second verse of the second stanza. The poet, previously a spectator, becomes an active participant and speaks directly to Apollo, to give him his solution or counsel regarding how to conquer Daphne. Clearly, now that Daphne has been rendered into a common prostitute by the preceding degradation, the only solution left is for Apollo to pay for her sexual favors, and the poet speaks directly to Apollo:

> Si la quieres gozar, paga y no alumbres.
>   Si quieres ahorrar de pesadumbres,
> Ojo del cielo, trata de compralla:
> en confites gastó Marte la malla,
> y la espada en pasteles y en azumbres.

As always, Quevedo chooses his lexicon carefully – while paying particular attention to the potential multiple meanings of words as one of the principal manifestations of his conceit style. With that objective in mind, he uses the verb "*gozar.*" This verb, when used in a non-sexual context, is synonymous with "enjoying," as in: "enjoying a person's company." However, when used within a sexual context, the verb is a vulgarism that implies the "taking of a woman's sexual favors for personal self-pleasure only."[21] It further has the connotation of "using" a woman for personal sexual gratification. Thus, the poet admonishes Apollo and lets him know that if he wants to "use" Daphne for his sexual enjoyment, he simply should attempt to "buy" her. Once again, Quevedo reinforces the prostitute label already placed on Daphne. This concept is found again in the second verse of the second stanza, as Quevedo emphasizes the "exchange" of money for sex. Simultaneously, the poet also continues the degradation of Apollo. A furthering of the degradation is achieved by a subtle comparison between Apollo's "light" (as the Sun) and the power of money to achieve the god's sexual desires. The end result is a reduction of Apollo's "light" to the level of importance of the light derived from a candle. Quevedo stays away from verbs and adjectives that are associated with the strength of the Sun's light: *"brillante, deslumbradora, resplandeciente, etc."*[22] Instead, Quevedo selects a verb that may be interpreted as the "standard" form of "to light" or as a verb that is commonly associated with candles and other domestic light sources at the time, thus his choice of the verb *"alumbrar"* could also be interpreted as a degradation of Apollo as the Sun – reduced to emitting the insignificant light of a candle or other similar object for providing light for daily use.

The rest of the second stanza presents the second illicit mythological love affair. It references the Mars-Venus liaison[23] that, from a mythological perspective, was driven by mutual lust among the protagonists. However, in this case, Quevedo portrays Mars as the suitor-lover, and degrades him by suggesting that his "conquest" of Venus was a result of giving her presents. Neither Cupid nor wooing technique is involved in Mars' conquest. Therefore, we are now able to ascertain a second and third common element among the mythological stories alluded. In addition to the "illicit" nature of the two stories, the following are also common elements: 1) Money or its equivalent (presents) are the key to achieving sexual favors and not the amorous skills of the lover nor the capricious interference of Cupid. 2) Since the Nymph and goddess are bought with either money or presents, they are both prostitutes—as only prostitutes are expected to be paid for sexual favors delivered to their clients, and said sexual favors are not commonly possible without the required payment.

Mars does not escape degradation in Quevedo's poetic treatment of this mythological love affair. The image presented by Quevedo ridicules Mars who, otherwise, would be considered fearsome as the god of war and the epitome of manliness as a potential lover (perhaps not "refined" but certainly "virile"). The metaphoric suggestion is that Mars either sold or, worst yet, pawned his armor and sword (clearly determining symbols for the god of war) to "buy" Venus presents of the "lowest" order: pastries, make-up, alcoholic beverages, and not presents of a "high" order: jewelry, perfume, silk and exotic fabrics, etc. The First and Third Type of ambiguities, as delineated by Empson, are achieved in relation to both Venus and Mars as antitheses of the myth supplanted by the degradation of the protagonists – while keeping the story line within recognizable distance of the original.

Immediately upon the conclusion of the second stanza, Quevedo reaches for yet another mythological story. In this case, it is Jupiter's metamorphosis into a "golden/gold" shower to be able sexually to posses Danae. Once again, the issue of "money to buy sexual favors" resurfaces, and the image of the female protagonist is transformed into one of prostitution. To achieve the latter, as Arrellano Ayuso has alluded (2003, 430), Quevedo chooses a verb that has alternative meanings that are resolved into one (Second Type of Ambiguity). The reader is forced to imagine the scene (there is a great deal of theatricality in this stanza): Jupiter transformed into a shower of golden rains upon Danae who, in turn, lifts her skirt to form a bucket-like object to catch as much of the raining gold as possible. However, the verbs selected and the additio0nal syntactical elements conspire to make an alternative interpretation more likely to be correct. The verb *"levantar"*[24] – in its reflexive form/Preterit: *levantóse* – not only serves to describe the means that Danae used to "catch as much gold as possible," it also serves to describe the actions that Danae would undertake if she were sexually welcoming Jupiter. This latter "purpose" is clearly reinforced in the following verse (4th verse of the second stanza): *"por recogerle en lluvia de dinero."* According to the *Collins' Dictionary: Español-Inglés/ English Spanish* the transitive verb *"recoger"* has many meanings: "To gather together, to pick up, to collect, to take in, to tidy up, to put away, to draw in, to fetch a person or thing, to include or contain within, to take into account, to reap as a result of, (reflex.) to withdraw, etc." Quevedo attaches the indirect object pronoun: *le* to the verb *"recoger."* The indirect object pronoun serves to indicate "for whom" or "to whom" the action of the verb is directed. The indirect object pronoun *le* may only be applicable to Jupiter, as the *"lluvia de dinero"*[25] functions as a direct object in the verse. Therefore, the reader arrives at the conclusion that there is simultaneity of purpose when Danae "lifts her skirt." There is a complete symbiotic relationship between the gathering of the raining gold and the granting of sexual access to Jupiter from Danae – these two purposes are inseparable and indistinguishable one from the other. We are again in plain view of a Second Type of Ambiguity. The transformation of Danae into another version of a prostitute is achieved, and the *modus operandi* is money once again.

The degradation of Jupiter is more subtle than the degradation of Apollo and Mars in the poem. First, the reader has to keep in mind that Jupiter is "first" among all the gods of the Roman Pantheon. As it is the case with Apollo, Jupiter (and, naturally, in his Greek persona as Zeus) has a long mythological history of "extramarital" love-affairs with, among others: Semele, Callisto, Leto, Elara, etc. (Grimal, 1996, 192-93 and 244-450). As was the case with Apollo, Jupiter/Zeus was not always successful in his conquests. For example, he was spurned by Thetis. While Jupiter/Zeus had used deceit in his mythological conquests, he did not resort to the pure buying of sexual favors from his amorous targets. In the Roman pantheon, Jupiter was considered the god of the sky, of daylight (as the father of Apollo) and of the weather – particularly of thunder and lightning, which he produced (Grimal, 1996, 244). The metamorphosis that Quevedo suggests in the poem requires that the reader also be aware of the mythological metamorphosis associated with Jupiter/Zeus's Danae and how she was "seduced." As controller of the weather, Jupiter had turned into a golden shower to seduce/posses Danae. In Quevedo's poem, the concept of "golden" to indicate the relative color of the mythological metamorphosis into rain becomes "gold." Since gold can only come from one's pocket or, in this poem, from one's money pouch, the gold does not "rain" from the skies; instead, it rains from Jupiter's money pouch. The simile is thus with a "common" purchaser of a prostitute's sexual favors. This brings Jupiter's divinity down to earth in a hurry!

The final stanza introduces the *dueña*, generally and in theory an older woman who served to accompany ladies so as to inspire respect from the opposite sex. Arrellano-Ayuso has already pointed out that *dueñas* were generally considered, among other things, perverse social manifestations (1998, 48). Quevedo's attacks on this social entity were implacable.[26] His "counsel" to Apollo to avail himself of a *dueña* further degrades the mythical figure. Quevedo uses the Second Type of Ambiguity by introducing the parallel: *dueña-estrella*, where the meaning is resolved into one of equivalence between the two terms. On one hand, *estrellas* (stars) have frequently been qualified as "go-between" as a result of the effect that the stars have on potential lovers, prompting the lovers into the affair. On the other hand, *dueñas* also performed "go-between" duties that, equally, facilitated the consummation of love-affairs. In the stanza, not even the stars could expect to be successful in love affairs without retaining a *dueña*. Apollo, as the god of the firmament, certainly had "ownership" of the stars; however, he also needs a *dueña* to conquer his own stars (representation of the ladies "guarded" by the *dueñas*). A further degradation of Apollo occurs when Quevedo assigns to Apollo the need for a *dueña* as a means of conquering Daphne.

Clearly, the figure and function of Cupid in this sonnet is only present in its allusion to the original mythical story narrated by Ovid. Cupid's arrows are substituted by a new, and more effective, type of arrow: money. In the world of the poem, there is only one motivator that functions in terms of sex. The cleverness, beauty and power of the mythological pantheon have been replaced by a degraded reality where there is no place for the refined, clever and persistent suitor that strives to conquer the loved one through his skills as a lover. The loved one has been transformed into a simple prostitute that is responsive to only "payment for services." Cupid, even in his capricious manifestations, has been exiled by Quevedo. What remains are but grotesque shadows, marionettes whose strings can only be moved if money is paid. Yet, the images created in this degraded world are not repulsive and carry a certain amount of sympathy conferred by the humorous manipulation of conceit language and linguistic ambiguities which we have attempted to show.

Notes

[1] The Spanish text reads as follows: "*El tiempo no ha sido benévolo y justo con don Francisco de Quevedo; para su fama—ese rumor común del mundo—ha recogido sólo la chispeante y desfatigosa nota juvenil de su obra, dejando en sombra y olvido lo más denso y humano de su pensamiento* (Scarpa, 2007, 12)." All translations of citations used in this study are mine.

[2] The Spanish text reads as follows: "*...No supieron sus contemporáneos, por señalar lo más escandaloso, que Quevedo fue un apasionado poeta amoroso*" (2007, 1).

[3] See Schwartz-Lerner, 2003, 369-70.

[4] See *El amor cortés en Quevedo*.

[5] Lía Schwarts Lerner correctly underscores that all satire establishes a dialectological relationship with its historical and social-cultural context. Very often, the reader who is familiar with Greco-Latin literary tradition quickly recognizes the dialogue that each text undertakes with its predecessor in the genre. Consequently, those literary critics that have been interested in satire (for example: Gilbert Highet in The Anatomy of Satire), have come to the conclusion that all satire is, basically, referential; it is not autonomous in the same way that a lyrical poem may be. The satirical "I" is often a thinly veiled mask that an author assumes to criticize the defects of the world and his/her society of the time (1978, 27-28).

[6] All quotes/references of Quevedo's poetic production are taken from Luis Astrana Marín's edition: *Don Francisco de Quevedo Villegas: obras en verso*. See List of Works Cited. All of Quevedo's poetic output is found in vol. 2. Quotes will be given by indicating the page number only.

[7] For more details concerning Daphne's metamorphoses and Apollo's pursuit, see *The Metamorphoses of Ovid*: 41-43. All references from Ovid are made from this edition (as shown in the List of Works Cited) and identified by the page number. In addition, for a concise summary of the myth, see Pierre Grimal, *The Dictionary of Classical Mythology*:128. (See List of Works Cited for bibliographical details).

[8] The only role played directly by Cupid in the poem takes place within the original mythological tale, and it is a "given" that the reader is expected to know this. Ovid narrates how Cupid is miffed with Apollo on two counts: (1) for not seeking his approval for his amorous adventures and, more importantly, (2) for his usurpation of the symbols of the bow and arrow so closely associated with Cupid's activities. Consequently, his mischief is put to work and he "hits" Apollo with a love arrow that renders him totally infatuated with Daphne. To complete his "mischief," Cupid then strikes Daphne with an "anti-love" arrow that makes her reject any and all potential suitors. Apollo is then "unable" to do anything other than to pursue Daphne to fulfill his desire, and she is left with the task of fleeing from him. Her rejection of all men, and particularly her rejection of Apollo, once "cornered," leads her to ask her father to metamorphose her into the Laurel tree to avoid being possessed by Apollo. Even then, Apollo continues to desire her and strokes the metamorphosed laurel as he laments his unfulfilled carnal love.

[9] All noteworthy Baroque writers in Spain had at their disposal a repertoire of classical texts and fragments that would be used to weave new figures, concepts and metaphors. These new concepts, figures and metaphors were achieved by an ingenious re-assembly of the original classical author's text so that a dual purpose was achieved: (1) It was clear that the new author had read the classical writer and (2) that his creativity was visible as a result of the stylistic "degrees of separation" achieved through his rhetorical skills: *disposito, elecutio and invention*. (Schwartz-Lerner, 1999, 6-7). Furthermore, with respect to Quevedo's rhetorical skills and the use of that skill in his poetry production, José María Pozuelo Yvancos tells us in his *"La construcción retórica del soneto quevediano"* ("The Rhetorical Construction of Quevedo's Sonets"): "Next to the genius and linguistic sharpness/depth found in Quevedo, we find a discursive rhetoric consciously based in the argumentative tradition of *invention* and in the use of premises from that other *invention* found in *elecutio*...(the translation is mine, 1999, 251)

[10] See Book IV, pages 98-99.

[11] Pozuelo Yvancos has already pointed out that Quevedo's architectonic design in his Poetry, never leaves any loose ends and has: "[...] *quizá lo que más singularice la construcción de sus sonetos de entre el resto de buenos sonetistas contemporáneos es la enorme trabazón a la que Quevedo somete los suyos, de forma que no queda eslabón suelto* (1999, 120)."Translation: *"...*perhaps what sets aside the construction of his sonnets from the rest of his contemporaries is the tightness to which Quevedo submits his; there are no loose ends."

[12] For an in-depth analysis of the Thomist philosophy as it relates to literary art in the XVI and XVII century in Spain, with particular emphasis on poetic justice leading to the sinful death of characters, see Jaime Leaños' "God, the Devil and Cupid..."

[13] The "destruction/degradation of the gods" finds its most complete representation in Quevedos's *Sueño del Juicio Final* or *La Fortuna con seso y la hora de todos*. The *Sueño* opens with a meeting of the gods called by a highly miffed Jupiter, and as each god enters the scene, he/she is degraded to the lowest possible level. Mars becomes a "Quijote of the deities;" Bacus is little more than a common drunk fumbling for words he cannot pronounce due to his drunkenness and uncontrollable drooling; Neptune, soaked and showing all his missing teeth, smells like rotting fish; Venus enters wearing many skirts and hoops that make an infernal noise, with a dire need of a shave; etc. See Francisco de Quevedo's *"La Fortuna con seso y la hora de todos in Obras Completas: Prosa*: 253-313.

[14] Apollo's amorous conquests are many; although his efforts were not always successful and, at times, he lost the contest to other gods and even to mortals. Among his conquests we find: the Nymph Cyrene that resulted in the birth of Aristeaus, a demigod; the Muses whose cult was closely linked to his own; Thalia, who provided him with sons, the Corybantes, demons that were followers of Dionysus; resulting from his union with Urania, she delivered the "musicians" Linus and Orpheous; and many more. See Grimal, 1996, 47-50.

15 In Spanish, augmentatives generally have a negative semantic significance or connotation.

16 The Spanish text reads as follows: *"Junto al negro, el rojo es el color predilecto de Quevedo. D. Alonso recorrió sus diversos tonos en varios poemas de Quevedo y los subrayó como el color predominante en su lírica* ...(1980, 436)."

17 We are using the term "deconstructing" to mean: "tearing down" and not in the sense popularized by Derrida's deconstruction theories.

18 Arrellano Ayuso calls this image "costumbrista." Meaning that it depicts a "frame" from the picaresque contemporary Spanish world known to Quevedo (1998, 44).

19 According to J. Neira (1980: 5-10), as cited by Arrellano-Ayuso: *"Afufa es lo mismo que huye apresuradamente arrastrando las faldas* (2003, 428)." [translation: *Afufa* is the same as "running away rapidly while dragging multiple skirts"].

20 My translation: nymph: has a double meaning, 'mythological being' and prostitute in the employ of a pimp to whom she pays...degradation of the myth through the use of the criminal underworld language.

21 According to Arrellano Ayuso, in the Golden Age of Spain the word *gozar* signified to copulate with a given woman, the subject for whom the verb was intended in the expression (1998, 45).

22 Translation: brilliant, blinding, resplendent.

23 The story of the affair of Venus and Mars appears in book IV of Ovid's *Metamorphosis*.

24 Translation: to lift.

25 Translation: rain of money.

26 The culmination of Quevedo's attack on the persona of the *dueña* is found in The*"Sueño de la Muerte* (192-220)." Since the *Celestina, dueñas* had served as 'go-between' with the objective of finding personal gain by "facilitating" the fall of the very ladies they were supposed to 'guard.'

The Ambiguity of *Eros* in Thomas Mann's *Death in Venice* and Other Writings

Bernhardt Blumenthal
La Salle University

Eros is a mischievous deity, unscrupulous, cruel—not a point missed by Thomas Mann: "It is a path of perilous sweetness," he reminds us, "a way of transgression, and must surely lead him who walks in it astray."[1] The artist who follows *eros* pursues an ambiguous course. It is the way of beauty and of shame, because it is the path of unbridled passion that leads to the abyss. Mann knew this well from his reading of Plato's *Phaedrus*: "when desire drags us irrationally towards pleasures and rules in us, its rule is called by the name of excess."[2] He put it this way: "We poets can be neither wise nor worthy citizens. We must needs be wanton."[3] None of this should surprise. After all *Eros* was born of the primordial Chaos, burgeoning forth from an egg laid by Night (Nyx), conceived with Darkness (Erebos). Ambiguously the final product of this incarnation is Brightness (Aither) and Day (Hemera).

Thomas Mann is no stranger to ambiguity. His characters live in the inhospitable middle ground between art and nature, body and soul, life and death. Mann's well-known bourgeois gone astray, Tonio Kröger, finds it quite difficult, in fact, to inhabit this ambiguous middle ground because he knows that "good work only comes out under the pressure of a bad life.... That one must die to life in order to be utterly a creator."[4] The artist, the connoisseur of beautiful things, captive to their voluptuousness, is headed from birth to the pit. Oscar Wilde, Mann's great Irish predecessor who tread the perilous path of beauty, tells us of Dorian Gray, for whom "there were moments when he looked on evil simply as a mode through which he could realize his conception of the beautiful."[5]

In fact, Thomas Mann knew quite early on, prior to similar revelations by modern physicists, that Chaos informs much of our grasp of the real. His great mentor, Goethe, who examined strata of rock, sometimes sharply layered, sometimes in formless heaps and sought to harmonize contradictions and find guideposts for his future investigations, had long pointed this out in his essay *Granite*: "Everything is ruin, chaos, and destruction."[6] Thomas Mann knew that there are phenomena of daily experience—snowflakes and sandstorms—that are so complex that we may not pass them through a linear equation, that we cannot predict the size and shape of future incarnations of such phenomena from their past formations. "Nature itself," he writes in *Doctor Faustus*, "is too full of obscure phenomena not altogether remote from magic—equivocal moods, weird, half-hidden associations pointing to the unknown—for a disciplined piety not to see therein a rash overstepping of ordained limits."[7] Jean-Yves Masson also observed Thomas Mann's infatuation with Chaos in his study of *Doctor Faustus*: "*Doctor Faustus* is a book written both from and against chaos."[8]

Once again we encounter Thomas Mann, the master of ambiguity, toying with both sides of the equation. He finds ambiguity confirmed in nature itself. Here is his conception of conical snails: "charmingly asymmetric specimens bathed in a pale rose or white spotted honey brown [they] had a notoriously poisonous sting....a fantastic ambiguity....a strange ambivalence....What a confrontation was there—poison and beauty."[9] Thomas Mann knew that Chaos, the ground from which Eros springs, informs reality long before physicists watching water drip from faucets and examining cloud formations in small planes realized that much of our immediate environment cannot be measured and is unpredictable. Thomas Mann notes the irregularity of much of nature in Adrian Leverkühn's experiments and observations in *Doctor Faustus*: "A similar pleasure he found in ice crystals; and on winter days when the little peasant windows of the farmhouse were frosted, he would be absorbed in their structure for half an hour, looking at them both with the naked eye and with his magnifying glass. I should like to say that all that would have been good and belonging to the regular order of things if only the phenomena had kept to a symmetrical pattern, as they ought, strictly regular and mathematical. But that they did not."[10] Thomas Mann, nonetheless, knows what an ice crystal is, just as he recognizes a leaf or a snowflake, although no two ice crystals are exactly the same. Thomas Mann knew as his mentor, Goethe, knew that although every leaf is different, the observer will recognize a leaf when he sees one because behind the most diverse phenomena there lies a general principle, a sort of Platonic archetype (Goethe's *Urphänomen*), which enables one to recognize a leaf when one sees it. Thomas Mann knew this long before Mitchell Feigenbaum pulled down a dusty translation of Goethe's *Theory of Colors* from a shelf in the Harvard library and read: "True observers of nature, however they may differ in opinion in other respects, will agree that all which presents itself as appearance, all that we meet with as phenomenon, must either indicate an original division which is capable of union, or an original unity which admits of division."[11]

The forms of the real, born of Chaos, which Thomas Mann refers to as "impish phenomena"[12] render experience ambivalent. The mathematics of the real world contemporary to Thomas Mann—one has in mind the seminal year 1905 and the publication of Einstein's *Special Theory of Relativity*—left Newtonian classical mechanics in shambles. The quirky things became real—time and space became relative to the speed of the observer. We eventually learned that reality is warped and that gravity is a function of mass. In fact, Adrian Leverkühn's musings about fern fronds and liquid drops lead somewhere, and Thomas Mann's "impish phenomena" became the building blocks of the real world.

In the context of ambiguities inherent in *Death in Venice* it should also be observed that Eros is principally the patron of male love (Aphrodite, the patroness of men's love of women). Thomas Mann describes the object of the aging writer's affection in the story, a boy of fourteen years, with the following words: "He took his seat, with a smile and a murmured word in his soft and blurry tongue...The lad had on a light sailor suit of blue and white striped cotton, with a red silk breast-knot and a simple white standing collar round the neck...above the collar the head was poised like a flower, in incomparable loveliness. It was the head of Eros."[13] Beauty and decadence is a theme identified by Thomas Mann and associated with Venice, a city literally sinking into the sea. Of Venice: "He remembered the autumn that he has passed there, and a wonderful love that has stirred him to mad, delightful follies."[14] Thomas Mann? No. Once again it is Oscar Wilde speaking of Dorian Gray. Quite obviously, the Irish and the German writers had similar views of the decadence of love engendered by *Eros* and of Venice as a showplace for that love.

Indeed, beauty is seductive, and the beauty pursued in *Death in Venice*, in particular, which Heinrich Detering refers to as "the at once exotically attractive and death-laden power of prohibited sexuality."[15] It is the voice of a lover who speaks to the artist from the lower depths. A certain ambiguity attaches to beauty; after all it is a product of the god born of chaos. No one knew this better than the poet Rilke "for beauty," he notes, "is nothing but the beginning of terror."[16] It is the desire to which the artist is drawn that deigns to destroy him. It is the passion that leads to love and to the abyss.

There is a principle in physics, referred to as the Second Law of Thermodynamics, which instructs us that the gift of time is death. According to this principle, heat transfers automatically in a closed system only from a hot surface to a cold one. In time structures break down, disorder increases, randomness multiplies and time—our time—moves inexorably only in one direction, that is, toward dissolution, destruction and death. Time like heat transfer is not reversible. This is the law of entropy and the ultimate source of all the contrariness and ambiguity in life. Gustave Aschenbach, the aging writer and central figure of *Death in Venice*, is the poster boy for the concept of entropy. He is a conscientious, disciplined artist whose life of tact and restraint eventually leads him to crave freedom, release, and forgetfulness. A dry, conscientious devotion to duty succumbs to ardent, obscure impulses, to vaulting unrest and to a thirst for distant scenes and new experiences. "It had been a life of self-conquest, a life against odds, dour, steadfast, abstinent;"[17] however, Aschenbach travels to Venice and falls in love with a fourteen year-old boy. He is smitten by *Eros*, pursues the wanton path of beauty and deconstructs. Aschenbach tries to mask the increasing entropy of his physical system by frequent trips to the barbershop. He has his hair dyed, his face powered and his lips glossed. He adorns himself with perfumes and makes lavish use of facial cream and cosmetics, dressing young with a bright red necktie and a sporty, brown straw hat with a gay striped band. The boy kept him enthralled. Nor is Mann alone in this. His contemporary, Constantine Cavafy, a Greek poet in far-off Alexandria was harboring the same sentiments and feeling the same urges:

> Something they said beside me
> made me look toward the café door,
> and I saw that lovely body which seemed
> as though Eros in his mastery had fashioned it,
> joyfully shaping its well-formed limbs,
> molding its tall build,
> shaping its face tenderly,
> and leaving, with a touch of the fingers,
> a particular nuance on the brow, the eyes, the lips.[18]

Eros has his way with artists; once captivated, the artist cannot renounce sympathy with the abyss.

The randomness of Aschenbach's life increases; the moral law falls into ruins. Entropy mounts. Aschenbach consumes overripe strawberries, contracts cholera, and falls gravely ill. His personal situation only mirrors the general conditions of the city caught up in a health epidemic. Aschenbach's pursuit of beauty, finally, leads him to the beach where in death his eyes are trained on the god-like appearance of the fourteen year- old boy. His troubled soul only reflects the deteriorating conditions of the beach scene: "The whole beach, once so full of color and life, looked now autumnal, out of season; it was nearly deserted and not even very clean. A camera on a tripod stood at the edge of the water, apparently abandoned; its black cloth snapped in the freshening wind."[19] Certainly, considerations about entropy, the deteriorating conditions of the environment, the loss of even a semblance of structure with the passage of time are appropriate. Eros is a hard taskmaster, a demanding god and consort of the damned.

Finally, *Eros* born of Chaos occasions us to consider once again the increasing disorder of Aschenbach's internal and external situation. The aging writer's troubles stem from his decision to break symmetry. When he entered the dining room of the resort hotel in Venice, the people assembled there represented a symmetrical pattern. He knew none of them; one individual was as indifferent to him as another. Aschenbach enjoyed at that moment the freedom of options. He broke that symmetry by alighting on Tadzio, trading the openness of possibilities for the stability of choice. In so doing, he sealed his fate, undoubtedly guided by the mischievous hand of *eros*.

Notes

[1] For the sake of readers who do not have access to German. I am citing works on the basis of readily available translations. *Death in Venice and Seven Other Stories* (New York: Vintage, 1963), 70.

[2] *Phaedrus* (Warminster: Aris & Phillips, 1986), 43.

[3] *Death in Venice*, 71.

[4] *Tonio Kröger*, in *Death in Venice*, 93.

[5] *The Picture of Dorian Gray* (New York: Penguin, 1985), 140.

[6] *Collected Works*, 12 (New York, Suhrkamp, 1983), 133.

[7] *Doctor Faustus* (New York: The Modern Library, 1992), 16.

[8] *La forme et le chaos dans Le Docteur Faustus de Thomas Mann* in *Faust ou la mélancholie du savoir* (Paris: Éditions Desjonquères, 2001), 186. My translation of: "*Le Docteur Faustus de Thomas Mann est un livre écrit à la fois à partir de et contre le chaos.*"

[9] *Doctor Faustus*, 20.

[10] *Doctor Faustus*, 22

[11] *Theory of Coluors* (Cambridge, Massachusetts/London: M.I.T., 1970), 293-294.

[12] *Doctor Faustus*, 25.

[13] *Death in Venice*, 28-29.

[14] *The Picture of Dorian Gray*, 157.

[15] *Das offene Geheimnis: Zur literarischen Produktivität eines Tabus von Winckelmann bis zum Thomas Mann* (Göttingen: Wallstein, 1994), 330. My translation of: "*die zugleich exotisch-lockende und tödlich-bedrohende Gewalt der verbotenen Sexualität.*"

[16] *The Selected Poetry of Rainer Maria Rilke* (New York: Vintage, 1982), 151.

[17] *Death in Venice*, 55.

[18] C. P. *Cavafy: Collected Poems* (Princeton: Princeton University Press, 1992), 55.
[19] *Death in Venice*, 72.

Eros and Ambiguity in Ukrainian Literature: The Case of Ivan Franko (1856-1916)

Leonid Rudnytzky
University of Pennsylvania

"Eros is a mighty daemon," as the wise Diotima said to Socrates. We shall never get the better of him, or only to our own hurt. He is not the whole of our inward nature, though he is at least one of its essential aspects.[1]

Acursory search for the themes of Eros and Ambiguity in Ukrainian literature yields but skimpy results, especially if it does not take into account literature written since the proclamation of Ukraine's independence in 1991. In comparison with other European letters, especially the Italian, French, Spanish, Austrian and German, Ukrainian literature is neither overly erotic nor exceptionally ambiguous. In surveying it, one is hard pressed to find titillating amorous scenes and equivocal moral or philosophical dicta. This is primarily due to the fact that two of its principal four characteristics are a pragmatic functionality and an all-pervasive spirituality.[2] Throughout the centuries Ukrainian literature has been, with minor exceptions, first and foremost, a literature with a mission serving an ideology or a cause. As a literature of a people located geographically on the Euro-Asian continent between East and West, it is often characterized by a clear-cut polarity which, for the most part, allows for no ambiguity. In addition, it is traditionally a deeply religious literature informed by an intense sense of morality and piety, which often tends to prefer Thanatos to Eros. However, upon closer examination, selected works of leading Ukrainian authors offer interesting insights into the nature of the Ukrainian national psyche; its vagaries and ambiguities in the realm of Eros. This paper explores the presence of Eros and Ambiguity in Ukrainian literature while focusing on the writings of Ivan Franko, especially his long narrative poem, *Ivan Vyshensky*, and attempts to skim over some of the post-modernist writing in contemporary Ukraine.

Written literature came into being when Christianity set foot on Ukrainian soil. With the baptism of Rus'-Ukraine under the rule of Grandprince Volodymyr the Great in 988, the so-called Church Slavonic language, became the literary language of the realm. Thus, the beginning of written literature in Ukraine is quite naturally religious. The earliest dated monument of Old Ukrainian literature is the *Ostromyr Gospel* (1056); predating it, however, is a rich oral tradition in which various Indo-European, especially Scandinavian, themes and motifs abound. The secular literature of that time is comprised mostly of translations, borrowings, various tales, proverbs, sayings and chronicles.[3] However, Christianity, especially the act of Baptism of Ukraine of 988, is the central event which dominates the early beginnings of Ukrainian literature, overshadowing all secular elements and events. It is, to use a Freudian term, the proto-experience (*Urerlebniss*) of the Ukrainian people, which has been preserved in many colorful depictions in literature, music and the plastic arts. The main historical sources for that period are the chronicles, the most important of which is known as *The Tale of Bygone Years*. In it we are told how Grand Prince Volodymyr sent out emissaries seeking information concerning different religions. Upon their return to Kyiv, these men described the Greek form of worship in most glowing terms, having been completely awed by its celestial splendor. If these reports are authentic, then Volodymyr's decision to accept the Greek religion, was made, partially at least, also for esthetic reasons. This is how the chronicler recorded the reports of the emissaries:

> We went to the land of the Greeks and they lead us to a place where
> they worship their God, and we knew not whether we were in heaven
> or on earth. For on earth there is no such splendor nor such beauty, and
> we are at a loss to describe it. We only know that God dwells there
> among men, and their service is fairer than the ceremonies of other na-
> tions. We can not forget such beauty, for every man, having tasted
> something sweet, is afterwards unwilling to accept that which is bitter;
> and so we can also no longer live here as pagans.

According to the chronicler, the official act of Baptism of the people of Ukraine took place in the city of Kyiv upon the Grand
Prince's return from Kherson, where he himself had received the
sacrament. First he ordered his twelve small sons baptized and
many boyars also received the sacrament at that time. This is how
the chronicler recorded the event:

> Then Volodymyr sent heralds throughout the whole city to proclaim
> that if any inhabitant, rich or poor, did not betake himself to the Dnipro
> river, he would become the Grand Prince's enemy. When the people
> heard these words, they were filled with joy and exclaimed in their
> happiness: "If this were not good, the Grand Prince and his boyars
> would not have accepted it." On the morrow, the Grand Prince went
> forth to the Dnipro with the priests. . . . and countless multitudes as-
> sembled. They all went into the water; some stood up to their necks,
> others to their breasts, and the younger near the bank, while adults
> waded further out, some of them holding children in their arms. The
> priests stood by and offered prayers. There was joy in heaven and upon
> earth to behold so many souls saved.[4]

In examining these reports, one is invariably struck (among other
things) by the marked psychological and cultural predisposition
to Christianity on the part of the ancestors of present-day Ukrainians, by their almost blind trust in their leader as well as by the
vivid description of the events narrated, which is not without literary merit. It is here, in the very early stages of its development,
that Ukrainian literature received the imprint of the Christian
spirit, which it has borne throughout the ages.

   It is therefore not surprising that in the letters of medieval
Ukraine, Eros was almost always mitigated by religious consid-
erations. It is said that, before his conversion, Volodymyr the
Great had several wives and hundreds of concubines and was

know as the "Fornicator Europae." Following his baptism, however, he led a chaste, virtuous life and was eventually proclaimed a saint of the Eastern Church. The interplay between religion and Eros is found throughout the literature of medieval Ukraine, both religious and secular, especially in such genres as the sermon, the lives of the saints, stories and tales of adventure, novels and poetry.

The seedbed of spirituality in Ukraine and the entire Slavic East was the Pechers'ka Lavra, the famous Kyivan Monastery of the Caves, founded in the Eleventh century by Ss. Anthony and Theodosius. One of its major publications, known as the *Patericon of the Kyivan Caves Monastery*, a collection of tales dealing with the lives of monks, authored by the bishops Simon and Polycarp in the Thirteenth century, is still a most valuable source of historic-cultural information. Here we find numerous examples of the struggle between Christian morality and life's temptations, some of which have clear erotic overtones.

One such tale features the life of Moses the Hungarian, who, having been taken prisoner during a war with the Poles, becomes the object of the ardent sexual desire of a Polish noblewoman. Having secretly become a monk, the hero struggles valiantly against the temptations of the flesh; he debates the pros and cons of monastic life with his pursuer and is eventually victorious. The psychological aspect of the plot of this tale is very well developed and the story has the flair of a novel of adventure. However, most of the tales comprising this collection are, according to Čyževskyj, written in a simple style without linguistic embellishment. On the ideological level, the notion of a complete fusion of the material and the spiritual lives of the monks of the Kyivan Monastery, which was the initial principal source of their spirituality, is replaced by a severe, unmitigated asceticism. Personal salvation now becomes the *sumum bonum* "pushing the ideals of service to the world and communal life into the background."[5]

We will discuss this agonistic conflict between asceticism and secular life, i.e., the *vita contemplativa* and the *vita activa* and examine the ambiguity inherent in it in our discussion of the works of Ivan Franko. At present, however, it is necessary to examine briefly the motifs of Eros and Ambiguity in the most famous secular work of Old Ukrainian literature, i.e., the anonymous epic poem written in the Twelfth century known as the *Tale of Ihor's Campaign* (*Slovo o polku Ihorevi*) for no introduction to or survey of Ukrainian literature can be considered complete without some reference to it.

The original manuscript of the *Slovo* was discovered in 1795 and was published, according to most scholarly accounts, in a rather Russianized, poorly edited version in St. Petersburg in 1800. During the Napoleonic war the original manuscript together with numerous printed copies perished in the Moscow fire of 1812. This subsequently generated skepticism about its authenticity providing a most bountiful source material for scholarly speculations well into our time.

Doubts about the authenticity of *Slovo* were first raised by the French scholar André Mazon in several of his publications in the 1940s.[6] It continues until today as evidenced by Edward L. Keenan in his study *Josef Dobrovský and the Origins of the Igor' Tale* published in 2003. Notwithstanding these assaults on the authenticity of the epic poem, for all intents and purposes it is generally considered the oldest Ukrainian secular, literary document and as such it occupies a most prominent place in the annals of Ukrainian literature. It is also the *locus classicus* of Ambiguity in Ukrainian literature, the product of two inimical ideologies. The epic *Slovo* has a pagan patina, but it is imbued with a Christian ethos. Pagan and Christian influences coalesce endowing the work with a magnificent sense of Ambiguity. Eros, on the other hand, is subdued in the poem; it makes a veiled, delicate appearance only in the prayer-lament of the wife of the hero, Yaroslavna, who awaits the return of her husband from captivity. Here is a brief sample of this poetic prayer:

> Early in the morning Yaroslavna weeps
> On the ramparts of Putivl, lamenting:
> "O Dnipro, son of Slavuta,
> You have pierced stone mountains
> Through the land of Polovtsi.
> You have carried the boats of Svyatoslav
> Down to Kobyak's chorts.
> Bring to me, O Lord, my beloved,
> That I not send to him my tears

To the sea early in the morning."
(translation L.R.)
Inter arma musae silent.

This Latin saying offers the reason for the paucity of Eros and Ambiguity in Ukrainian literature in the following centuries. Internecine wars, Tatar invasions, religious strife and polemics had a negative impact on the development of Ukrainian literature. We can only agree with Čyževskyj, that "the period extending from the end of the thirteenth to the end of the fifteenth centuries represents a distinct pause in the development of Ukrainian literature, but such pauses have occurred periodically in the spiritual, cultural and literary life of Ukraine. While the 'wasted years' in the history of our people may evoke feelings of regret, we should bear in mind that periods of stagnation are always followed by epochs of vigorous blossoming."[7]

With some exceptions, the periods of Renaissance and Reformation in Ukrainian literature do not have much to offer in terms of our topic. The presence of Eros in poetry is mitigated by religious fervor, which continues well into the period of the Baroque. The motifs of *memento mori* and *carpe diem*, present in all Baroque literature, do fuel some ambiguity which, however, is always resolved by the religious ethos of the time.

Eros and Ambiguity make their presence known in the Classic-Romantic Age of Ukrainian literature. Ivan Kotlyarevsky (1769-1838) in his "mock-heroic" poem *Aeneid*, that travesties Vergil's *Aeneid*, establishes the beginnings of Eros and Ambiguity in modern Ukrainian literature. Although a parody of Vergil's masterpiece, Kotlyarevsky's version is a completely original work. It is the first major piece of imaginative literature written entirely in the vernacular, thus, marking the beginning of modern Ukrainian literature and language. Eros and Ambiguity inform the content of this epic poem. The former is especially emphasized by the racy, colorful, at times, vulgar burlesque-like language, and the latter is derived from its symbolic-satirical content. In Kotlyarevsky's poem, Virgil's Aeneas and his Trojan warriors become Ukrainian Cossacks and the Greek gods the oppressive Russian landlords. This is the beginning of the type of Ambiguity derived from the notion of ethnic and psychological distinctiveness between

Ukrainians and Russians which permeates the gamut of Ukrainian life and letters.[8] Kotlyarevsky also initiates the process of "Ukrainization" of foreign literary themes and motifs endowing them with local color, placing them into a Ukrainian environment giving them an unmistakable Ukrainian character. This process reaches its zenith with Ivan Franko's children's tale *Lys Mykyta* (*Mykyta the Fox,*1890), which, on a deeper level, is a biting satire of life in Austrian Galicia in the Nineteenth century. The following two quotations from the *Aeneid*, the first three cantos of which were published in St. Petersburg in 1798, can serve as examples:

> Aeneas was a lively fellow,
> Lusty as any Cossack blade,
> In every kind of mischief mellow,
> The staunchest tramp to ply his trade.
> But when the Greeks, with all their trouble,
> Had burned down Troy and left it rubble,
> Taking a knapsack, off he wheels,
> Together with some reckless puffins –
> Singed lads, who looked like ragamuffins –
> And to old Troy he showed his heels.[9]

Homage paid to Eros informs the entire poem. Lines such as "A dark-eyed beauty, sweet and active/ Delicious, shapely and attractive," uttered by Aeolus, the god of winds, or Dido's curses of Aeneas who having had his fill of her, leaves unceremoniously, can serve as examples of the ever-present Eros:

> For me the sun's fair light is darkened;
> Apart from him no light I know.
> Ah, Cupid, impish brat of anguish,
> Take pleasure now to see me languish –
> Would you had died and saved these aches!

As in Vergil, this unrequited love of an abandoned woman ends in self-immolation: "She loved Aeneas so, that she/Could die in flaming agony;/Her soul in Limbo's shades awoke."

Kotlyarevsky's works influenced both Classicism and Romanticism in Ukraine. The former, contrary to most classical literature of Western Europe, is often de-eroticized. A telling example here is Petro Hulak-Artemovsky's (1790-1865) translation of Goethe's ballad "Der Fischer," ("The Fisherman"), in which the translator eliminated all the erotic motifs featured in the original. Kotlyarevsky also influenced the early works of Taras Shevchenko and other Ukrainian Romanticists.

Eros and Ambiguity are an integral part of Shevchenko's life and works. It was Ivan Franko who best assessed the poet's importance for Ukrainian life and letters by relating the following contrasting biographical facts which crystallize the contradictions and ambiguities of his existence:

> He was the son of a peasant and became a prince in the realm of the spirit.
> He was a serf and became a great power in the realm of human culture.
> He was an uneducated layman and paved new, lucid, and free paths for professors and scholars.
> He was burdened ten years with the musket of a Russian soldier and has done more for the freedom of Russia than ten victorious armies.
> Fate has treated him unsparingly during his life and yet was unable to transform the gold of his soul into rust, his love for mankind into hatred and scorn, his faith in God into pessimism and despair.
> Fate was generous to him with suffering, but it was also not miserly with joys, which flowed from a wholesome spring of life.
> And not until his death did it grant him the best and the most valued possessions—unpassing fame and eternally flowering joy, which his works continue to inspire in the hearts of millions of people.
> Such was and is Taras Shevchenko for us Ukrainians.[10]

Indeed, Shevchenko's importance to the Ukrainian people cannot be overstated. His fiery poetic verse remains even today a crucial factor in the preservation of the Ukrainian national identity. He is often seen as a symbol of Ukraine's past glory and a guarantor of her future. The duality of Shevchenko's being, as shown in the Franko quotation above, as well as the Ambiguity surrounding his image created by his poetry is brilliantly detailed by George G. Grabowicz in his seminal study *The Poet as Mythmaker: A Study of Symbolic Meaning in Taras Ševčenko*.[11] Grabowicz writes: "The mythical nature of Ševčenko's poetry is unmistakable. Through his own psychological and existential circumstances, his genius and, not least of all, the cultural readiness for his message, he was able to establish a unique and timeless resonance with the conscious and unconscious feelings of his people. ... Through this too he gave his people the ability to rediscover themselves and with that to gain a sense of reborn vitality. But that gift...was not without its drop of poison: the basic structural component of the myth, the apotheosis of communitas and the negation of structure, made for a questionable socio-political legacy."[12]

It seems especially appropriate to write about Ivan Franko on the heels of the One Hundred and Fiftieth anniversary of his birth, which was celebrated in Ukraine and outside its borders throughout the year 2006. This anniversary has once again focused attention on the poet and prompted the re-publication of several of his works as well as the publication of numerous studies about him. Of great significance are also the plans that have been made regarding future Franko scholarship. On the initiative of Viktor Yushchenko, the president of Ukraine, a 100 volume critical edition of Franko's works will be prepared for publication during the next decade together with a multi-tome *Ivan Franko Encyclopedia*. These are but two academic projects that were conceived during the jubilee year; to be sure, there are many others of varying degrees of significance.

Together with Taras Shevchenko (1814-1861) and the nation's premier dramatist-poetess, Lesya Ukrayinka (1871-1913), Ivan Franko comprises the leading triumvirate of Ukrainian literature. He is, without doubt, the number two Ukrainian author, for those who believe in listing writers in a hit-parade fashion. However, in spite of the adulation accorded to him, especially in his native Western Ukraine, the name Ivan Franko is hardly a household word in the cultural circles of the West. His *oeuvre*, as well as the entire body of classical Ukrainian literature, remains little known outside the Ukrainian linguistic realm. The reasons for this rather curious and complex phenomenon, I have suggested elsewhere,[13] and they shall not be repeated here. One can only hope that in the coming years this *status quo* will change; Franko and his work merit wider international recognition.

Blessed with a prodigious, photographic memory, an almost computer-like ability to recall and correlate data instantly, as well as with an extraordinary analytical talent, Ivan Franko was a man of amazing versatility and productivity. In his native Ukraine, he left an indelible imprint on every major area of human endeavor, especially in the realm of the humanities. His literary and scholarly legacy is a veritable treasure trove for students of literature and language, culture and history, anthropology and folklore, economics and political science, and many other academic disciplines. Franko had an encyclopedic knowledge of world literature and philosophy, acquired through his voracious appetite for reading, and an indomitable Faustian drive in his pursuit of social justice for the Galician (West Ukrainian) peasants and national sovereignty for his native Ukraine. He was among the first leading Ukrainian intellectuals to advocate complete political independence for the nation, thus breaking with the federalist tradition (with Russia) advocated by such trenchant thinkers as Mykola Kostomariv (1817-1885) and Mykhaylo Drahomanov (1841-1895), who was young Franko's mentor in political and social matters.

Franko was the author of lyric, epic, and narrative poetry; he wrote satire, both in verse and prose; he published many short stories, novellas and full-length novels, he authored comedies, dramas, critical essays, scholarly studies, book reviews as well as newspaper articles and political pamphlets, and, lest we forget, he wrote not only in Ukrainian, but also in Polish, German and Russian. Among his most important contributions to Ukraine's culture are his translations from world literature. If one were to collect all of his works in this area and to arrange them chronologically, one would compile a comprehensive, well-annotated anthology of world literature, ranging from various ancient Oriental and Greek masterpieces to early twentieth century German and Austrian authors.

In a life fraught with repeated arrests and imprisonments, bitter career disappointments, tragic love affairs, an unhappy marriage, prematurely deteriorating physical health and a concomitant mental decline, Franko often found a reaffirmation of his existential purpose in writing poetry. He described some of his works as entities born of pain and suffering, because like Goethe, who once asserted, "All my works are fragments of a great confession," Franko was essentially a confessional poet. Writing for him was a cathartic experience; he often managed to transform ugly and cruel reality into striking and ennobling beauty through the prism of his artistic temperament.

A deeper truth about people, including poets and thinkers, is sometimes revealed through the appellatives bestowed upon them by the public. Ukraine's poet laureate, Taras Shevchenko, for example, is universally known as "Kobzar" (the Bard), not only because this is the title of his principal collection of poems, but also because he embodies the emotional side of Ukrainian poetry. Indeed, it would be fair to state that Shevchenko's oeuvre is the heart and soul of the Ukrainian nation, while Franko's is its mind and its intellect. Not counting the label, "revolutionary democrat," bestowed upon him rather inappropriately[14] by Soviet scholars, Ivan Franko is known exclusively by the two appellatives: "The Stone-hewer" and "Moses"—taken from his two famous poems, "Kamenyari" ("The Stone-hewers, 1878)   and "Moysey" ("Moses."1905).[15] However, to limit Ivan Franko to these two designations is to do him an injustice. He could (and perhaps should) just as well be referred to as the "Great Conquistador," in accordance with his poem "Konkistadory" ("The Conquistadors," 1904). Here are the opening lines of the work in Percival Cundy's translation:

> Across the stormy ocean,
> While billows seethe and roar,
> Our fleet sails onward, fighting,
> To reach an unknown shore. . .

And having landed in the unknown land, the conquistadores burn their vessels, for there is no return for them to the past. The last lines of the poem summarize their devil-may-care attitude:

> We die or else we conquer!
> This is our battle cry.
> The world belongs to heroes,
> The devil take all fears!
> We win by blood and labor
> A home for coming years.[16]

All three poems deal with the problem of leadership and the search for a better life. In the "Conquistadors" the collective is the dominant factor; in "Moses" (1905) it is the lone individual that is of paramount importance.[17] In both cases, however, the action of the protagonists is confined to a pre-set task, a definitive, predetermined goal: to remove impediments on the path to the future—in "The Stone-hewers," to find the promised land—in 'Moses." In "The Conquistadors," the problem is formulated in an unambiguous, almost Kierkegaardian *Either / Or* manner. The ethos of this poem is more heroic, martial, almost imperialistic, and there is no conflict here between the leader and the masses, as is the case in "Moses." A *sui generis* integration has been achieved here; the leader and his followers have established a congenial *modus vivendi* with their fate; the entire society seems to have matured. In common, however, with the other two poems, there is the motif of struggle for a better future, presented here in a rather upbeat optimistic way. In "The Conquistadors," perhaps more so than in any other of his works, Franko exhorts his compatriots to conquer new worlds, worlds of the intellect, for themselves and to burn the ties that bind them to the dark epochs of the past.

Ivan Franko's intellectual legacy is universal as to its make-up and inexhaustible as to its content. To be sure, his collected works contain many ambiguities and contradictions. Working constantly under pressure, he was often unable to let his creation mature, to remove all its flaws, to attain stylistic perfection. Yet the moral and ethical dimensions of his writings remain firm and inviolable – he was always true to himself, he championed humanistic values, and he was always aware of his duties and obligations to his fellow man. The latter feature of the poet's mind is most palpably expressed in his famous frequently quoted dictum offered here (in a rather non-poetic translation) by the author of this article:

> Each of you should know that upon you
> Rests the well-being of millions,
> And that for the fate of millions,
> You will have to give account.

This stanza is, in fact, a simplified poetic rendition of Kant's Categorical Imperative, which in its most basic formulation states that the 'maxim' implied by a proposed action must be such that one can will that it becomes a universal law. The spirit of this formal moral law in Kantian ethics informs many of the Ukrainian poet's writings. We find it rather explicitly present in the long narrative poem "Ivan Vyshensky," in many of his poetic collections, and implicitly in several of his novels and short stories.

These and other qualities of the mind of Ivan Franko (such as courage, sincerity and truthfulness), which he possessed perhaps even to an excessive degree, have made him a teacher of his people and the mentor of several generations of Ukrainian poets and scholars.

The word Eros, not counting any Ukrainian synonyms, appears over forty times in Franko's original works as well as in his translations, especially those from literatures of antiquity. In the latter category we find the following titles of poems translated: "What a Scoundrel, this Eros," "Eros Threatened," "Eros for Sale," "Eros Hidden," "Eros Wounded," "The Slave of Eros" and "They Caught Eros."[18]

Plato's concept of Eros as an acquisitive love, based on an insuperable need to possess the desired object, informs Franko's lyrical poetry, especially his *Zivyale lystya (The Withered Leaves,* 1891), the source of which is an unhappy love affair, one of many in his life. This collection is comprised of lyrics ranging from the simple amatory to the fiercely erotic. Some of these verses are set to music, as for example, the following two stanzas, entitled "My Despair":

> If at night, by your window, you happen to hear
>   A voice that is sobbing and weeping,
> Do not glance in alarm at the casement, my dear,
>   But turn once again to your sleeping!
>
> For it is not an orphan, who motherless strays;
>   And it is not a beggar who's spying;
> It is just my despair that laments all its days,
>   And my love inconsolably crying.[19]

This love poetry features an idealized image of woman akin to Goethe's "das ewig Weibliche," and both Goethe's *Faust* and the *Sufferings of Young Werther* have left an indelible imprint on this collection:

> I bow to you because you wooed me not
> But in my breast extinguished the wild fire
> Young love would hail as real;
> And in my lonely, melancholy lot
> Engraved upon my heart a high desire,
> A feminine ideal.[20]

In this collection, Eros, as postulated by Plato, i.e., a powerful force that draws man toward the good, the true and the beautiful, vies for supremacy with Thanatos; *Liebestod* motifs anticipating Wagner and the themes of undying love and immortality inform the poem.[21]

Eros, as an intensely subjective act of the human spirit, also makes its presence felt in Franko's prose, his major novels as well as short stories. Of special interest is a literary gem of realistic prose entitled "Lesyshyna chelyad'" (Lesykha's Servants, 1877). It depicts a slice of the life of a peasant family, the head of which, Lesykha, is a "hard and stingy widow" of an alcoholic wife beater. Lesykha, "who knows how to devour another person's soul, just like rust knows how to devour iron," brutally dominates the lives of her daughter, Horpyna, and her daughter-in-law, Anna. Lesykha's son Hnat, the husband of Anna, is an insensitive ne'er do-well with thieving tendencies, whom the old woman uses to control those around her. Two additional members of the household are an old beggar, who does odd chores around the house and takes care of the apiary, and a young orphan boy, Vasyl, an inept cowherd whom Lesykha has regularly flogged for not doing his job properly. Vasyl is known as "the Hummer" because, while herding cows, he constantly hums to himself incomprehensible songs -- his only defense mechanism against the old woman's mistreatment and cruelty.

The focus of the narrative, however, is on the two young women, Horpyna and Anna. Like Vasyl, they too seek solace in song. In spite of Lesykha's objections, they sing folksongs while working in the field during the day, and at night they dream of idealistic love. Interspersed throughout the narrative, these songs act as a leitmotif revealing the yearnings and sufferings of the two young women and the hopelessness of their situations. At the same time, these songs, together with the brief glimpses of the lovely rustic milieu and of moonlit summer nights, create a powerful contrast between the natural beauty of the Ukrainian landscape and the ugliness of the human condition, as set forth by the author in a most realistic, almost naturalistic manner. Hence, for the two young women, song becomes a second existence and Eros a means of transcending the misery of everyday life. Franko's *Lesykha's Servants* aesthetically coalesces Eros and Ambiguity, while offering insightful glimpses into the deepest recesses of the female soul.

Ambiguity reaches its zenith in Franko's narrative poem *Ivan Vyshensky*, which is a drama of the human soul and its quest for salvation. The work is divided into twelve cantos. Its protagonist, a historical figure, was a mighty champion of the Orthodox Church who, through his polemical writings and eloquent speeches, generated strong opposition, especially among the Cossacks, to Roman Catholicism, the Union of Brest (1596) and western influences in general. Franko had a keen, unabated interest in the life and works of Ivan Vyshensky (c.1550-1625). He published five studies on him and much of this research found its way into the poem. Franko admired Vyshensky's patriotism, his fiery rhetoric and his zeal to combat social evils, but he was puzzled by the theologian's predilection for asceticism and by his mystical world view. Unable to resolve satisfactorily the Vyshensky enigma through scholarly analysis, Franko apparently decided to come to terms poetically with the subject that had eluded his empirical efforts. In the poem, Vyshensky is an old man, who having renounced all worldly things, has opted to spend the rest of his life in monastic contemplation on the island of Athos. The salvation of his immortal soul is his only raison d'etre.

In Canto V of the poem, we find Vyshensky at peace with himself and having overcome the world (so he believes), his soul rejoices in the raptures of his imminent salvation:

> Gone from here's the small, the petty,
> That disturbs the soul with feelings,
> And distracts away attention
> From the one – and greatest – goal.
>
> All that's left is themes eternal,
> Themes eternal, great and holy,
> On eternal themes, and holy,
> Fix your sight, my striving soul!

Vyshensky's religious fervor increases. He has renounced all personal desires and has transcended himself. Immured in his living tomb and separated from the world he is enveloped by a phantasmagoric vision and the ecstasy of seeing himself in the harmony of the cosmos hurtling toward a mystical union with God:

> Like a choir, great chords surround him –
> Golden oceans, opal rivers –
> And the tones that all comprise them,
> Fill the earth and sky with sound!
>
> And the hermit's soul goes flowing,
> Past those harmonies almighty,
> Down a swan that plows the ocean,
> Swung by waves; now up, now down.[22]

Eventually, however, the outside world intrudes into his ascetic existence. Life in various forms tempts him. A spider weaving his web conjures up all kinds of thoughts in his mind. Then suddenly, borne by winds, cherry blossoms evoke distant memories, powerful thoughts and doubts:

> Can it be Ukraine still calls me,
> My beflowered, happy Eden,
> My grim Hell of blood and hardship –
> Can it be she calls me still?

While seeking to assuage these doubts through fasting and prayers the final temptation appears to the hermit in the form of a scroll lowered to him in a basket containing his weekly rations. This scroll is a letter from Cossacks who have come to take him back to Ukraine so that he may once again lead them in battle against the enemy. Their impassioned pleas upset Vyshensky even more than his previous encounters with the spider and the cherry blossoms. Now he must choose between personal salvation and the salvation of millions of his countrymen, but he is unable to act. He implores God to send him a sign but nothing comes. At last when the evening descends on the island, he rereads the letter from the emissaries and "bedamps the script with tears." Finally he knows the truth: the true Christian puts the spiritual welfare of others before his own salvation:

> And what right did you possess here,
> Oh conniving, wretched mortal,
> To place first your own salvation,
> There, where millions could die?

The truth is thus made known to him harshly, unequivocally. He rediscovers the true spiritual reality and reawakens to life. He realizes, that according to Christ's teaching, his first duty is to his fellow man, and he tries to stop the slowly disappearing vessel which carries the Cossacks back to Ukraine:

> Wait! Wait, stay! Don't leave without me!
> I'm alive! And like I used to, -
> I still love Ukraine, I'll give her, -
> All she needs! My love, my life!

But this realization comes too late. – Or does it? The Cossacks do not hear him. They do not return. The poem ends with a beautiful fugue-like Ambiguity. Ivan Vyshensky, enraptured, crossing himself three times devoutly steps out of his mountainous cavern onto the path of light formed by the rays of the sun.

> And the world before him faded.
> Save that dazzling road all-golden,
> And that barque, far far before him, -
> And he stepped. And disappeared.

> And inside the lifeless cavern,
> Just a cross of wood lay gleaming, -
> Crumbling husk of dreams, illusions;
> And the ocean's ceaseless roar.

The Ambiguity of the poem's ending resonates with the words of John D. Caputo found in his essay "In Praise of Ambiguity." Caputo states, "whatever is important, valuable, significant is ambiguous – love and death, God and suffering, right and wrong, the past and the future. … ambiguity is like the blackness of the night sky, which makes the stars glow more brilliantly and leaves us wondering what else stirs in those dark depths from which they shine forth."[23]

Eros and Ambiguity abound in Ukrainian literature during the first three decades of the twentieth century. In this period, which later became known in Ukrainian as "Rozstrilyane vidrodzhennya" (the "Executed Renaissance"),[24] Ukrainian literature reaches unprecedented heights, only to be totally devastated by Stalin's reign of terror in the 1930s. Active at that time, hundreds of brilliant poets, writers and dramatists, were either killed or exiled to Siberia, and their writings were assigned to oblivion. One group of poets, known as the neo-classicists of Kyiv, is of special importance. Their best known representative, Maksym Rylsky (1895-1964) survived the purges by writing paeans to Stalin and the Communist Party. His earlier poetry can serve as an example of Eros in early twentieth century Ukrainian literature.

> Fragrant roses adorned our wedding bed,
>> The image of Cythereia blesses it from the corner.
> We will bring the goddess honey-sweet figs,
>> Dark, strong wine and young doves.

> The sun conceals itself in the sea, the roses smell more intoxicating.
>> Hands search for hands, greedy lips for lips …
> Give us the strength, goddess, to be beautiful in love
> And in a bewitching night to conceive a wise son.

Eros in Rylsky's work vacillates between the world of the senses and the world of the spirit. It is a desire and aspiration which is neither purely human nor divine yet always transcendent. As in the work of Ivan Franko, it is derived from the Platonic concept of the dualism of existence as developed in Plato's *Symposio*. Another example of his classic, restrained treatment of Eros is found in the poem *The Kiss*:

> I caught up with her in a dark thicket.
> Already lying among the fragrant grasses,
> She fended me off with her resilient arms.
> She finally grew quiet – and a wondrous wonder happened:
> Her lips cursed me and all my kin,
> Like a crimson flower, she stretched out her goblet
> To me, filled with sweet exhaustion.
> Her strong and shapely legs tired from running
> Looked like white marble under the mute moon,
> And in a quiet voice, raspy and wondrous,
> She proclaimed: "Cruel victor!
> To fall in this battle was closest to my heart.[25]

Even in his advanced age, having survived Stalin's terror by making compromises with the devil, Rylsky continued to worship beauty. For him, the act of writing poetry became a form of escapism from the dreary reality of Soviet existence.

The introduction of the doctrine of Socialist Realism as the only permissible form of art, for all intents and purposes, banned both Eros and Ambiguity from Ukrainian literature. Totalitarian in nature and intolerant to outside ideas, Socialist Realism became a powerful tool of communist ideology. Literature as a result became propagandistic, puritanical and sterile. Authors, who deviated from Party guidelines, suffered grave consequences. It was not until the "Thaw Period," under the reign of Nikita S. Khrushchev, that literature once again regained its authenticity and its proper place in the fabric of Ukrainian life. Especially the so-called *Shistdesyatnyky*, the Generation of the Sixties, which includes such poets as Vasyl Symonenko (1935-1963), Vasyl Stus (1936-1985), whose life was cut short by Soviet persecution, Lina Kostenko (b. 1930), Ivan Drach (b. 1936), Yevhen Sverstyuk (b. 1928), as well as Dmytro Pavlychko (b. 1929), all of whom are still active today, contributed immensely to this revival. Their courageous treatment of such themes as individualism, patriotism, religion and freedom, among others, invigorated Ukrainian literature, infusing it with a powerful creative momentum. Of special significance is also the novel *The Cathedral* (*Sobor*, 1968) by Oles' Honchar (1918-1995), who while a faithful adherent of Socialist Realism, nonetheless managed to restore some dignity to Ukrainian prose. Art, for Oles' Honchar was "the last refuge of freedom," and this credo informs the ethos of his *Cathedral*. Eros and Ambiguity are an intrinsic part of the narrative. The former manifests itself as "pure and holy, ... a feeling that will always be the song of life in art." The Ambiguity of the novel is derived from the failed attempt of the author to reconcile the glorious Cossack past with the dreary Soviet present.[26]

In the late 1980s and especially after the independence of Ukraine, Ukrainian literature changed radically. With the demise of the Soviet Union and the advent of freedom of expression, Eros became unbound; it lost its Platonic character and, in many works, acquired pornographic features. The motif of Ambiguity, as expressed in contemporary Ukrainian letters, however, continues to be based on an insecure national identity and uncertain selfhood caused by the split mentality besetting the population of present day Ukraine.

Eros and Ambiguity reentered the Ukrainian literary scene in the 1980s with the Bu-Ba-Bu literary group formed in 1985 by three young writers—Yuri Andrukhovych (b. 1960), Viktor Neborak (b. 1961) and Oleksandr Irvanets (b. 1961).[27] Bu-Ba-Bu stands for *burlesk* (burlesque), *balahan* (mayhem) and *bufonada* (buffoonery), and the trio truly lived up to the name of the group. Their influence on Ukrainian youth of that time, on literature, culture, especially pop-culture, was indeed revolutionary. It can be compared to the impact made by the Beatles on the world of music in the 1960s. Their boisterous showmanship, acerbic and often sardonic criticism of the *status quo*, and their reckless disrespect for "traditional" Soviet-Ukrainian values helped create a counter-culture which has impacted the current postmodernist literary movement in Ukraine.

In his novels and speeches delivered all over Europe, Andrukhovych has established himself as a leading literary voice of contemporary Ukraine. Indeed, he is, probably, the best known Ukrainian writer outside the borders of his native land; many of his works have been translated into German, English and other languages. A truly postmodernist treatment of Ambiguity and Eros is offered by Viktor Neborak, especially in his poem "The Flying Head" and "The Urban God Eros," which are characterized by linguistic innovation, experimentation and the influence of

Rock music.[28] However, the case for the tragic existential Ambiguity of contemporary Ukraine is best made by the poet, dramatist and novelist Oleksandr Irvanets in his novel *Rivne/Rovno.(Stina).Nibyto Roman* (Rivne/Rovno. [The Wall]. An Alleged Novel), published in 2002. Already the title of the work indicates its basic philosophical thesis – while the Soviet Union is dead, it is not buried. The *homo sovieticus* is very much alive. The specter of Stalinism still haunts Ukraine, divided into East and West and suffering from, what the Ukrainian literary critic and essayist Mykola Riabchuk calls "the post-Soviet schizophrenia."[29]

Other contemporary writers, who have gained a great measure of popularity (or, as the case may be, notoriety) and whose works are informed by Eros (which , at times border on pornography), are: Oksana Zabuzhko (b. 1960) especially with her best-selling novel *Polyovi doslidzhennya z ukrayinskoho seksu* (*Field Work in Ukrainian Sex*), which has gone through eight editions since its first publication in 1996 and has been translated into eight languages; Yuri Pokalchuk (b. 1941), whose short story, "The Temple of Poseidon," can serve as an example here,[30] and numerous other authors of the so-called Generation of the Eighties.

However, for our purposes, the prose of Valeriy Shevchuk (b. 1939), a member of the Generation of the Sixties, is of special importance. In his philosophical-psychological novels, which have established him as one of Ukraine's leading prose-writers, Shevchuk seeks to come to terms with Ukraine's post-Soviet reality, the authenticity of life, religion and happiness through the prism of mostly self-created mythological and pseudo-historical events. His newest novel, *Sribne moloko* (Silvery Milk, 2002)[31] set at the end of the Seventeenth century and written in the manner of a Baroque tragi-comedy, is a masterful fusion of Eros and Ambiguity. The protagonist of the novel, Hryhoriy Komarnytsky, a wandering cantor-teacher, author of a popular erotic Ukrainian folksong, is a kind of anti-Don Juan who, often against his own will, is embroiled in love affairs with the women of the various villages he visits. As a result he suffers severe often cruel punishment meted out by the cuckolded husbands and the village authorities, and sometimes the women themselves. He modifies the dictum of Torquato Tasso, i.e., "woman leads man to Paradise, but brings him to Hell," to describe his own condition: "woman does not always lead man to Paradise, but always to Hell."[32] These sentiments notwithstanding, the novel's episodes of sublunary love create a type of magical realism. The plethora of spiritual heights and depths, the preponderance of intellectual and emotional dialogues, the simultaneous presence of humorous and tragic events as well as moments of pleasure and suffering expressed in a remarkably rich, often archaic language endow the novel with a magnificent, baroque patina, while the almost surrealistic setting of the moonlit skies above the Ukrainian villages, enveloped by the silvery milk (the leitmotif of the novel), enhances the reign of an all-embracing Eros with its promise of ultimate redemption.

Perhaps the most striking portrayal of Ambiguity in world literature is offered by Franz Kafka in his novel *Der Prozess (The Trial, 1925).* It suffices to quote but a few sentences from the commentary on the famous parable contained in the novel that begins with the words, "… before the law stands the doorkeeper…." Kafka's priest comments: "…the right perception of any matter and a misunderstanding of the same matter do not wholly exclude each other." And later in the text he continues: "The scriptures are unalterable and the comments often enough merely express the commentators despair." And finally, he tells the protagonist Joseph K.: "it is not necessary to accept everything as true, one must only accept it as necessary." "A melancholy conclusion," said K. "It turns lying into a universal principle."

Nowhere in the entire body of Ukrainian literature do we find such sentiments of all-pervasive agnosticism and utter despair. In Ukrainian letters, Eros and Ambiguity are always a source of hope. The reason for this is, perhaps, the profound religious ethos which informs most of the great works of Ukrainian literature.

This albeit superficial and rather brief survey traces (admittedly somewhat sporadically) the evolution of Eros and Ambiguity in Ukrainian literature from the end of the first millennium to the present. The aesthetic presence of Eros and Ambiguity in literary works leads one to conclude that Ambiguity is an intrinsic characteristic of the Ukrainian mind. As reflected in Ukrainian letters, its presence manifests itself in the everyday life of contemporary Ukraine. Ukrainians, as a rule, always know what Ukraine should not be; they are never quite certain however (with some rather idealistic or utopian exceptions) what it really should be. This tragic ambiguity is rooted in the history and geography of the country. Located between East and West, and occupied for centuries by its neighbors from both sides, the notions of national identity and statehood (or rather the lack of it, as the case may be) lie at its core. Thus Ukrainian literature, perhaps like no other, is a true mirror of the Ukrainian soul. Ambiguity in Ukrainian literature is frequently mitigated by Eros with its many shades of meaning but mostly based on the Platonic concept as developed in the *Symposio* and *Repubblica*. Perhaps Carl Jung put it best when he analyzed the nature of Eros and its intrinsic Ambiguity in the following passage:

> Eros is a questionable fellow and will always remain so, whatever the...legislation of the future may have to say about it. He belongs on one side to man's primordial animal nature which will endure as long as man has an animal body. On the other side he is related to the highest forms of the spirit. But he thrives only when spirit and instinct are in right harmony. If one or the other aspect is lacking to him, the result is injury or at least a lopsidedness that may easily veer towards the pathological. Too much of the animal distorts the civilized man, too much civilization makes sick animals. This dilemma reveals the vast uncertainty that Eros holds for man. For, at bottom, Eros is a superhuman power which, like nature herself, allows itself to be conquered and exploited as though it were impotent. But triumph over nature is dearly paid for. Nature requires no explanations of principle, but asks only for tolerance and wise measure.[33]

This interplay between Eros and Ambiguity provides depth and beauty and mystery to a literature that has been the mainstay and custodian of the Ukrainian national identity.

Notes

[1] C.G. Jung.

[2] For further discussion of the salient features of Ukrainian literature see: Leonid Rudnytzky, "Notes on the Nature of Ukrainian Literature," in *Ukraine at Crossroads*, edited by Nicolas Hayoz and Andrej N. Lushnycky, (Bern: Peter Lang, et al.) pp. 213-232.

[3] For a thorough analysis of early Ukrainian literature see: Dmytro Čyževs'kyj, *A History of Ukrainian Literature (From the 11ᵗʰ to the End of the 19ᵗʰ Century) Second Edition with an Overview of the Twentieth Century* by George S.N. Luckyj (New York: The Ukrainian Academy of Arts and Sciences and Ukrainian Academic Press, 1997), pp. 17-225.

[4] The original Old Slavic name of the *Primary Chronicle* is *Povist' vremyanykh lit*; in English it is principally known as *The Tale of Bygone Years*. The work is a history of the Kyivan Rus' from c. 850-1110. It is thought to have been compiled in Kyiv in 1113 by a monk named Nestor, hence it is also known as *Nestor's Chronicle*.

[5] Čyževskyj, pp. 170-171. For additional examples see also: *The Hagiography of Kievan Rus'* translated with an introduction by Paul Hollingsworth. (Cambridge: Harvard University Press, 1992), and Oleksandr Aleksandrov, Starokyivska ahiohrafichna proza – XI-pershoyi tretyny XIII st. (Odessa: AstroPrint, 1999). See also his: *Das Paterikon des Kiever Höhlenklosters* (Eidos Verlag: Munich) 1964.

[6] Mazon, André. *Le Slovo d'Igor*. Traveaux publiés par l'Institut d'Études slaves, vol. 20. Paris: Droz, 1940. "L'auteur probable du Poème d'Igor." *Comptes rendus des séances – Académie des inscriptions & belles-lettres* (April-June 1944): 213-20. "Le Slovo d'Igor." *The Slavonic and East European Review* 27, no. 69 (1949): 515-35. See also the Review Article of Keenan's study by Andriy Danylenko "The Latest Revision of the *Slovo o polku Igoreve*, or Was Jaroslav of Halyč Really Shooting From His '*Altan*' in 1185?"in *The Slavonic and East European Review* vol. 82, no. 4 October 2004.

[7] Čyževskyj, p. 235. The interplay of paganism and Christianity in *Slovo* was first pointed out by G.P. Fedotov in his *The Russian Religious Mind: Kievan Christianity, the Tenth to the Thirteenth Centuries*. (Cambridge: Harvard University Press, 1966), vol. I, pp. 315-362.

[8] This Ambiguity is especially apparent in the works of Nikolai Gogol (Mykola Hohol, in Ukrainian). As shown in Edyta M. Bojanowska's excellent study, *Nikolai Gogol: Between Ukrainian and Russian Nationalism*. (Cambridge: Harvard University Press, 2007.) She writes: "Gogol's fiction on Russia offers a national rebuke rather than apotheosis. ... While folkloric stylization and historicity, the hallmarks of his nationalism, distinguish Gogol's image of Ukraine, his image of Russia has no such layering. ... Gogol's Russian nationalism was not a deeply held and sincerely held conviction, but rather contrived aspect of his public persona. ... While professing complete conformance to various popular orthodoxies of Russian nationalism, Gogol often subverted them. ... Gogol's relation to Ukraine was less conflicted ... Gogol celebrates Ukraine as a nation on the Herderian model: united by organic culture, historical memory, and language." pp. 369-370. Further cases of this type of Ambiguity characterizing the Ukrainian mentality are found in the works of many Ukrainian nineteenth century writers and intellectuals, especially Mykola Kostomarov (1817-1885). See *Towards an Intellectual History of Ukraine: An Anthology of Ukrainian Thought from 1710 to 1995*. Edited by Ralph Lindheim and George S.N. Luckyj. (Toronto, et. al.: Toronto University Press, 1996.)

9 All quotations from Kotlyarevsky's *Aeneid* are taken from *The Ukrainian Poets 1189-1962*. Selected and Translated into English Verse by C.H. Andrusyshen and Watson Kirkconnell. (Toronto: University of Toronto Press, 1963), p. 37ff.

10 Franko's original German text of this statement is found in: *Ivan Franko Beiträge zur Geschichte und Kultur der Ukraine. Ausgewählte Deutsche Schriften des Revolutionären Demokraten 1882-1815*. E. Winter and P. Kirchner, eds., (Berlin: Akademie-Verlag, 1963), p. 175. This volume contains most of Franko's works and letters written originally in German.

11 Grabowicz, (Cambridge: Harvard University Press, 1982).

12 Grabowicz, p. 161-162.

13 See Albert A. Kipa and Leonid Rudnytzky, "Lessing in Ukraine," *Lessing Yearbook XXXII, 2000* (2001), p.171, and Rudnytzky, "The Undiscovered Realm: Notes on the Nature of Ukrainian Literature," in *Ukraine at a Crossroads*, Nicolas Hayoz and Andrej N. Lushnycky, eds. (Berm, Berlin et al.: Peter Lang, 2005), pp. 215-232.

14 "Was Franko a democrat? Was he a revolutionary? Both words may have different meanings. There will be no disagreement about accepting Franko as a democrat. . . .On the other hand, his qualifications as a revolutionary are rather doubtful. He was, of course, an opponent and severe critic of the existing political and social system. But he never engaged in underground conspiratorial activities, nor did he preach violent revolt. His arrests are not an argument to the contrary, because they were due to the malpractice of the Polish-controlled administration and judiciary in Galicia. In his maturity at least, Franko always advocated evolutionary methods in politics." See Ivan L. Rudnytsky's review article, "A Publication of the German Writings of Ivan Franko," *Slavic Review* XXVI (1967), No. 1, 141-147.

15 In contrast to these epithets, Franko referred to himself poetically in such simple terms as: "a son of the people," "a stone-cutter," "a mason," or "a blacksmith," the latter being his father's trade.

16 Clarence L. Manning (ed.), *Ivan Franko: The Poet of Western Ukraine. Selected Poems. Translated with a biographical Introduction by Percival Cundy* (New York: Philosophical Library, 1948), pp. 254-255.

17 For a comparison and contrast of the two poems see my "Ivan Franko u poshukakh ukrayinskoho ya," *Visnyk NTSh, International Edition of the Shevchenko Scientific Society*, No. 36 (Fall-Winter 2006), pp. 25-27.

18 All quotations from Ivan Franko's works, unless otherwise indicated, are to the fifty volume edition: *Ivan Franko: Zibrannya tvoriv u pyadesyaty tomakh* (Kyiv: Naukova Dumka, 1986), vol. 9 pp. 290 ff. For a selection (three volumes) of Franko's imaginative prose works translated into English see the series "Ukrainian Fiction in English," translated by Roma Franko, edited by Sonia Morris, Language Lanterns Publications, 2006. www.languagelanterns.com.

19 *The Ukrainian Poets*, p. 213.

20 *The Ukrainian Poets*, p. 221.

[21] Bohdan Tykholoz, *Eros versus tanatos*. (Lviv: Ivan Franko Lviv National University, 2004).

[22] The English translation quoted here is by Roman Orest Tatchyn. See my essay "Ivan Franko's Dramatic Poem *Ivan Vyshensky*: An Interpretation" in *Ivan Franko – Mystets i myslytel': Zbirnyk dopovidey dlya vidznachennya 125-richchya narodyn i 65-richchya smerty Ivana Franka*, edited by E. Fedorenko (New York: Shevchenko Scientific Society, 1981), pp. 178-212.

[23] *Ambiguity in the Western Mind*, edited by Craig J.N. de Paulo, Patrick Messina and Marc Stier (New York, et. al.: Peter Lang, 2005) p. 15. See also Nicholas Rudnytzky, "Ivan Franko and Lazar Baranovych: A Case of Certitude in Ambiguity," *The Ukrainian Quarterly*, vol. LXII, No. 3-4, 2006, pp.288-297.

[24] The term was coined by Yuri Lavrynenko with the publication (1959) of an anthology of literature from that period.

[25] See Maksym Rylsky, *Autumn Stars: The Selected Lyric Poetry*, translated from Ukrainian with a translator's introduction and notes by Michael M. Naydan. (Litopys: Lviv), 2008 pp. 165, 207.

[26] See *The Cathedral*, by Oles' Honchar, translated by Yuri Tkach and Leonid Rudnytzky. Edited and annotated by Leonid Rudnytzky (St. Sophia Religious Association of Ukrainian Catholics: Philadelphia, 1989).

[27] For a concise analysis of the Bu-Ba-Bu phenomenon see Mark Andryczyk's "Bu-Ba-Bu: Poetry and Performance" in *Journal of Ukrainian Studies*, vol. 27, nos. 1-2: 257-272.

[28] See Victor Neborak *The Flying Head and other Poems* translated with an introduction and notes by Michael M. Naydan (Lviv: Sribne Slovo) 2005.

[29] Riabchuk explores Ambivalence and Ambiguity in contemporary Ukraine as a socio-political phenomena in his books *From Little Russia to Ukraine: the Paradoxes of a Belated Nation-Building* (2000), *TheDilemmas of the Ukrainian Faust. The Civil Society and "Nation-Building"* (2000), *The Zone of Alienation: Ukrainian Oligarchy Between East and West* (2004) all in Ukrainian. Also important are his numerous articles written in English: "Ambivalence to Ambiguity: Why Ukrainians Remain Undecided?" www.wilsoncenter.org/kennan, "Ukraine: One State, Two Countries?" http://www.iwm.at/t-23txt8.htm.

[30] *Ukrainian Literature: A Journal of Translations* vol. 1 (New York: Shevchenko Scientific Society) 2004, p. 157-168. The literary scholars Solomea Pavlychko and Tamara Hundorova have made a significant contribution to the understanding of Ukrainian feminism and postmodernism. For additional analysis of Eros in contemporary Ukrainian literature see "Erotic Assemblages: Field Research, Palimpsests, and What Lies Beneath" by Maryna Romanets in the *Journal of Ukrainian Studies* 27 nos. 1-2 (Summer-Winter 2002), pp. 273-285.

[31] Valeriy Shevchuk, *Sribne moloko* (Lviv: Kalvaria; Kyiv: Knyzhnyk) 2002. See also his "The Moon's Cuckoo from the Swallow's Nest" in *From Three Worlds: New Writing from Ukraine*, edited by Ed Hogan, Askold Melnyczuk, Michael Naydan, Mykola Riabchuk, Oksana Zabuzhko (Moscow and Birmingham: GAS; Boston, Massachusetts, 1996), pp. 100-136.

[32] Shevchuk, p. 127.

[33] C. G. Jung "The Eros Theory." in *Two Essays on Analytical Psychology.* Princeton: University Press, 1977, 28.

Divided Loyalties: *Eros* and Ambiguity in Freud; Attempts at Resolution and their Discontents

Bruce Lapenson
North Carolina Central University

F reud, like Marx, provided an insightful diagnosis of the ills of our human condition. Marx was not shy about a solution, while Freud said very little on this account.[1] Some writers while admitting Freud stopped at the micro level,[2] still take great pains to decipher a resolution to the problems of social life using Freud as a theoretical basis. Such attempts unintentionally admit of the ambiguity in Freud, and their endeavors try to make him much less so. Those who engage in these difficult projects are well-intentioned and their efforts are potentially useful. I will make use of a number of these efforts to suggest that Freud forces his readers into a divided and therefore ambiguous position regarding interpretations of a solution for social ills.

The purpose of this essay is to explore Freud's concept of Eros and its ambiguity. I will focus the analysis on three texts, Philip Rieff's *Freud: The Mind of the Moralist*, Jeffrey Abramson's *Liberation and Its Limits*, and Abraham Drassinower's *Freud's Theory of Culture*, that make sustained arguments which attempt to prescribe what Freud may have regarding a central message for social life, political life, and individual happiness. A necessary first order of business is to explain what I mean by "double individuals," the central thesis concerning divided loyalties, and Freud's understanding of the terms Eros and narcissism.

DOUBLE-INDIVIDUALS

By "double individuals," is meant an implication gleaned from Freud's statement:

> A good part of the struggles of mankind centre round the single task of finding an expedient accommodation – one, that is, that will bring happiness – between this claim of the individual [for individual liberty] and the cultural claims of the group...³

The individual is always a part of civilization and a particular culture, as this is inescapable, as well as one who wishes to enjoy life continually.⁴ The "claims of the group" are promoted by restrictions, which encourage moral behavior. The "...original personality which is still untamed by civilization..."⁵ may rebel against the group claims in the hopes for a better life, but the super-ego "...troubles itself too little about the happiness of the ego."⁶ The individual is thus "double" being that she/he belongs to themselves and the culture. Especially troubling for the ego's claims to happiness is the Freudian belief that this culture is internal as well as external. Equally troubling for culture is the perennial existence of the "original personality." If one had to choose per the question, 'Which of the id or super-ego was Freud most concerned with?', whichever side was claimed a very strong argument could also be made for the other view. When Freud entertains that we are hostile to civilization, he quickly dismisses the potential claim that we'd be better off (happier) without civilization.⁷ At the same time, Freud knew well the destructive potential of cultural claims:

> When once the Apostle Paul had posited universal love between men as the foundation of his Christian community, extreme intolerance on the part of Christendom towards those who remained outside it became the inevitable consequence.⁸

He knew also of the trouble that cultural dictates create for the individual:

It was discovered that a person becomes neurotic because he cannot tolerate the amount of frustration which society imposes on him in the service of its cultural ideals...[9]

DIVIDED LOYALTIES

The central thesis of this essay makes the claim that our double individual orientation results in a divided loyalty and a troubling ambiguity. Freud's fears concerning the id and the super-ego make his over-arching argument complex. One thinks of both the individual and society as vulnerable to human nature and that which we create to control it (civilization). Adding greatly to the dilemma Freud lays out is his nearly complete inattention to a prescription. We are left with pondering how much id and how much super-ego will be conducive to a happy and productive individual life and a peaceful society. Complicating matters further is the perennial and inescapable narcissism of humans. Of course the individual would choose more id than super-ego, and of course the individual would choose more super-ego than id for his peers. The problem as Freud pointed out is "...everyone else has exactly the same wishes as I have..."[10] While the original personality has its bias the current one has the opposite bias, but as "...society is perpetually threatened with disintegration,"[11] it is clear in Freud that the original desires never really leave us, hence our loyalties are divided between self and community.

EROS

Eros to Freud means one of two major groupings of instincts whose particular aim is "...to bind together..."[12] Freud refers to Eros as the love instinct, but does not confine it:

But we do not separate from this [sexual love]... self-love... love for parents and children, friendship and love for humanity in general... devotion to concrete objects and to abstract ideas.[13]

Eros to Freud is nearly everywhere – he speaks of communities as libidinally bound[14] and also other social units (groups) as such.[15] Libido, the energy of Eros, is capable of being invested by the ego in any external object. But, as Eros seeks to bind and preserve larger and larger social units the other major instinct, Thanatos or death instinct seeks "...to undo connections and destroy things."[16] While it is logical to assume the two instincts as coming to conflict, the situation is more complex to Freud. The two are also capable of alloying. Aggression (Thanatos) against a group that is perceived to be a threat to community stability (Eros) aims to restore the perceived loss of security and/or pleasure derived from a stable environment, but may actually be rooted in the ever present death drive. Here, we see aggression or Thanatos working, presumably, in service of Eros, but in reality, the opposite may be true; Eros may be an excuse or smokescreen for Thanatos. In short, Freud creates a structure for perception beset with complexity, we can't be sure if Eros is genuine or in service of its adversary, rendering resolution of human conflict difficult and impermanent. In such a theoretical structure ambiguity would be hard to get around.

NARCISSISM

Freud depicted the origin of love "...in attachment to the satisfied need for nourishment."[17] He also defined primary narcissism as the state "...in which at first [in the ego] the whole available quota of libido is stored up."[18] The former quote suggests that love is not selfless or altruistic by nature, but follows from the natural or primary needs of the self. The latter quote relates to an even earlier state in which "...the child does not distinguish between the breast and its own body..."[19] Love, therefore, is possible only when an external object is noticed, and reaches its furthest state from primary narcissism "...when a person is completely in love..."[20] However, all of this becomes more complex when Freud conceives of love as checking narcissism,[21] and the ego ideal as "...heir to the original narcissism in which the childish ego enjoyed self-sufficiency..."[22] The former passage is provocative since it suggests that love provides a limitation on that from which it originated. The latter statement evokes a similar reaction as moral conscience and repression is seen as tied up with a primitive state where such things did not exist.

The complexities of *Eros*, narcissism and double-individuals must be taken on in any work on Freud. We can argue that attempts at explication are also attempts to make Freud linear or non-complex and where such endeavors come up short we find ambiguity. Three texts, chosen for their varying interpretations of Freud, will be analyzed with regard to the ambiguities in Freud's use of Eros as the instinctual force of private and public bonds.

AUTONOMY, DETACHMENT, AND RESIGNATION

Philip Rieff's well-known *Freud: The Mind of the Moralist* begins with the author proclaiming that Freud left us with no message: "[Freud] accepts contradictions... nevertheless his doctrine contains intellectual and moral implications that, when drawn, constitute a message."[23] Rieff also states that "...no ultimate advice may be expected from Freud."[24] Rieff's interpretation of Freud pictures the individual, painfully aware of the difficulties of social life and of psychic life, reluctantly realizing a need to conform to cultural morals and ideals, and therefore falling back on the only place she or he can maneuver somewhat freely, their individual personality. However, this too takes a continual stoic endurance to perpetuate.[25] Rieff's focus on the individual and the content he offers may seem contradictory to his belief that Freud offered ultimate advice, but the point falls in line with his individual focus:

His [Freud's] is a very intimate wisdom, tailored to the patient and that occasion.[26]

We see here that to Rieff, we cannot, if we follow Freud, expect universal wisdom since each individual's life is unique. Rieff's view of Freud as emphasizing the "...anti-political individual seeking his self-perfection in a context as far from the communal as possible"[27] as well as characterizing Freud as "[t]he prophet of disengagement..."[28] is consistent with the over-arching focus on the individual as the last refuge for living with some degree of autonomy. In all of this, however, where is the super-ego?

Rieff acknowledges the "conservative" aspects of Freud:

[Freud] is the architect of a great revolt against pleasure... he exhibited its futility. It is... toward the reality principle that Freud turns us...[29]

Rieff understands the predicaments of life that Freud discussed as exemplified in his belief that strict rules regarding social life are causes of neurosis but to discard them would be unwise. He knew that to Freud fidelity and incest taboos were instruments of repression but Freud did not advocate lifting them.[30] However, Rieff also believed that Freud feared "...our deeper inclinations toward submissiveness and domination"[31] as more disruptive to Eros than cultural repressions. Rieff goes so far as to state that Freud saw sensuality (sexuality) as liberating us from authority. Rieff interpreted Freud as advocating both stoicism and endurance and individual freedom. His view of the necessity of morals in Freud does not seem to be central, whereas individual freedom seems to be. He states that Freud "...intimates that we are ready for a new beginning... [from] the old systems of repressive authority..."[32] This favoring of a "...detached conformity..."[33] is not an appealing portrayal of the super-ego. It smacks of 'I do not like this but I will go along with it.' By contrast Freud feared aggression too much to advise a weaker moral conscience which a reluctant conformity would likely foster. Freud stood in the corner of sublimated Eros, an aim-inhibited instinctual gratification which does a better job of bonding individuals together than aim-directed drives. The former acts are done with the super-ego in mind.

Rieff's anti-political Freud may seek to maintain as much freedom from those things, e.g., politics which would dominate his/her expenditure of libido, and limit the individual's freedom:

Freedom is... a metaphor, for Freud, when applied to any form of society; it can be properly said to exist only within the person... The quest for *social* freedom is... a contradiction in terms.[34]

To Rieff, political life for Freud as for most of Western political thought cannot escape limiting the individual. Every governmental ideology becomes authoritative although to various degrees, but Rieff's Freud is barely if at all a seeker of the communal. It can be argued that a reluctant conformity – as long as the individual ego has achieved some feeling of autonomy – encourages Eros, for certainly Freud knew of the gratification that is possible through subliminated libidinal satisfaction and the implication that this feeling of well being was an inducement or necessary condition for Eros (bonding) in a community.[35] But, Rieff's readers do not come away with a positive depiction of the super-ego. One can't help but feel overwhelmed by political and other authorities, and one is tempted to call Freud a libertarian – following Rieff – and government, politics a necessary evil. Following such a depiction, how long would social order maintain? Eros is not just about private love to Freud, but he is quite clear that Eros seeks to bind much larger numbers of people together.

Ironically, Rieff's Freud is somewhat optimistic. Though "Therapy prepares a mixture of detachment and forbearance, a stoic rationality..."[36] sounds pessimistic or less than appealing, Rieff does appeal to the love and desire or need for as much individual autonomy as possible existing in all humans. Paul Roazen intimated as much:

> Behind all Freud's awareness of men's inner coercions... is an Enlightenment dream of freedom.[37]

Rieff's appeal goes further in his assertion that to Freud, the modern's "...identity is for him to choose."[38] As noted previously, unpacking a thinker is intentionally or not an attempt at non-contradiction of portrayal, which furthers Rieff's theoretical appeal with regards to his Freud. I will explore in a later section if Rieff's effort succeeds in making Eros in Freud unambiguous, i.e. if he draws Freud without divided loyalties.

A COMMANITARIAN FREUD

Jeffrey Abramson, in *Liberation and Its Limits*, is more optimistic than Rieff while arriving at a much different political possibility. Abramson explores the erotic ties of parent and infant as enriching and enlargening the self of both. Though he admits that Freud never explored the political implications of these early attachments, Abramson theorizes that they form a basis for "...meaningful common identity..."[39] and "...the virtues of fellow-feeling and friendship, of citizenship and allegiance to a common good."[40] Abramson believed, however, that Freud offered the individual a "...limited kind of liberation,"[41] which, since he (Freud) possessed a "...commitment to distance from others..."[42] could not find liberation in larger social units. This distance from others recalls Rieff, but whereas he sees it as integral to our only possibility for freedom, Abramson believes that it is in attachment to community bonds that we feel most rewarded. However, taking even Rieff's Freud who advises a reluctant acknowledgement and adherence to the social super-ego, raises a question regarding how anti-political or committed to distance Freud actually was.

Abramson's possibilities for Freud imply a greater or more friendly commitment to a super-ego than does Rieff. Accordingly, the vision of community in Abramson seems to establish a less precarious social bonding. The emotional rewards accompanying advancements in character achieved through striving toward a common good, friendships, and the other commanitarian values may preserve a strong moral and ethical environment. Rieff's somewhat socially alienated and politically uninvolved independents are not pictured in Abramson. Abramson does, however, point out that Freud's depiction of groups and political community, while held together by Eros, lacks an "...active, self-enriching participation with others in a common life."[43] This point fits in with Abramson's attempt to flesh out political possibilities in Freud. Freud does not make the super-ego sound appealing:

> In the severity of its commands and prohibitions it troubles itself too little about the happiness of the ego...[44]

Freud's depiction of Eros in groups is many times more unappealing:

> It is always possible to bind together a considerable number of people in love, so long as there are other people left over to receive the manifestations of their aggressiveness.[45]

Binding people together of course results in rules and regulations, formal and informal, which make manifest a group super-ego. Freud is clear that men by nature would rather do other things than follow laws and informal dictates or procedures. By contrast, Abramson's vision of community possibilities depicts humans as bound but satisfied. Questions come up here regarding how Abramson deals with primary narcissism as a disrupter of communitarian groupings, how committed to individual distance Freud was, and if, as Abramson points out, Freud rejected a world view, how can a shared communal life not defy this?

LIFE WITHOUT ILLUSIONS

Abraham Drassinower, in *Freud's Theory of Culture*, argues that, according to Freud, humans must encounter rather than deny death, and thereby enable themselves to experience Eros, "...the open expanse of life."[46] To Drassinower, "Thanatos is a refusal to love what will die,"[47] thereby inducing us to live with illusions such as immortality, which keeps the individual in the past, in the mode of infantile helplessness due to which we remain enmeshed with authority in order to alleviate pain and suffering. The wish for immortality and the negation of one's inevitable death recalls Freud's view that religion renders one "...[in] a state of psychical infantilism..."[48] To Drassinower, we thus become subjects of a super-ego which "...bonds us to the love of an ideal to which we are helplessly inferior."[49] This ideal, composed of the impossible aspirations presented by authority figures,[50] regards the possibility of a maturity in which, having encountered death in an affirmative way, we can feel, however fleeting, joy in living (Eros).

Drassinower suggests that humans can foster an alternative super-ego, described as "...an ascendancy of the demands of care rather than destructiveness..."[51] and "...a duty to endure life and respect the otherness of the other..."[52] He implies that Freud believed that a more positive or better super-ego is predicated on individual ego strength, possible only if psychic and intellectual dependency is overcome. This possibility depends on the painful acceptance of our mortality. The question of the solidity of this new super-ego comes to the forefront here, as accepting otherness can certainly be vulnerable to creating an inadequate community bond. It is always wondered, especially in Freud, how much liberal treatment or orientation to others is allowable prior to the community bond beginning to loosen. One can envision the id feeling less restricted in Drassinower's interpretation of Freud and wonder if the super-ego of care can maintain.

Drassinower makes the point that, to Freud, discontents can be decreased but not eliminated and that the resultant perpetual struggle of living maintains the positive erotic quest within us.[53] In other words, the resolution of discontent would in essence deaden people. This can be linked to the belief in immortality as rooted in the wish for a magic bullet, which destroys or renders less significant the pain of our mortality. Such a state might foster a decrease of activity and meaning and a concomitant lessened satisfaction with life. The benefits of the inability to resolve struggle are clear; however, it isn't apparent how the acceptance of death would make humans less aggressive, Freud's central concern.

EROS AND AMBIGUITY

Rieff's portrayal of the individual in Freud as the only focus of freedom falls far short of resolving ambiguity in Freud's depiction of erotic bonds. The problem is not so much that Rieff's reluctant super-ego is unappealing as Freud tended to focus on the destructive and uncaring aspects of moral conscience also. Of much greater concern is where Rieff goes with Freud. He positions Freud as something of a libertarian and thereby goes beyond Freud's implication that freedom can be as destructive as political and moral restrictions. Rieff's "...new beginning..."[54] which he felt Freud hinted at involving some degree of greater individual freedom would have been viewed warily by Freud. Rieff sees this freedom as highly internal, a striving toward the perfection of the self, but accompanied by a "...deliberate detached conformity..."[55] Freud's concern that "[c]ivilization has to use its utmost efforts... to set limits to man's aggressive instincts..."[56] gives pause to the weakening of communal bonds made possible in Rieff's interpretation. On the other side, the detached conformist may eventually seek a better community, one of connectedness in which the individualistic lack of such longs for the erotic ties of a larger group, creating a feeling of external freedom as a group member. Such a person would rebel against detachment because the external society was alienating as atomized persons became the nature and rule of its social environment.

This picture of possibilities when contemplating Rieff exemplifies the uneasiness of Eros in Freud. We long for freedom, but we also long for bonds. While the latter longing may not be primary in humans, and its origin may be rooted in narcissism or ananke, it is still desired. According to José Brunner, "...the child's recognition of the parents' control over his needs and wishes also turns a possible loss of their love into a dreaded prospect."[57] As adults, we seek the love of the external also. There is some identification with an external object than an individual seeks and which is a component of her/his identity. These may be groups, large or small and or individuals, and the purpose is always at base, one's own pleasure, however sublimated, but this does not make the need to bind any less true. Speculating on the wish for an unrestricted id, Freud commented that we would quickly oppose our own thoughts on the lifting of restrictions upon realizing that all others wished for the same.[58] In such a situation we realize the good of law and order, governments, and social customs, all of which are important to Eros.

The previous points do not intend to portray a simple and wholly good super-ego, which Rieff misses, and which makes Eros possible, but do show that erotic desires are not confined in modern life to the area of individual freedom. Of great import though is the double individual aspect of our longing for both personal freedom and the recognized need for conformity. Both needs may be in service of Eros, but both may also be overcome by the wish to undo.

Abramson presents a more appealing super-ego or the possibility for such in Freud than Rieff. Abramson is aware that he's used a piece of Freud in ways that the latter did not, but still his argument is provocative. The infant-parent bond is not a one-sided act, regarding pleasure, but involves the satisfaction of both participants. Indeed, Abramson reminds that late Freud theorizes Eros as a category of instincts which seek to bind. These points, to Abramson, provide a premise in Freud for communitarian endeavors that Freud never discussed. Abramson is well aware of how un-Freud his argument is, exemplified especially by his view that Freud preferred distance for the self from others as important to individual identity. Evidence for the notion of distance in Freud can be found in *Group Psychology and the Analysis of the Ego*, when starting with the point that self-love instigates a wish to make others like us.[59] Of course we often cannot make others images of ourselves, and so difficulties emerging out of a life in common are not rare. The point in *Civilization and Its Discontents* that mankind has made the least progress with social life,[60] compared to medical and environmental advances can also bolster Abramson's claim that psychoanalysis championed the uniqueness of each self, since community life was much harder to improve. Though Abramson seems to be telling us where Freud could have gone, we can analyze his point about distance i.e. where he thinks Freud is stuck. Despite the difficulties of a life in common presented as a major thrust in *Civilization and Its Discontents*, the main message of the text is the necessity of Eros, of binding and strong communal bonds.[61] Psychoanalysis may have favored the individual, but macro-level Freud, at least in the text in question, did not focus on individual distance from others. The ambiguity, though, is palpable when one considers that in the final chapter Freud both warns us that the super-ego cares nothing for happiness and he also wishes for Eros (bonds) to meet and overpower the forces of Thanatos. The crucial point here is that erotic bonds cannot exist without forming a super-ego of some ethical or moral content. Freud wasn't as committed to social distance as portrayed, but is at the same time wary of community bonds.

Abramson sees his differences with Freud regarding groups, politics, and communal bonds:

> [To Freud] Eros is the gravest source of... the "authoritarian personality"... [b]ut Freud cannot adequately account for the fact that politics sometimes goes well... and that when it does Eros enriches rather than impoverishes personal character.[62]

According to Abramson, Freud's view of a solid community "...has little to do with active, self-enriching participation with others in a common life."[63] Of course, Abramson is correct here, but Freud would be mistrustful of communities because their claims to shared moral visions would inevitably instigate the repressed aggression in their members to surface. Freud was wary of any moral or political content emerging from communities because "...the psychical reaction – formations..."[64] holding back aggression weaken in groups toward outsiders, though such groups become aggressive under the guise of protecting their common identity.[65]   Alan Bass argued that Freud rejected a worldview because it eventually functions as a defense and deflects new situations or realities that must be encountered if the ego is to be healthy.[66] Bass' point can be seen in light of Freud's wariness of community agreements as they could also function defensively and result in the harmful isolation of new ideas. Again, this does not equate to Freud favoring the autonomous detached individual as the best that human societies could encourage. Instead, Freud leaves his readers in a place of ambiguity with regards to a resolution of the tendencies of Eros; we must bond and in the bond is the seed of its undoing. Abramson's possibilities for Freud therefore do not make him less ambiguous with regards to Eros, but instead offer a possible Freud that could have been. If Freud had entertained such a path it is hard to see it not being contradicted or compromised by what we know he did say.

Drassinower seems on target when he envisions Freud's message of acceptance and endurance of the continual struggles of life. *The Future of an Illusion* also lends support to Drassinower's claim that Freud cajoles man to live without illusions.[67] However, Drassinower's belief that Thanatos is a refusal to love what dies (life, others, ourselves), but in not refusing we emerge caring of others and accepting of differences seems somewhat optimistic regarding Freud. Drassinower may believe that the acceptance of mortality may make humans less divisive since the wish for immortality – often embodied in the religious – has tended to divide. Freud didn't seem to go this far in *The Future of Illusion*, but even if Drassinower is merely extending Freud toward a possible logical conclusion, Freud remains skeptical of democratic sounding theories. The acceptance of difference might tip the tenuous balance of a moderate individual freedom within a social structure of limits. To Freud, democracy could be dangerous because of its demoting of authority.[68] It also isn't clear how accepting differences would sublimate the aggressive instincts especially if a weakening of authority or community structure resulted. Such lack of clarity or explanation is increased by Freud's lack of sustained discussion regarding his prescription of culture's major task.[69] Freud seemed to think that a life minus religious illusions would enhance man's rational powers, which was necessary for attacking problems, but he never went so far as theorizing that we would automatically love or care about each other more.[70] Like Abramson, Drassinower's provocative insights render a possible extension of Freud, but in Freud, Eros seems eternally vulnerable to unleashing its opposite, and the prescribed sides of the balance that he implied, most importantly their degrees of strength, cannot be isolated since Freud, in his cultural work, mainly diagnoses. The individual remains, also with a divided loyalty, to self and to society; the bond is practical, but also restricting and confining, while its undoing is liberating but also disorienting and eventually destructive. Freud left us in this place, even though we have to admire those whose efforts present possible Freuds.

Notes

[1] Philip Rieff, *Freud: The Mind of the Moralist* (Garden City, New York: Doubleday & Company, Inc., 1961), xx.

[2] Jeffrey B. Abramson, Liberation and Its Limits (New York: The Free Press, 1984), 122.

[3] Sigmund Freud, *Civilization and Its Discontents*, trans. and ed. James Strachey (New York: W.W. Norton & Company, 1961), 50. Freud spoke of "double individuals" on p. 65 of the text cited here.

[4] Peter Gay, ed. *The Freud Reader* (New York: W.W. Norton & Company, 1989), 692-693.

[5] Freud, 50.

[6] Freud, 108.

[7] Freud, 49.

[8] Freud, 72-73.

[9] Freud, 39.

[10] Gay, 693.

[11] Freud, 69.

[12] Sigmund Freud, *An Outline of Psycho-Analysis*, trans. and ed. James Strachey (New York: W.W. Norton & Company, 1949), 18.

[13] Sigmund Freud, *Group Psychology and the Analysis of the Ego*, trans. James Strachey (New York: Bantam Books, 1965), 29.

[14] Freud, *Civilization and Its Discontents*, 65.

[15] Freud, *Group Psychology and the Analysis of the Ego*, 35.

[16] Freud, *An Outline of Psycho-Analysis*, 18.

[17] Freud, 70.

[18] Freud, 20.

[19] Freud, 70.

[20] Freud, 21.

[21] Freud, *Group Psychology and the Analysis of the Ego*, 71.

[22] Freud, 52.

[23] Rieff, xx.

[24] Rieff, xx.

[25] Rieff, 359.

[26] Rieff, xx.

[27] Rieff, 280.

[28] Rieff, 266.

[29] Rieff, 355.

[30] Rieff, 359.

[31] Rieff, 175.

[32] Rieff, 359-360.

[33] Rieff, 360.

[34] Rieff, 279.

[35] Freud, *Civilization and Its Discontents*, 57-58.

[36] Rieff, 359.

[37] Paul Roazen, *Freud: Political and Social Thought* (New York: Alfred A. Knopf, 1968), 298.

[38] Rieff, 240.

[39] Abramson, 30.

[40] Abramson, 138.

[41] Abramson, 123.

[42] Abramson, 122.

[43] Abramson, 129.

[44] Freud, 108.

[45] Freud, 72.

[46] Abraham Drassinower, *Freud's Theory of Culture* (Lanham, Maryland: Rowman & Littlefield Publishers, Inc. 2003) 30.

[47] Drassinower, 30.

[48] Freud, 36.

[49] Drassinower, 6.

[50] Drassinower, 149.

[51] Drassinower, 159.

[52] Drassinower, 160.

[53] Drassinower, 53.

[54] Rieff, 359.

[55] Rieff, 360.

[56] Freud, 20.

[57] José Brunner, "Oedipus Politicus," in *Freud: Conflict and Culture*, ed. Michael S. Roth (New York: Alfred A. Knopf, 1998) 84.

[58] Gay, 692-693.

[59] Freud, *Group Psychology and the Analysis of the Ego*, 42-43.

[60] Freud, *Civilization and Its Discontents*, 26, 37-38, 68-70, 72-73, 111-112.

[61] Freud, 111-112.

[62] Abramson, 60.

[63] Abramson, 129.

[64] Freud, 70.

[65] Freud, 72-73.

[66] Alan Bass, "Sigmund Freud: The Question of a Weltanschauung and of Defense," in *Psychoanalytic Versions of the Human condition*, eds. Paul Marcus and Alan Rosenberg (New York: New York University Press, 1998).

[67] Gay, 711-714, 717.

[68] Freud, 74.

[69] Freud, 50.

[70] Gay, 711-712, 714, 717.

A Deceptive Ambiguity: Revisiting Scheler's Philosophy of Love and Religious Activity

Thomas Carroll
National University of Australia

C OMING TO TERMS WITH LOVE

Eros, after all, was a mischievous little imp with arrows, a fellow of surprises who delighted in striking those who expected it least.[1]

Love informs the very fabric of our lives as individuals and social beings. Prior to an *ens cogitans* or an *ens volens*, according to the German philosopher Max Scheler (1874-1928), the human is a loving being, *ens amans*;[2] we live on the basis of our love. Nevertheless, love is one of those weasel words; a universal human phenomenon understood and valued by all, yet elusive under scrutiny, whose precise meaning is difficult to pin down; at times full of surprises. Characterized as "an Austro-Hungarian Empire uniting all sorts of feelings, behaviors and attitudes, sometimes having little in common,"[3] love is prototypically ambiguous. Though the Catholic phenomenologist Jean-Luc Marion deplores the "silence of love" within current philosophical discourse, introducing *The Erotic Phenomenon* (2007), he adds the caveat that when it is spoken of by philosophy it is mistreated or betrayed: "one would almost doubt whether philosophers experience love."[4] In a 1982 interview Emmanuel Levinas reasons to his infrequent use of this term: "it is a worn-out and ambiguous word."[5] Writing in *Assorted Opinions and Maxims* (1879) Friedrich Nietzsche observed:

> '*Love.*' – The subtlest artifice which Christianity has over the other religions is a word: it spoke of *love*. Thus it became the *lyrical* religion. [...] There is in the word love something so ambiguous and suggestive, something which speaks to the memory and to future hope, that even the meanest intelligence and the coldest heart still feels something of the luster of this word.[6]

Later, discussing the issue of punishment in *On the Genealogy of Morality* (1887), he claims: "all concepts in which an entire process is semiotically concentrated defy definition; only something which has no history can be defined."[7] Certainly love has a history within Western thought. Despite the fact the Jewish phenomenologist also shuns this religious philosophical baggage, exemplified in the playful childlike Greek god *Eros*; it is precisely this which prompts further uncertainty and fuels our speculative interest. The claim "Christianity in its origins is not systematic"[8] is apparent when examining the nature of love within the Gospel tradition, which seeks belief through the reader's *metanoia*, "conversion of heart," by narrating the parables, stories and sayings of Jesus. As the principle of God's action and the believer's response lived in community, love lies at the heart of Christian life; however philosophically speaking, it is difficult to understand a "new commandment" to love which moves in several directions towards God, neighbor and one's enemies, and by implication oneself; not to mention the difficulty in commanding love in the first place. The more theologically nuanced Johannine understanding "God is love" only exacerbated this situation, with God loving us first and from within this relationship, the one who loves knows God. The syncretism of early Christianity compounds this scriptural indistinctness with the emergence of two competing notions of love, the Platonic *eros* and the Johannine *agape*.[9] Saint Augustine of Hippo, the "greatest Christian thinker," supplely employs the Latin equivalents *amor* and *caritas*;[10] essentially undifferentiated each can be good or evil according to the object loved, sought for its own sake. As such "love is a kind of craving (*appetitus*)," an inclination or a movement which draws us out of ourselves;[11] as interpreted by Scheler: "Augustine expressly made love the *original* power of movement of the divine as well as the human spirit."[12] Understood as an "ordered love" from Augustine onwards, in which we love God for himself and each other in and for God, this movement of love prompts the feelings of the heart and directs our understanding. Following his initial phenomenological contribution "The Idols of Self-Knowledge" (1911);[13] these Greek notions and related philosophical issues were initially taken up in Scheler's next book length article, "On *Ressentiment* and Moral Value-Judgment"(1912), subtitled "A Contribution towards a Pathology of Culture;" known as *Ressentiment,* it was later republished in a compilation of essays *On the Overthrow of Values* (1919,1923). This explored the nature of Christian love against the backdrop of the atheistic, humanistic and subjective trends of his day. Acclaimed by German Catholics and the broader intellectual community alike, familiar with the thought of both,[14] Scheler's ingenious interrogation of Christianity's ardent critic with its saintly exponent earned him the appellation "The Catholic Nietzsche."[15] Within this questioning his friend Martin Heidegger observes: "Augustine and Pascal acquired new meaning – new answers to and against Nietzsche."[16] Writing in "On *Ordo Amoris* and Its Confusions" (1914-15 and 1916), considered the *leitmotiv* of his thought,[17] Scheler indicates the direction of his nascent philosophy of love, the driving force behind this critical exchange: "*Our heart is primarily destined to love,* not to hate." Moreover, identifying the possibility of alternative forms of "*pseudo-* love" he observes: "Even the *man of ressentiment* originally loved the things, which in his present condition he hates."[18]

Considering the cultural and intellectual mix of the past century, the post modern "celebration of plurality,"[19] which prompted a reappraisal of this received bifurcation of love, Denis de Rougemont questions rhetorically what will remain of love once liberated from "our restrictive religious heritage" and now burdened with an unbridled sexuality.[20] More to the point he asks "from what should we 'liberate' love?" suggesting the real obstacle to understanding love are ourselves! Moving from current generational self-indulgence, he posits the surfacing of a "more convivial vision of community" informed by a "new ethic of love" whose goal is the "full and authentic freedom of a real person: *the control, not of others, but of oneself.*" Concluding *Deciphering Eros* (2005) Paul Gifford similarly calls for a more adequate "image of human potential" grounded in the dignity of personal freedom.[21] Nevertheless these ruminations only tell half the anthropological story; often unforeseen consequences accompany love. An unsettling experience for those who we see themselves as being in control, especially of those personal and intimate activities which constitute who we are; where the logic of "one size fits all" doesn't fit. Highlighting this lack of clarity the novelist Siri Hustvedt cautions: "to pretend ambiguity doesn't exist in sexual relations is just plain stupid."[22] Equally misguided is to ignore its presence in other human situations, nowhere more so than the human restlessness in religious activity; Scheler claims: "*Inquietum cor nostrum, donec requiescat in te,* is a basic formula for all religious acts."[23] As beings capable of love, "in the matters of the heart we acknowledge an abiding uncertainty."

Though such emotive phenomena have been dismissed as instinctual and irrational by many, Scheler's God centered and love orientated "*value-personalism*"[24] reflects another approach, one worth revisiting; summarized in his 1921 Preface to the Second Edition of *Formalism in Ethics and Non-Formal Values*:

> What is of moral value, in my view, is not the "isolated" person but the person originally and knowingly joined with God, directed toward the world in love, and feelingly united with the whole of the spiritual world and humanity.[25]

Acclaimed "a phenomenon of genius"[26] and "the most brilliant German thinker of his day,"[27] Scheler presents an enigmatic figure within contemporary thought, whose relatively minor if not forgotten status remains a conundrum. A Catholic philosopher of the heart, he specialized in the phenomenological study of our affective life, feelings and value judgments, understood as non-rational not irrational, within the ambit of what it is to be human; only humans can be surprised, laugh and weep. Recognized as "the greatest philosopher of love in the twentieth century,"[28] this chapter revisits Scheler's univocal concept of love as it evolved within his interrogation of Nietzsche, his religious and philosophical affiliation with Catholicism[29] and its community based medieval, Augustinian Pascal orientation[30] between 1899 till around 1923; as such his philosophy of love is approached accumulatively as it emerges in more than one early work. First applied to "the study of man" by the founder of philosophical anthropology,[31] the expression "deceptive ambiguity," while characterizing his Catholic faith, has particular relevance concerning the value orientation of religious activity, "*amare in Deo,*" wherein the loved religious value of the Holy can become confused, displaced or substituted; Scheler claims: "*Thus man believes either in a God or in an idol. There is no third course open!*"[32] First identified by Nietzsche, this tragic situation of value confusion, on both individual and cultural levels, reveals the vulnerable side of religious activity as a human phenomenon; potentially illusory, it is not as straightforward as we believe. The best selling novel *The Name of the Rose* (1980), written by the medieval specialist[33] and semiotician Umberto Eco, captures the spirit of this confusion, as the fictional Franciscan friar William of Baskerville observes:

> Yes, there is a lust for pain, as there is a lust for adoration, and even a lust for humility. If it took so little to make rebellious angels direct their ardor away from worship and humility toward pride and revolt, what can we expect of a human being?[34]

CONTEMPLATING A VULNERABLE ACTIVITY

> What binds all things to order, governing earth and sea and sky is love. If love's rein slackened all things now held by mutual love at once would fall to warring with each other ... O happy race of men, if love that rules the stars may also rule your hearts![35]

"The last of the Roman philosophers and the first of the scholastic theologians,"[36] Boethius is a figure facing both ways. Raised in the same philosophical abode as Augustine, he was "deeply Augustinian;"[37] however eclectic by disposition, he also absorbed the contemporary Neo-Platonism and available Plato and Aristotle read in the original Greek; his translations and commentaries were an indispensable resource for later generations. This philosophical diversity informs his contemplation (*speculatio*) of love, especially in two poems from his classic *The Consolation of Philosophy*.[38] A dialogue with lady Philosophy, written awaiting execution, he questions why am I here? Living with the choices he made, "often disturbed by destructive affections,"[39] this meditation on evil as privation and the unreliability of fortune which combines Christian doctrine and Greek philosophy, remained a seminal influence. Moreover the *Consolation* identifies the unifying function of love as he connects ontology with theology "under the power of returning love;"[40] a tradition which would prompt Heidegger's critical attention.

An ubiquitous theme in classical and medieval thought, few would disagree with the twelfth century theologian and mystic Richard of Saint-Victor as he begins his treatise *Of the Four Degrees of Passionate Charity*; inspired by the biblical song of love (a medieval favorite): "I am wounded by love. … This is a joyful subject and very fruitful; one that will not weary the writer or fatigue the reader.[41] The Victorine's recognition of the many-sided nature of love, along the "path of love" from the human being to service of neighbor and ultimately towards union with God, reflects the "great preoccupation"[42] within the monastic schools and emerging universities of this time. Approached philosophically, "the problem of love" for these Christian scholars involved a systematic study of the nature of love itself, wherein its versatility was reflected in different expressions applied to "love for God and the divine love for man and human love."[43] Employing the metaphor of mirror (*speculum*), the Schoolmen amalgamated the bipolar relations within the created world under the umbrella of love: "The book of nature reflects the book of the soul; love reflects knowledge, knowledge reflects love. And all, like a many-faceted gem, reflect the grace of compassionate charity;"[44] a connection later addressed by Scheler in "Love and Knowledge" (1915).[45] The later *Amoris divini et humani antipathia* (1629) written by Ludovicus of Leuven reflects this systematic mirroring in its eighty four chapters on love; chapter seventy four is entitled *Speculatio amoris*. "Love's panorama" presents sacred love and the human soul both pointing at their image in a mirror, whereby the soul is carried by God above all discourse and reasoning to reflect on the Absolute,

"God is the very nature of incomprehensibility."

Eco's popular novel, written as "an act of love,"[46] provides a window into this fascinating world. Ingeniously contrived within a fictional fourteenth century monastic setting, the location for an important religious debate, typical for the time, he combines in narrative form a murder mystery perpetrated by monk on monk which underlies the search for a "forbidden manuscript" (the last remaining copy of Aristotle's second book of the *Poetics* on comedy) within an account of the existing religious practices and mores, controversies and heresies; drawn together as the now elderly German monk Adso of Melk tells his own "love story," detailing his youthful experiences (sexual, religious and intellectual) as a novice, along with his impressions gained in the company of his English tutor William while visiting a prosperous Benedictine monastery in North Italy. As a medieval tale of love and lust within a religious environment, "they believed in God but traded with the Devil," Eco's novel illustrates the possible consequences arising from value confusion within religious activity; as in the dialogue, concerning disordered heretical activities, between the young novice and the elderly Cistercian Ubertino of Casale when the Cluniac asks:

> What is love? There is nothing in the world, neither man nor Devil nor any thing, that I hold as suspect as love, for it penetrates the soul more than any other thing. Nothing exists that so fills and binds the heart as love does. Therefore, unless you have those weapons that subdue it, the soul plunges through love into an immense abyss.[47]

Furthermore, in the novel's 1986 film adaptation by Jean-Jacques Annaud, during another conversation with his novice on this same topic William points to the apparent ease wherein genuine religious feelings and activity can be subverted and displaced by irreligious ones: "the step between ecstatic vision and sinful frenzy is all too brief." While Ubertino thoughtfully instructs young Adso "you must learn to distinguish the fire of supernatural love from the raving of the senses;" there is no sense of any puritanical denial of the sensual life within the medieval mind.[48] Moreover as recognized by the Protestant personalist Rudolf Eucken, not only was the sensuous nature viewed as "an essential part of religion," but "the mingling of the sensuous and the spiritual is represented in the main by Roman Catholicism."⁴⁹ Paradoxically, this medieval confluence of divine and human, spiritual and sensuous factors within the nature of love conceals the potential for confusion; detailed by Scheler's appropriation of a disordered "*ordo amoris.*"

From the perspective of a "phenomenology of a cultural tradition,"⁵⁰ the pertinent issue for this new mindset as it absorbed the issues of previous eras was not one of contrasting one type of sensibility with the other as if mutually exclusive but rather integrating them; culminating in the monumental achievement of Scholasticism. Referring initially to the Aristotelian organization of the sciences (*trivium*) taught in monastic schools, it came to represent the systematic cultivation of every branch of human knowledge and the formulation of the truths of the Christian religion integrated within one harmonious whole; in the struggle against Modernism Pope Leo XIII advocated the revival of this philosophical approach in *Aeterni Patris* (1879). Binding everything together was the premise: the truth unfolded by reason cannot contradict the truths revealed by God. An approach used to great effect by Saint Thomas Aquinas, it originates from Boethius' Aristotelian understanding of order which guided his teaching practice and directed his theoretical differentiation between sciences, especially theology and philosophy. A discipline which naturally questions the latter answers these by its use of reason (*ratio*) to examine, order and explain; understood in the context of a *speculatione divina*,⁵¹ Boethius moved beyond dialectical argumentation in his *Consolation* to contemplate the Divine loving governance of the cosmos: "what binds all things to order, governing earth and sea and sky is love (*amor*)."⁵² This God centered metaphysical ordering in love equally applies to our ethical values and norms, informing all human relations, international, social and personal, such as marriage and friendship. However, in her song Philosophy also recognizes the human potential for rebellion against this ordered love; exemplified in Boethius' tragic circumstances. From the twelfth century onwards scholars complemented this philosophical approach, by creatively expropriating the thought of another late fifth century figure, the anonymous

Syrian mystic and monk called Pseudo-Dionysius,[53] who thoroughly Christianized the Neo-platonic concept of hierarchy, especially in their contemplation of ontology;[54] as such reality was ordered and hierarchic.[55] Underlying this systematic approach was the Johannine inspired understanding of love, in which being was lovingly and purposefully created by the Personal God *ex nihil.* Everything created, heavenly bodies, material objects, values, clergy etc. was essentially ordered rather than chaotic and thereby accessible to philosophical scrutiny. Such hierarchical thinking enabled the schoolmen to formulate the multiform nature of love, identifying its power, diversity and passion; they were able to recognize the difference between God and each kind of being within this order of "returning love" without positing any *"distance* or *estrangement* from God." Scheler reflects this Pseudo-Dionysian position when he claims "the formal structures of society, organic and inorganic nature, and the heavens" are constant and mirror "a *stable hierarchy* of powers and *existences"* and a *"hierarchy of values."*[56] In "Ordo Amoris" he states: "Only God can be the apex of the graduated pyramid of the realm of that which is worthy of love, at once the source and the goal of the whole."[57]

While exploring the fictional monastery library, after a fleeting sexual encounter with an unknown peasant girl, Eco has the novice Adso stumble across a treatise *Speculum amoris* by the fictional Maximus of Bologna "on the malady of love.[58] Highlighting love's vulnerability, this reference not only identifies the medieval interest in the multiform nature of love but also recalls its specific genre of *speculum* literature,[59] which sought to include encyclopedic knowledge of a particular topic within a single work, a summary survey such as Roger Bacon's *Speculum alchimiae* or Saint Albert Magnus' *Speculum astronomiae.* By means of this exhaustive process of mirroring, scriptural and patristic thought was amalgamated within an "integral and balanced humanism."[60] For the scholars of the twelfth century, "love was not only to be experienced; it was also to be set in order;" however given humanity's Fallen state the ordering of love, *ordo amoris,* was rather a matter of "reordering" our flawed human love: "He has ordered charity in me." (Song 2:4).[61] This integrative approach towards love and the related study of human feelings[62] was apparent in Medieval

Latin and vernacular literature, which mirrored the juxtaposition between sacred and secular, ordered and disordered, rational and irrational. As a cultural phenomenon, it was apparent in the popularity of Ovid's *Ars Amatoria* during a time of great religious renewal following the Gregorian reforms; typified by the ill fated love affair between Héloïse and Abelard, this era also witnessed the emergence of a theology of marriage along with the ideal of courtly love; all the subject of the audio CD *Speculum Amoris: Medieval Love Lyrics of Mysticism & Eroticism* (1994), a recent compilation of medieval songs propagating the various facets of love. Tract *Dulcis amor* (7) comes from the twelfth century *Carmina Burana*, "the most famous anthology of medieval lyric yet discovered;"[63] popularized by the musical setting of Carl Orff (1936). Also known as the *Burana Codex*, this manuscript collection of songs on religious themes, moral or satirical songs, love songs and drinking songs as well as religious plays was discovered in 1803 in the Bavarian Benedictine Archabbey at Beuron.

As an emergent "phenomena of *consciousness*" disclosed in religiously inspired metaphysical thinking and ethical valuation, priority is given to the latter where "*medieval thinking*" for Scheler merged with "emotional thinking," wherein "*valuating 'prefeelings'* largely determine the unitary formation of meaning."[64] Primarily known for *The Problem of Human Life* (1890), it was the Nobel laureate's next publication *The Truth of Religion* (1901) which consolidated Eucken's influence over his young protégé, under whose supervision Scheler completed his doctorate (1897)[65] and *Habilitation* (1899).[66] Their shared esteem for Augustine's philosophical legacy, especially his study of human nature and religion as a related concern, fuelled an abiding interest in the religious, sensuous and communal spirit of the medieval world. A recent convert to Catholicism (1899) living through the turbulence of Modernism, an early exponent of the phenomenological attitude[67] and later coping with life in chaotic Weimar Germany, paradoxically an era of extensive historical interest in the origins of Christianity, Scheler turned to this lovingly ordered worldview for inspiration: "Every love is love for God, still incomplete, often slumbering or self-infatuated, often stopping, as it were, on its way."[68] While interest in Catholic figures such as Augustine and

Pascal, according to a contemporary Hans Jonas, was a "hot topic" in the German universities during the 1920's,[69] Scheler was not an Augustinian scholar and reliant on secondary sources. As such the medieval *ethos* provided a suitable lens for viewing the Augustinian patrimony which according to Heidegger, Scheler "dressed up in phenomenology;"[70] this qualifies the claim, "no philosopher of the 20th century has professed so great a dependence on Augustine as Max Scheler."[71] Critical of Augustine's over reliance on Neo-Platonic thought, he nevertheless identified Europe's formative cultural and intellectual influence as being "overwhelmingly Augustinian, based on love, action and the in-building of God's kingdom into the world."[72] Scheler returns to this decisive influence as he addresses "Christian Love and the Twentieth Century" (1917):

> We now see clearly the full significance... of the humanitarian erasure of the *first part of the commandment of love*. Once the common reference of all men to *God* is denied, and with it the final, deepest and most effective interconnection of souls, their link in and through God, it is *impossible* to go on assuming any *hierarchy* of values to which our love should be directed in varying measure according to definite laws of preference.[73]

A MIXED LOVE AFFAIR

> I find myself in an immeasurably vast world of sensible and spiritual objects which set my heart and passions in constant motion. I know that the objects I can recognize through perception and thought, as well as all that I will, choose, do, perform, and accomplish, depend on the play of this movement of my heart.[74]

Disorganized, passionate and intellectually "always on the run," Scheler's philosophy of love evolved in tandem with a personal life structured around the playfulness of his own affections, particularly his affiliation with Catholicism: "a heart restless and divided."[75] A "hands on" philosopher, his extensive treatment of the emotional life detailed in his major 1913 phenomenological publications *The Nature of Sympathy* and *Formalism in Ethics and Non-Formal Ethics of Values*,[76] reflects in part his own questionable moral and religious value preferences. Twice dismissed from

University teaching because of public scandal arising from his ex-tra-marital relations with students and three times married, it was a mastery projected in his philosophy but never achieved in his personal life. A figure of ambiguity, remarking on the complexity found in the human being, Scheler could well have had himself in mind: "man has too many ends!"[77] Unlike his sainted religious philosophical inspiration, his personal restlessness remained un-resolved; as critics observed: "Scheler projected his own self too much into his philosophy and, conversely, he did not live up to his philosophical principles in his own life."[78]

For over two thirds of his short life Scheler lectured and wrote from "an avowedly religious standpoint," a recognizable figure within Catholic circles; after a lengthy period away from univer-sity teaching, this reputation was sufficient for his appointment as professor of philosophy in 1919 at the Sociological Institute within the re-established University of predominantly Catholic Cologne. As an aspiring Catholic philosopher Scheler influenced a genera-tion of young realist phenomenologists from Munich and Göttin-gen, later converts to the Catholic faith and prominent philosophers; Edith Stein was canonized a saint (1986) and his friend Dietrich von Hildebrand was informally called by Pope Pius XII "the 20th Century Doctor of the Church." Regarded "a star in the *Catholic literary revival* in Munich,"[79] Scheler contributed numerous articles to *Hochland* (1900),[80] considered Germany's leading Catholic review, founded by his Bavarian journalist friend Carl Muth. This pattern of energetic activity continued in Co-logne through his involvement with the *Katholischer Akademischer Verband,* an organization which sought to combat anti Catholic German intellectual prejudices: "habits of mind conditioned by a long history."[81] Living in the "land of the Reformation," where confessional division informed national consciousness, these asso-ciations sought to counteract the traditional Catholic *"ghetto men-tality"* spawned from the cultural experience of *Kulturkampf,* "the struggle for civilization against obscurantism."[82] As such, Scheler assumed a Catholic identity, particularly necessary for this time: "one of the theologically most eventful and personally tragic peri-ods of Roman Catholicism."[83] While largely immune from this he-retical movement, "when the Encyclical was penned there was no

Modernism in Germany,"[84] Germans were none the less affected by collateral damage, the escalating antagonism "between tendencies which set catholic against catholic."[85] Within certain Catholic circles, Scheler's marginal involvement with a new movement for reform, *Reformkatholizimus,*[86] would have been regarded with suspicion. Founded during the 1890s by Catholic intellectuals such as F.X. Kraus, Hermann Schell and his friend Muth this movement sought the renewal of Catholic thought from within by orthodox means and positively engaged their contemporary culture, its issues and trends. Furthermore, given his personal association with the supposedly modernist Baron Friedrich von Hügel, a former student of his mentor Eucken, all of which seemed to point in a certain direction; "a Catholic, but of course not an ultramontane one."[87] His friend Heidegger, another lapsed Catholic, confirmed this assignation when identifying Scheler's philosophical path "'catholic' as a universal-historical world power, not in the sense of the Church;"[88] elsewhere he observed: "Nowadays, in Germany, through Scheler, the Catholic movement of Modernism also goes back to Augustine."[89] Mindful of category mistakes, Scheler was certainly an advocate, but definitely not an apologist, for a particular understanding of Catholic thought of an Augustinian Pascal orientation. As a matter of principle he shunned all forms of indoctrination, especially the prevalent NeoThomism or "church philosophy."

Nevertheless, appearances can be deceiving as Scheler observes in his 1923 Foreword to *Christianity and Society*: "At no time of his life and development could the author call himself a 'believing Catholic' according to the strict standards of the theology of the Roman Church.[90] Precariously positioned between competing personal influences and values, his actual religious life as a practicing Catholic remained questionable; "at times it appeared forced," observes his mentor, remarking elsewhere "the religious stirrings for him easily take on a forced and dark nature."[91] However, like Nietzsche who claimed in his autobiographical *Ecce Homo* (1888) to "have no experience of actual *religious* difficulties,"[92] Scheler enjoyed religious activities, "expressive action" in liturgical and cultic forms; however the "purposive conduct," the sense of moral responsibility and ethical behavior associated with such activity,[93] let alone its deeper faith commitment remained ambiguous to say the least; As such, his religious life mirrors the apparent ease whereby loved religious values can be confused or displaced. Recalling Pascal's phrase "search groaning," Scheler wandered within an uncertain religious terrain: "[his] need for salvation and his endless search for God took him along ever new paths sprang from the guilty entanglements of his erotic life."[94]

The genesis for this ambiguous confusion is revealed during his "religious conversion," characterized as "*agape* prompted by *eros;*"[95] a mixed affair over several years which led to his eventual baptism as a Catholic in 1899. Born a Jew in Catholic Munich, with a docile Protestant father and a domineering obstinate Jewish mother, Scheler was raised in an entirely secular environment, absorbing the religious spirit of neither parent. It was as a curious fifteen year old that his religious love affair with Catholicism began, an attraction prompted by his youthful fascination with the colorful spectacle of Bavarian Catholic devotion, "the fragrance of the incense and the baroque splendor of the candlelight celebrations" mixed with a sexual subversive element, the presence of attractive young Catholic servant girls from his uncle's house who secretly introduced him to these festivities in the first place;[96] this same relative Ernst Fürther introduced the writings of Nietzsche to his teenage nephew. This Catholic sense of communal celebration united in religious love, initially experienced in Munich was later reinforced during adult life through his association with the Benedictine Archabbey at Beuron.[97] The "Beuron experience"[98] not only recalls Scheler's participation in its religious *ethos* and liturgical life which only confirmed his earlier experience of the communal dimension of Catholic religious activity, one which simultaneously elicits an emotional response from the individual participant, but also identifies the location during the winter of 1916 where the prodigal son sought reconciliation with the Church, his "second conversion." A centre of Catholic liturgical renewal, the Archabbey attracted many contemporary intellectuals, including young phenomenologists such as Scheler and his friends.[99] Within this religious community he experienced the personal integration of the religious and philosophical influences in his life; the latter initially received through the guidance of an

Augustinian priest, the chaplain at his local *Gymnasium*, who introduced his young student to the philosophical foundations of Christian love and its communal expression as understood by Saint Augustine. This priest's religious example serves a key role in Scheler's later philosophy of religion.[100]

Scheler's loss of Catholic faith, questionable to begin with, was also a gradual process marked by factors equally mixed; his increasingly intermittent Catholic practice, vacillating between spiritual abandonment occasioned by erotic excess and renewed religious fervor following repentance, his third civil marriage in 1924 and the escalation of his overt criticism of "Catholic ideology"[101] with its closed forms of "*dogmatic thinking*," outlined in *Problems of a Sociology of Knowledge* (1924); all prompted Scheler's "slow and painful realization that even my anti-scholastic and anti-Thomistic version of Augustinianism was really incompatible with the dogmatic philosophy of the Church."[102] On a sociopolitical level, his increasing frustration with the ineffectiveness of Catholicism as a community building force within post-war Germany, "the Christian commandment of love is one of edification and *organization*,"[103] fuelled his critical reappraisal and rejection of the basic tenet of Christianity, "a spiritual, personal God omnipotent in his spirituality;"[104] culminating in the eventual repudiation of his Catholic faith: "I can no longer claim to be a 'theist' in the usual sense."[105] However, consistent with the value orientation associated with sphere of the Absolute, common to human beings, a religious substitute for the Holy was now required which he found in "his own private religion of the impotent evolving God."[106] The God of religious faith, the "Divine Person," was replaced by a conceptual idol, the neutral "Divine" within a radical religiously inspired meta-anthropology. Herein the human being becomes the locus for the "becoming God" in a bizarre reversal of the Incarnation and classic dualism; an impotent "spirit" and directive "life" merge within a pantheistic anthropomorphic process of "*Deitas;*" the subject of religious aphorisms. His forthcoming publication *Philosophical Anthropology* (never published) would examine the "history of man's self-understanding and his relation to sub-human nature and the deity."[107] Concerning the reversal of his thought Staude observes "the Catholic Nietzsche withdrew into the mists of Schellingian pantheism."[108] However, another contemporary the Catholic theologian Hans Urs von Balthasar characterized the potential for subversion within the evolution of Scheler's thought as a whole, from the Christian inspired "eternal in man" into the "eternal man."[109] Perhaps greater clarity may be gained with the now completion of Scheler's *Gesammelte Werke* (1954-1997). Resigning from university teaching in late 1927, he relocated from Cologne to Frankfurt to take up a new position in its University. Expectations for a new beginning were short lived; aged fifty four Scheler died from a sudden heart attack on May 19, 1928. Perhaps the final deception was his Catholic burial in Cologne's South cemetery; the celebrant unaware of his denial of faith. His grave bears no religious signage.

THE HEART OF THE MATTER

> Christian 'love' is a particular kind of spiritual act, which is by its very essence primarily orientated toward the spiritual person (of God and men)...[110]

Nietzsche introduces *On the Genealogy of Morality* (1887) with the scriptural adage "where your treasure is, there will your heart be also," adding: "*our* treasure is where the hives of knowledge are."[111] Returning to the genesis of our values, Nietzsche revaluated these by a "*critique* of moral values, *the value of these values should itself, for once, be examined.*"[112] Employing this highly innovative approach, he pin pointed the fundamental flaw in the Christian morality of love (charity), namely its evolution from the non-religious reactive sentiment of *ressentiment*: "Jesus of Nazareth, the embodiment of the gospel of love" initiated the "slave's revolt in morality when *ressentiment* itself turns creative and gives birth to values."[113] As such, the master of suspicion and consummate critic, sought the end of Christianity "at the hands of its own morality (which cannot be replaced);" achieving the juxtaposition between philosophical "meaninglessness" and "moral value judgments."[114] Devaluing the loving artifice of Christianity, Nietzsche simultaneously recognized the emotive power of love over "the meanest intelligence and the coldest heart," and its inherent ambiguity, the possibility of value confusion and deception; as observed earlier in *Human, All Too Human* (1878): "Can *all* values not be turned round? and is good perhaps evil? and God only an invention and finesse of the Devil? Is everything perhaps in the last resort false?" Concerning our valuations, if we are capable of being deceived, he argues "*must* we not be deceivers?"[115] Although human beings possess a wonderful, if not deceptive capacity for valuation; as "born winged-insects and intellectual honey gatherers" in a constant flurry of acquisitive activity, beings who value and know they do so, Nietzsche claims "we are unknown to ourselves," because we have never looked: "Who *are* we, in fact?"[116] This connection between values and humanity remained a pivotal concern for both Nietzsche and Scheler. By this historical critical reassessment of value formation, their related feelings and religious metaphysical foundations in *On the Genealogy of Morality*, Nietzsche repositioned the study of values within mainstream philosophical discourse;[117] an exchange first undertaken by Scheler in *Ressentiment* (1912); utilizing the Catholic philosophical resources which inform his emerging philosophy of love. By his likewise critical response, the Catholic Nietzsche not only defends the value of Christian love, "a particular kind of spiritual act," but in so doing ingeniously subverts the Nietzschean polemic, overturning the current values of the humanitarian *ethos*, with its accompanying denial of God, as itself a product of *ressentiment*. Recently another Catholic Bavarian engaged Nietzsche's value critique as a means of approaching the issue of Christian love; at the beginning of his first encyclical *Deus Caritas Est* Pope Benedict XVI asks the rhetorical question: "Did Christianity really destroy *eros*?"[118] Perhaps the Holy Father had the following passage from *Twilight of the Idols* (1888) in mind: "it was only Christianity, with *ressentiment against* life in its foundations, which made of sexuality something impure: it threw *filfth* on the beginning, on the prerequisite of our life."[119]

> There can be no doubt that the Christian ethos is inseparable from the Christian *religious* conception of God and the world.... At the very least, Christian morality must be tied to Christian religion by the assumption of a spiritual realm whose objects, contents and values transcend not only the sensory sphere, but the whole sphere of *life*.[120]

The "thinker of the *Eternal in Man*,[121] Scheler's philosophy of love reflects this Christian worldview, wherein human beings understood as personal loving beings relate to each other and fulfill their very essence and ultimate destiny in a freely realized loving relationship in God; as loving beings we are religious. Confronting Nietzsche's atheistic diagnosis of value confusion Scheler returned to a Christian medieval understanding of love, personal and communal, along with its integral anthropology; in so doing he recognizes a continuity rather than opposition between *agape* and *eros*. These are absorbed within a personal understanding of love, an activity arising from our spiritual nature, "a spiritual intentionality which transcends the natural sphere;" elsewhere he states "love is *the* fundamental spiritual act; it is an irreducible and spontaneous movement."[122] However as with the schoolmen, the natural, sensual and vital dimensions within the human experience are integrated rather than denied or denigrated within an ordered understanding of love: "Love loves and in loving always looks beyond what it has in hand and possesses."[123] As such, Christian love is distinguished by the God initiated personal "*direction of its movement:*"[124] "Now the very *essence* of God is to love and serve."[125] Scheler's Augustinian inspired recognition of the dynamic tendency in love to proceed in either direction, in the opinion of Herbert Spiegelberg, marks his originality concerning the phenomenon of love;[126] it also reveals the potential for "*pseudo-love.*"

Responsible for introducing "the analysis of emotional life to the phenomenological movement,"[127] humans are emotional beings capable of desire and attraction, experiencing different levels of sensations and feelings, such as fear, sympathy, friendship and love, understood on the basis of "*an original* emotive intentionality"[128] disclosed in our consciousness. In response to the question "how is reality given?" Scheler answered "through feelings:"[129] "*All feelings* possess an experienced relatedness to the person."[130] As such, this personal connection links the objective hierarchy of values (sensible, vital, intellectual and religious) with our experience of emotions and feelings, given prior to conceptual representation: "the recognition of a *cultivation of the heart* as an autonomous concern, completely independent of the cultivation of understanding."[131] Considered non-rational rather than irrational, Scheler draws on the Pascalian assertion "the heart has *its* reasons," wherein he claims there is an "*ordre du Coeur*, a *logique du coeur*, a *mathématique du Coeur;*" an ordering as objective as deductive logic.[132] In rejecting the usual empirical or intellectual reduction of "*the whole emotional life*" to sensibility, by means of phenomenology Scheler approaches our emotional life, along side the rational though differentiated, as constitutive parts within the whole human being; there is no question of either/or. Popularly known for his *Pensées* (1670), Scheler begins and ends "Love and Knowledge," (1915) with references to Blasé Pascal's earlier "Conversations on the Passions of Love"(1653);[133] containing the kernel of his Christian anthropology later developed in the *Pensées*, which confirms its authenticity, Pascal "validated and further extended Augustine's chain of thought." In probably his last Catholic essay, "The Meaning of Suffering (1923), Scheler also cites this early work: "Pleasure is good and suffering bad. Man needs no proof of this. The heart feels it."[134] While "man was born to think," Pascal also recognizes we are "born with a sense of love in our hearts, which develops as the mind is perfected;" within this coincidence between "love and reason" Scheler reads a deeper meaning, namely "love first *discloses* objects, which appear to the senses and which reason later judges."[135] Furthermore, while love might be our most natural passion, writing in "Conversations," Pascal recognizes we are capable of being confused as to the value of what best fills the vacuum within ourselves as "the most beautiful creature God ever made." Interestingly Scheler's other explicit reference to the earlier mentioned Greek expressions was in his essay "Love and Knowledge" (1915) where he favors another expression of supposedly Augustinian origin, "*amare in Deo*," which he makes his own.[136] Marion reflects a similar preference for Latin when he claims: "Making love in advance perhaps does not depend upon me, but *loving to love (amare amare)* does."[137]

"Marching forth from his Benedictine retreat to attack the windmills of modern European civilization,"[138] Scheler's philosophy of love evolved within a broader context: the emergence of a massive religious cultural phenomenon at the beginning of last century, the erosion of belief; which initiated "the age of atheism"[139]and its variants, humanitarianism, naturalism and individualism. The calamitous years of European hostility 1914-1918 and the cultural disintegration left in its aftermath only confirmed Scheler's diagnosis of the era's deleterious condition, "its immense *désordre du coeur*,"[140] which required a cultural rejuvenation of the heart of Christian love as the only means of reconstruction. Characterized by a shift in religious consciousness spanning a relatively short two hundred years, this began as a private affair, such as when an intellectual elite of like minds gathered together in the Paris salon of the atheistic materialist Baron Paul d'Holbach, and progressed to a cultural phenomenon of radical godlessness shared by millions of ordinary human beings constitutionally unable to believe or appreciate in any way the existence of the Judeo-Christian God. How was this remarkable feat accomplished? Obviously a complex issue, but in no small part was this achieved by paying attention to something we all share and recognize, our emotional life. No longer the province of philosophical abstraction within talk fests among intellectuals, a new breed of atheists emerged who directed attention to our human condition as such, understood as the source of religion, and to something we all understand, namely the values which inform our emotional life, not only positive feelings of love, but also reactive feelings of pity, revenge and *ressentiment*; well expressed by Ludwig Feuerbach: *"Man feels nothing towards God which he does not also feel towards man. Homo homini deus est."*[141]   This religious disintegration of Europe was recognized by disparate figures such as Cardinal John Henry Newman and Friedrich Nietzsche;[142] the so-called "patron saint of postmodern philosophy."[143]

> Christianity is essentially a matter for the heart...The main teachings of Christianity only relates to the fundamental truths of the human heart; they are symbols....To become blessed through faith means nothing other than the old truth, that only the heart, not knowledge, can make happy. That God became human only shows that humans should not seek their blessedness among eternity, but instead found their paradise on the earth;... It [humanity] recognizes in itself "the beginning, the middle, the end of religion. [144]

Following his Christian confirmation in 1861, the "little pastor" became increasingly disillusioned with the value of religion: later characterized as "the product of the people's childhood."[145] Writing above in 1862, Nietzsche reveals his disenchantment, subverting the emotive language of the heart to disclose Feuerbach's atheistic anthropological reduction of religion undertaken in "that dangerous book," *The Essence of Christianity* (1841), received as a birthday present: "The beginning, middle and end of religion is MAN."[146]   Losing faith around 1865, the youthful Nietzsche exchanged religious certainty for its opposite: "Strife is the perpetual food of the soul, and it knows well enough how to extract the sweetness from it."[147]   As with Scheler, humanity remained pivotal in Nietzsche's value philosophy. Writing in his unfinished "On Truth and Lies in a Nonmoral Sense"(1873)[148] he outlines a severely naturalistic picture of this condition, living alone and adrift in an irrational world devoid of a benevolent God. A mere cosmic accident, humans are ill equipped either to comprehend what is going on or to do much about it. While Nietzsche's philosophical indebtedness to Arthur Schopenhauer following his accidental reading of *The World as Will and Representation* (1818) in 1865 goes without saying; his "great teacher's *nihilism*" became increasingly untenable, "he *said 'no'* to life and to himself as well."[149] Rejecting his nihilistic pessimism, Nietzsche also questions "Schopenhauer's religio-moral interpretation of men and the world," especially his confusion "over the *value of religion with respect to knowledge*."[150] Nothing and no-one escaped Nietzsche's critical attention; as revealed in his most philosophical work, *Human, All Too Human* (1878), which marks Nietzsche's radical break with Modernity as his astute, critical and severe observations on so many fronts of human experience inexorably moved to a single conclusion: the interpretative and evaluative foundations of Western civilization are vacuous, lamentably "human, all too human."

Introducing *Ecce Homo* (1888) Nietzsche claims: "*Human, All Too Human* (1878) is the memorial of a crisis."[151] The nature of this crisis came in moment of sudden insight, outlined in his 1886 Preface to the first volume of *Human, All Too Human*: "Renouncing everything I once revered? renouncing reverence itself" and having grasped the "sense of perspective in every value judgment" he realized "*the problem of the order of rank*" was his problem.[152] This is later confirmed in *On the Genealogy of Morals*, when Nietzsche announces what amounts to be a second critical phase; having addressed "the *problem of values*," it was necessary to decide "the *rank order of values*;"[153] this work ends with his first published reference to *The Will to Power. Attempt at a Revaluation of all Values*.[154] Desperately ill, it would not be an overestimation to claim Nietzsche's later life was haunted by "the shadow-existence of the *Revaluation*;"[155] a philosophical task of encyclopedic proportions. Writing in *The Anti-Christ* (1888), planned as the first volume of *The Revaluation of all Values* Nietzsche claims: "What sets *us* apart is not that we recognize no God, either in history or in nature or behind nature – but that we find that which has been reverenced as God is not 'god-like' but pitiable, absurd, harmful, not merely an error but a *crime against life*."[156] An indication as to the meaning of the latter is provided in *Will to Power* (1901): "But *what is life?* ... My formula for it is: Life is will to power."[157] While post-Cartesian philosophy is characterized by the gradual emancipation from Christian religion; Nietzsche's comprehensive philosophy sought to achieve a complete break, accomplished from within by means of internal criticism. For Heidegger, Nietzsche thinks nihilism as the "inner logic" of Western history.[158] Considered the "last metaphysician," the "will to power" is no mere human willing; rather it is the mode of Being now ruling everything that is, and following the "death of God," the basis of human resourcefulness. Formulated by Jacques Derrida, for Nietzsche "the entire history of religion and philosophy can be regarded as a 'history of metaphors and metonyms.'" As such Derrida argues: "We have no language – no syntax and no lexicon – which is removed from this history."[159] The genealogical devaluation of values is a prelude to the inevitable "advent of nihilism," which anticipates the arrival of "*new values*;"[160] revaluation provides the means for a "courageous becoming- conscious and affirmation of what has been achieved."[161] In other words, the diagnosis itself becomes the revaluation: "*That the highest values devaluate themselves;*" adding in a note "It is *ambiguous*."[162] With uncharacteristic optimism, he projects a new theory of value to fill the void occasioned by devaluation: "The new values must first be created – we shall not be *spared* this task!"[163] As "free spirits," philosophers become adventurers and circumnavigators of that inner world called "man," that "higher" and "one [above] the other" likewise called "man." Interestingly given Nietzsche's anti Christian project, perhaps another instance of subverting from within, these later themes find a certain resonance with thought of two prominent Catholic authors who similarly addressed the anthropological context of ordered values. As Nietzsche sharpened his critical understanding of revaluation by undertaking an extensive program of background reading, especially during the last three years of his troubled life, he reacquainted himself with a Catholic philosopher, first read in 1878;[164] well regarded by Nietzsche, Pascal was considered a personal example of how Christianity can corrupt even the "most supreme and honest of men."[165] Furthermore, in 1885 Nietzsche read "for relaxation" another Catholic figure not so well regarded, as he approached Augustine's *Confessions* (ca 400) with the eye of "a radical physician and physiologist." Typical of his personalized idiosyncratic reading, Nietzsche dismissed Augustine's "passion for God"[166] by *ad hominem* remarks, attacking his values and attitudes, reducing his religious and metaphysical statements to psychological and physiological motives or causes: "Philosophical value zero! *Vulgarized* Platonism – a way of thinking which was invented for the highest aristocracy of the soul, and which he adjusted to suit slave natures. Moreover, one sees into the guts of Christianity in this book."[167]

Nietzsche's critical access to Christianity was through the lens of another. While the French word *ressentiment* became synonymous with his philosophy; this reactive sentiment was first used by another Schopenhauerian, Eugen Dühring's *The Value of Life: A Course in Philosophy* (1865),[168] to identify the genesis of justice; whereas for Nietzsche "the *last* territory to be conquered by the spirit of justice is that of reactive sentiment!" Moreover, Scheler's discussion of this sentiment, in response to Nietzsche's highly original use, enables him to identify the potential for confusion and ambiguity within our valuations. While both recognize *ressentiment* as a factor in the genesis of morality, especially its formative influence in our value preferences; Nietzsche exaggerated this, claiming "to know the conditions from which those values have sprung and how they developed and changed." "A self-poisoning of the mind" *ressentiment* is literally a re-feeling of an original feeling of bitterness or indignation, initiated by a conflict with another's values, accompanied by an experience of "weakness" or "powerlessness;" characteristic of the "master-slave" relationship. These experiences have definite causes and consequences, arising from the systematic repression of certain emotions, such as revenge, hatred, malice and envy, all normal components within our human nature.[169] As such, a direct connection exists between their repression and the emergence of value delusions; wherein the emotional discomfort occasioned by *ressentiment* is reassigned to an external cause against which we react. By means of this phenomenological analysis Scheler ingeniously subverts Nietzsche's original characterization of Christian love "as the most delicate flower of *ressentiment*," arguing his original hostility towards the influence of Christian love represents such a value confusion or delusion. Essentially, the feeling of *ressentiment* presupposes the recognition of higher values against which we react, such Augustine's experience of restlessness; the source of its philosophical significance. For Scheler, Christianity was not *ressentiment* ridden, but rather the modern humanitarian *ethos*, with its accompanying denial of God and religious community, is such an instance of disordered love and value confusion, born of ignoble weakness and the denial of vital values, in favor of values of utility. Furthermore, for these authors valuation does not occur in isolation, *in vacuo*; as a human activity this presupposes a something "other" against which that which is valued, an "in relation to a what?" Whether a Personal God, a "tablet of virtues," a list of rules or norms etc., valuation is contextual and historical; especially when accessing the ordering of values. While recognized problematic by Nietzsche, his life filled nihilism prevented its resolution; whereas for Scheler, Pascal and Augustine our valuations are grounded in a God centered form of hierarchical ordered love. Nevertheless, both Nietzsche and Scheler understand these ordered valuations as revelatory, they disclose who we are as human beings.

Unlike Nietzsche's "God is dead" humanism, built on a vague promissory "will to power," Scheler's response to "What is man?" and "What is man's place in the nature of things?,"[170] a unifying theme throughout his philosophical development, was "colored by the anthropology of Christianity"[171] until 1923: "*Our heart is primarily destined to love.*" Adopting Pascal's insight, he furthermore claims: "*Whoever has the* ordo amoris *of a man has the man himself;*" namely, the direction of our ordered love reveals the "basic line of our heart (*Gemüt*) running beneath our empirical many-sidedness and complexity."[172] Living during the Modernist crisis, and looking for an alternative to the prevalent Neo-Scholastic rationalism, Scheler turned to the Augustinian Pascal orientation, with its combined emphasis on intuitive interiority and the primacy of "the reasons of the heart;" as his contemporary the Jesuit Erich Przywara remarks: "Augustinianism set out from the restless tension of the creature; Thomism thinks rather of the creature as proceeding from and external to the self-existent God."[173] Considered the greatest proponent of the "philosophy of the heart,"[174] Augustine introduces his *Confessions* by citing Psalm 34:3 "*Whisper in my heart, I am here to save you,*" to which he responds "my soul is like a house, small for you to enter, but I pray you to enlarge it.[175] Within Christian iconography Augustine holds a heart, symbolizing both the direction of his thought and his mystical experience. Understood as "the personal core" of the human being, the "heart" discloses the affective dimension of human experience, especially in the exercise of free will and personal choice; the *cordis affectus* of the twelfth century Cistercian tradition. However, as Augustine well recognized, human love and the judgment of value in our personal choices can be confused and misdirected, characterized by his own "restless heart" (*cor inquietum*); revealing humanity's darker side Scheler cites with approval Pascal's inversion "Our Heart is too spacious."[176] While the motivational or driving impulse (*Triebimpuls)* which arouses our attention may diminish, the activity of love is boundless, fulfilling itself in what is found worthy of love, "*what* we grasp as *worthy of love*": "Love loves and in loving always looks beyond what it has in hand and possesses."[177] In this context, "the *sursum corda* may assume fundamentally different forms at different elevations in the various regions of love," revealing the emotional dynamism in our loving search for God and moral goodness: "*Inquietum cor nostrum donec requiescat in te* – God and only God can be the apex of love."[178]

Within its human context, Christian love is understood as receptive, as being God given; the legal axiom *"nemo dat quod non habet"*
best expresses this Augustinian understanding. Scheler shares as
this understanding as he concludes his essay "Repentance and
Rebirth" (1917): "Love stirred within us. At first we thought it our
love – the love of God – our love of him. We came to know it for
his love – the love of God. His love of us."[179] However, as both
Nietzsche and Scheler recognize, the potential exists, both individually and culturally, for our loved valuations to be confused or
misdirected: "Even the *man of ressentiment* originally loved the
things which in his present condition he hates."[180] Scheler characterizes this deceptive ambiguity as *"infatuation" (Vergaffung)*,
and represents the confusion of our "ordo amoris;" it captures the
experience of being enraptured by some finite good, regardless of
the overall direction of our personal choices which constitute our
heart; such behavior is delusive.[181] Within religious activity, a
valued good understood as absolute through delusion is called an
"idol;" a situation characterized by the experience of "dissatisfaction," occasioned by the lack of proportion between the personal
activity and the intentional object, equally applicable to the individual person and the community, reflected in its cultural *ethos.*

> "Man" as the being of "highest value" among earthly beings and as a
> moral being becomes comprehensible and phenomenologically intui-
> table only on the presupposition of the idea of God and *"in the light"* of
> this idea! We can even say that, correctly viewed, he *is* only this move-
> ment, the *tendency* and the *transition* to the divine.[182]

A Catholic phenomenologist, Scheler appreciated the diversity
and complexity of our love as human beings, wherein we attain
our individuality, distinctiveness and unity of life: "The fullness,
the gradations, the differentiations, and the power of his love cir-
cumscribe the fullness...and *range* of contact with the universe.[183]
Against Nietzsche's one dimensional naturalism, he saw human
nature as multidimensional, capturing our inherent complexity:
"Man would undermine his own being if he cultivated only the
spiritual and intellectual powers at the expense of his lower, vi-
talistic, emotional nature."[184] As a unity of life, we are natural and
social beings whose material, rational, emotional and personal

dimensions must all be respected; avoiding the traditional oppositions, these dimensions function simultaneously. However, the personal qualitatively distinguishes humanity, recognized through a variety of resources namely rational, cultural and religious, traditionally understood as reflecting "spirit;" this is integrated with the other dimensions designated as "life." While *"indefinability,"* characterizes humanity,[185] the personal is constitutively "open," understood as an unceasing dynamic movement towards values; associated with this is our personal "self-transcendence," whereby the human being "can *transcend all* life and can *transcend* oneself;" in fact, the person is the "intention and gesture of 'transcendence' itself."[186] Reacting to the modernist blight of immanentism, Scheler views this personal transcendence as ultimately moving towards God as Divine Person; as such the human person is a "God-seeker:"

> Therefore the idea of "person" as *applied* to God is not an anthropomorphism! God is rather the only *complete* and *pure person.* And what we may call a human person is only an incomplete "person" conceived in terms of a simile.[187]

Seeking the "eternal" in man, Schelers' phenomenological anthropology is both *"theomorphic,"* wherein the human person is "the *tendency* and the *transition* to the divine"[188] and *"cosmomorphic,"* where humanity is understood as "microcosm, an actual embodiment of the reality of existence in *all* its forms."[189] This is further detailed by means of two distinctive features of Scheler's thought; which are employed to great effect in his understanding of religious activity. As a hierarchical thinker, our emotional life is viewed as "a highly differentiated system of natural revelations and signs," wherein the levels of our emotional life and corresponding experience possess "an inherent meaning."[190] Revealing his indebtedness to Augustine and Pascal, Scheler sees an "original relatedness" between our stratified emotional life (sensible feelings, feelings of life, pure psychic feelings and spiritual feelings)[191] and the objective hierarchy of values, wherein the latter are given immediately in emotional activity prior to conceptual representation; one commentator observes: "the intentionality of affectivity is irreducible to that of cognition or volition."[192] In these circumstances Augustine's insight is confirmed: "love is not blind."[193] These ideas have particular significance for understanding religion, wherein Scheler uses the prompting of the human heart, "from those sources in man where divine and merely human streams connect"[194] in understanding the nature of religious activity; he literally absorbed the spirit of the beatitudes: "Blessed are the pure in heart, for they will see God." (Matthew 5:8). Approached from this human perspective of *"in lumine Dei,"* religion and love as sides of the one coin.

The recognition of "spheres of consciousness" within human beings marks a further distinctive Schelerian insight.[195] With the resourceful complexity within human awareness in view, these are considered *Urgegebene,* foundational phenomena within consciousness whose existence is assumed and was never submitted to critical appraisal. Irreducible to each other, they are "co-original" and possess an original identity and order; Scheler identified five spheres in the following order: the social, external, inward, the inanimate and the Absolute; "A *new* order, a new absolute layer of being,"[196] this sphere was initially detailed in his first two phenomenological publications. When combined with his "epistemological principle of self-evidence," (especially concerning the sphere of the Absolute it makes as little sense of "proving" its existence as proving the existence of the external world, the self or one's fellow beings),[197] these naturally accessible "spheres of being and their related objects" contribute to an integral understanding of consciousness and especially provide Scheler in "Problems of Religion"(1921) with the theoretical basis for his phenomenological study of religious activity as a natural phenomena; based in our shared human access to the sphere of the Absolute. Nevertheless, revealing the influence of a medieval understanding of love as communal and in view of the social character of being human, Scheler appreciates an experiential priority is given to the other, *"the social sphere of the 'with-world' (Mitwelt)* or the sphere of human togetherness, "I and Thou;" *"Where there is an 'I' there is a 'we', or 'I' belong to a 'we'."*[198] By means of the "Robinson Crusoe" experience, he discloses our innate awareness of communal *"belonging"* in persons who live in complete isolation through the experience of the "non-fulfillment" of certain intentions, such as loving, promising, thanking, all of which are directly related to the other person as "bearer of values;" this personal restlessness, the emptiness of our hearts reveals our human relatedness and mutual solidarity. Given our social nature as individuals, being conceived in a loving relationship and born into family life, there are four corresponding types of collective being, namely the mass, life-community, society and person-community (*Gesamtperson*), i.e. family, Church and nation; the latter concept reflects the influence of Ferdinand Tönnies and his distinction between "living community" (*Gemeinschaft*) and artificially constructed forms of being together, "society" (*Gesellschaft*).[199] In this context, the Catholic Church is considered distinctively personal. Interestingly, Scheler develops Eucken's earlier use of the "I-Thou" notion in his *The Truth of Religion* (1901),[200] originally used by Feuerbach in a discussion concerning the nature of the God-head; "*The mystery of the Trinity is the mystery of participated, social life – the mystery of I and Thou.*"[201] Originally employed to great effect concerning the issue of inter-subjectivity in *The Nature of Sympathy* (1912); this use certainly predates that of his contemporary the Jewish philosopher Martin Buber in his classic *I and Thou* (1922) which details his dialogical philosophy. This social priority informs the significance given to the religious community, the Church, as a constitutive element within religious activity; it is within the religious community we first receive access to the gift of God's love.

The ordered value orientation of Scheler's understanding of love, viewed as an independent though variable personal activity within an integral understanding of what it is to be human, anticipates the direction taken by contemporary thinkers such as Jean-Luc Marion who also advocates love as univocal, "the indivisibility of the single garment of love" whose story is "only told in *one way*"[202] or Pope Benedict XVI who claims in his encyclical *Deus Caritas Est* (2006): "'love' is a single reality, but with different dimensions."[203] Ultimately all three recognize that as human beings we are the recipients of the precious gift of love "which God lavishes upon us and which we in turn must share with others."[204]

LOVING IN GOD

> The love of God in its highest form is not to have love "for" God, the All-merciful - for a mere concept, in effect; it is to *participate* in His love for the world (*amare mundum in Deo*), and for Himself (*amare Deum in Deo*); in other words it is what the scholastics, the mystics and Saint Augustine before them, called "*amare in Deo.*" If we wish to ascribe the highest of moral qualities to God, in the infinite mode of being, we can only do so by following Saint John and Saint Augustine, in treating love as the inmost essence of God Himself, and *identifying* Him as Infinite Love.[205]

Since Clinias of Crete claimed "all Greeks and barbarians believe in the existence of gods" as fact,[206] philosophers have scrutinized the nature of religion, its claims and significance within society. Living in an "age of collapse" and "sensitive and receptive to the winds of many a doctrine that swept Germany in the first quarter of the twentieth century,"[207] as well as to his own traditional Catholic resources, Scheler offers a very original appreciation of religious activity in its own right, as a means toward the philosophical (and implied cultural) rehabilitation of religion. Though his essential phenomenology of religion was undertaken well into his career: "To seek religion, not in the sense merely of piety or inner adherence to existing positive religion, but in the sense of new faith-inspired thinking about the objective realm of religion;"[208] the foundations were prepared much earlier within his philosophy of love. A difficult and enigmatic text to approach, *On the Eternal in Man* (1921) contains an assemblage of several pre-existing essays, written independently between 1917 and 1920, and includes "Problems of Relgion"(1921), purposefully written for this publication; this remains the primary source for his thought on religion. Envisaged as the first volume of a three part series entitled *Religious Renewal,* a second volume was announced in 1923, comprising two earlier essays "*Ordo Amoris*" and "Love and Knowledge;" while this never eventuated, the connection between religion and love should be obvious from their content. Furthermore, the former operates as an Archimedean fulcrum throughout Scheler's *Gesammelte Werke* or at least until 1923; though he certainly retains interest in religion after losing his faith. The originality of specifying the "essence of religion" from within its own resources undertaken in "Problems of Religion," first impressed the young Talmudic scholar Levinas studying in Strasburg in 1923; perhaps not so surprising given the essay's positive influence on his tutor, the Alsatian professor of Protestant theology and young phenomenologist Jean Héring, author *Phé-nomènologie et philosophie religieuse* (1925).

Notwithstanding an "unconscionable number of 'view-points"[209] regarding religion, writing in his 1923 Preface to *On the Eternal in Man*, new opportunities also emerged during the post-war European crisis, such as a *"loosening of traditional rigidity* of thought;" a factor Scheler attributes to its positive reception.[210] Given the necessarily complex and ambiguous nature of religion, which in many respects mirrors the human condition, he sought a middle path, certainly one less traveled at the time but gaining popularity within a small circle of contemporary theorists of religion,[211] focusing attention on religious activity itself; specifically the "irreducible elementary phenomena in the mystic experience of divinity." Understood as *"amare in Deo,"* this unobtrusive but critical expression allowed Scheler, following Augustine, to regain the essentially theistic perspective critically denied by Nietzsche; mirroring his phenomenological realism, this religious intimacy supplies "the meaningfulness of monotheistic religious experience and its intentional object."[212] Characterized an "enthusiastic philosopher"[213] by his contemporary Alfred Schutz, who as a public speaker could easily engage, entertain and retain his audience's attention; this similarly captures Scheler's lifelong interest *in God* and *concerning God, (en theo)*; notwithstanding the radical transition from traditional theism to a bizarre dualistic pantheism, his 1926 claim remains pertinent: "The meaning of man's life is first of all God."[214] By means of this philosophical project, "the search for God in man within community," Scheler endeavored to redress the humanitarian erasure of the *"first part of the commandment of love"* and the consequent demise of the religious community and denial of "any *hierarchy* of values to which our love should be directed in varying measure according to definite laws of prefer-ence."[215] A twofold restorative process of retrieval and appropriation provided the means: *"For 'back to X' is the essential form of religious renewal.*"[216] Returning to the Augustinian tradition which first drew attention to the anthropological religious context wherein the personal nature of God was disclosed, experienced and understood; this was absorbed within his own *value personalism* and phenomenological understanding of "experience;" which he used to "avoid the extremes which have plagued the philosophy of religion."[217] Given their reliance on "extra-religious factors," such as intelligence, ethical activity or a subjective emotional experience, both Thomism and Kantianism provided an inadequate basis for understanding religious activity; reduced to either rationalism or fideism. Perhaps his attitude is best expressed by Pascal: "If we submit everything to reason our religion will be left with nothing mysterious or supernatural. If we offend the principles of reason our religion will be absurd and ridiculous."[218] While the Protestant Friedrich Schleiermacher, writing in *On Religion: Speeches to Its Cultured Despisers* (1799) engendered a particular interest in religious experience as a universal phenomenon, grounded in the emotive experience of "feeling" by the religious subject, it was the American pragmatic philosopher and psychologist William James in his *fin de siècle* classic *The Varieties of Religious Experience* (1902), who was responsible for the promotion of a philosophical interest in the emotive life as a means to understanding religion: "it is the feelings, acts and experiences of individual men, in their solitude" not theologies or stifling church rituals, which provide the key to understanding the spiritual life and religious activity.[219] However, James failed to appreciate the distinctive religious character, reducing it to the human: "But religious love is only man's natural emotion of love directed to a religious object."[220] Taking distance from the connotations of individual subjectivism associated with "experience," in view of his own realism as it integrated Husserl's understanding of intentionality, this word assumes a new significance: "*Experience is an 'intentional' act in which an experiencer is directed toward an experienced object.*"[221] Understood as mutually constitutive, incorporating a "consciousness of an object" as well as a subject, Scheler broadened the parameters within which experience is approached, avoiding a "*too narrowly exclusive a concept of experience,*"[222] one which accessed the collective experience of the religious community, hitherto unnoticed by philosophers. By means of his phenomenological study of religious experience, "a new faith-inspired thinking about the objective realm of religion," Scheler reestablished the primacy of the loved religious object (God) within the religious community, understood as sharing God's love with others, as determinant for the integrity of religious activity. In so doing, a distinctive triadic structure is disclosed, based on the tenets of his *value personalism*, which incorporates the individual believer as person, the religious community, "community-person" (*Gesmatperson)* or "love-community" (*Liebegemeinschaft*) and the Divine Person, the religious object characterized as: "Only a real being with the essential character of Divinity can be the cause of man's religious propensity."[223] This personal structure within religious activity, and only in religion because of its object, identifies Scheler's extraordinary originality, whereby he transcends the traditional bipolarity associated with religious experience, necessarily incorporating the religious community. Writing in *The Nature of Sympathy* (1913): "a personalist view of human brotherhood entails theism (according to our account, whereby person and whole exist on their own, yet also for one another, though never *merely* for one another, since both exist together for God as a Person, and it is only 'in God' that they can exist for one another)."[224] There can be no private religious activity; as a human phenomenon, this personal activity necessarily includes the experiential priority of the religious community. Given the connection between "person" and "act," both individual and communal, the more inclusive expression "religious activity" is preferable to the already nuanced "religious experience;" whoever heard of a community experiencing something, yet communities can and do act. While this structure received no explicit attention from Scheler, by employing C.S. Peirce's "rope" mode of argumentation[225] it emerges from within the various threads of his though when taken together.

By means of this distinctive structure Scheler challenged the received theories of his day which all failed to recognize the irreducible character of religious activity: *"religious experience and its object form a closed and irreducible whole."*[226] "We had the experience but missed the meaning," T.S. Eliot's well known phrase from

Four Quarters (1943) encapsulates Scheler's criticism of these philosophical explanations, which focused either on the experiencing subject, as in Protestantism, or its objective theological meaning, as in Catholic Neo-Scholastic rationalism, to the exclusion of the other; let alone the prevalent anthropological atheism which reduced religion and its object to a mere human phenomenon. Furthermore, these theories failed to recognize its inherent meaningfulness was given "in" the actual activity: *"religious experience and its object form a closed and autonomous whole,"*[227] elsewhere he calls for the *"originality and non-derivation of religious experience."*[228] Understood as revelatory, this personal activity of love provides access and awareness of the loved personal "other" and Divine "Other," which otherwise would be lacking: "love is not blind."[229] Again citing the authority of Augustine, the claim "all knowledge of God is knowledge *from* God" is axiomatic for this activity, providing the locus for the loving disclosure and revelation of the Divine Person; a gift given and received in love.

> The religious act is unable from its own resources, or with the help of thought, to *construct* what hovers as an objective idea, notion or intuition before the human performer of the act. He must somehow *receive* the truth he "intends," the salvation and felicity he "seeks,"... Where the soul does not – however indirectly – touch God, and touch him knowing and feeling himself touched by God, no *religious* relationship can subsist.[230]

As a means of exploring this claim, Scheler elaborated a set of *"diagnostic"* criteria[231] to identify genuine religious activity as an *"essential class of acts."* Differentiated from other forms of activity, religious acts are characterized by the movement of *"world transcendence;"* as such only the Divine Person can fulfill the intention of the religious act, with the accompanying the experience of *inadequacy* when it is replaced by any finite object or "idol." Regarded as non-economical and non-self referential, this activity resists as with any personal relationship the logic of calculation or *quid pro quo.* Confirmed by his "Beuron experience" he claims: "every religious act is simultaneously an *individual* and a *social* act;" employing the traditional expression, *"Unus Christianus, nullus Christianus"* he applies this to all religion.[232] Therefore in religious activity we experience ourselves being lovingly directed towards the Divine Person as the highest value of the Holy within the religious community; furthermore, nothing can be produced, manufactured, either individually or culturally, that can fulfill this religious intention:

> The most conclusive, though merely negative sign of a religious act, as distinct from all other acts of the mind or spirit, is an attendant insight into that fact that *of its essence it cannot be fulfilled* by any finite object belonging to or itself forming, the "world." In this sense Augustine's dictum, *Inquietum cor nostrum, donec requiescat in te,* is a basic formula for all religious acts.[233]

Identifying the reasonableness of religious activities within the parameters of human condition,[234] James was a "precursor" of some of the philosophical attitudes later associated with the phenomenological movement. [235] However, Scheler was critical of his failure to sufficiently refer to the religious object, let alone attempt an underlying "Divine ontology" and dismissal of the impact of the religious community, "James' universal *subjectivism* is a child of Protestantism."[236] In contrast, the Catholic Scheler emphasized the study of the *"nature* and *essential structures"* of religious objects and the "forms of religious acts appropriate to those experiences" as an essential prerequisite for an adequate understanding of religious activity wherein individual persons are summoned to the *"purely religious* intimacy in God of *amare in Deum in Deo,"*[237] received by means of personal example, the *homo religious* or Saint, lived in the religious community.

Prior to the medieval times, the notion of a purely individual religious activity was largely unknown. Though distinguished from the modern "turn to the subject," the emerging focus on the individual's self-awareness and self-consciousness within religious activity represents one of the distinctive features of this age;[238] whereby the individual human soul through the shared act of religious love was provided access "to a new *direct relationship to God* (not mediated by the world and its order)."[239] To understand this religious relationship, Scheler focused on mysticism, the traditional religious context for such a loving disclosure by means of its spiritual and non-discursive approach to "union of the soul

with God." As such mystical "union," the unmediated, transforming experience of the individual human soul with the Divine,
represents a unitary experience based on mutual otherness. Contrary to any naturalistic or pantheistic type of experience wherein
there is a fusion of identity between believer and God, "true mysticism of the spirit" for Scheler "always retains at least a consciousness of the ontological gulf (*intentionale Daseinsdistanz*)
between the human being and God as a "limit" of approach.[240] As
with the Medievals, this understanding of mysticism embraces the
human natural connection with the "*lower order of Nature;*" accordingly Saint Francis of Assisi functions as Scheler's "model,"
revealing the essential connection between the various dimensions
within human activity.[241] By his personal mysticism of love, St.
Francis *expanded* the Christian experience of love for God and
neighbor to include "*all lower orders of Nature.*" This "*heresy of the
heart,*"[242] preferring the emotional and natural elements in formu-
lating Christian experience, constituted a profound break with the
prevailing scholastic rational emphasis of the time. Citing the
testament of Thomas of Celano concerning the religious activity of
St. Francis, Scheler claims: "He called all creatures his brothers,
and in a *strange way, wholly denied to others*, he looked with the
heart's keen insight into the inmost being of every creature."[243] As
such, mysticism is not only an inward experience but one lovingly
directed towards other persons, the Divine person and through
them the natural world. As an activity, it is received within a religious community, one which supports the individual believer, as
during the "dark night of the soul" when Saint Teresa was as-
sisted by the routine of community life shared with other religious
sisters or when Saint Augustine received the gift of his mystical
experience in the company of his sainted mother Monica. From
within this religious activity, "loving in God," a loving of all
things with the love of God, we receive a new perspective, namely
the religious perspective wherein the believer sees the world *in
lumine Dei* without nevertheless seeing God himself. As distinctly
personal, mysticism leads to the "purely *religious* intimacy in God
of *amare Deum in Deo.*"[244] It is this loving religious intimacy in
God which informs the human access to the natural knowledge of
God; the distinctive religious "logic of discovery" which is for-

mulated by Pascal: "You would not seek me had you not already found me."[245] From this Christian position, the desire for God informs our human consciousness evidenced from the loving "experience of the heart."

Against the current trend of immanentism, religious activity necessarily involves an essential "distance:" "the 'distance' of the persons and their respective and reciprocal awareness of separateness is kept in mind."[246] In these circumstances Scheler responds to Schopenhauer's humanist reduction of Christian love to sympathy, a form of humanitarian fellow feeling: "All love (ἀγάπη, caritas) is compassion or sympathy"[247] along with its distinctive religious overtones : "sympathy and pure love are expressed in Italian by the same word, pieta."[248] Undertaken in his original study of love in *The Nature of Sympathy* (1913), Scheler accepts Schopenhauer's recognition that "fellow feeling is a phenomenon of the metaphysical order;"[249] sympathy operates between the poles of two individual beings, who literally "feel with" each other.[250] The philosophical significance of "feeling with" lies in the experienced disclosure of an "essential *difference* between persons;"[251] one which involves an emotional participation in the other's feelings, an intentional reference to another's experience. As such, sympathetic activity, discloses the constitutive and reciprocal *"distance"* between persons;[252] for Scheler this points not only to the "Otherness" of the Divine Person but also to the essential social character of human experience as a lived priority; within this emotive social experience he differentiates several levels, beginning with emotional identification, vicarious emotion, fellow-feeling and the love of humanity and finally "non-cosmic personal and Divine love."[253]

> It is love of the divine and holy, a love which has to move towards its goal before it recognizes itself as the response to a *pre-existent* love directed toward the loving soul, that God has located, in the final analysis, that mysterious driving-wheel which sets in motion all our cognitive knowledge of him as a person.[254]

Whereas sympathy is responsive towards the other person, religious love is essentially directed to the Divine Person, a spiritual emotion arising from a "movement of the heart," towards this

Person as bearer of value of the Holy. Scheler rejects the prevalent naturalistic theories as inadequate because they fail to recognize the essential *"transcendence"* of love as a spiritual act. Within human experience, as we have seen, there is a movement which is experienced in relation to an essential hierarchical "order of values:"[255] moving from the lowest values of the agreeable-disagreeable to the highest, values of the Holy-Unholy. These are approached by means of this loving movement within the sphere of the Absolute, wherein access is attained to the Divine Person. "Exclusively the province of the religious act,"[256] "faith," "awe" and "adoration" reflect distinctively personal religious attitude; necessarily personal, faith is directed towards the person as bearer of the value, the *homo religious;* within its Christian context it is faith "in" the person of Jesus Christ. However, we encounter a difficulty insofar as the person and its acts can never be an "object" in knowledge: "the personal in man can *never be disclosed to us as an 'object.'* Persons cannot be objectified, in love or any other act."[257] The person can only be "known" in the context of a revelatory *"participation"* in the being of another received through the act of love. In the religious love of the person, as with any form of love, a person can be silent.

> You cannot choose between having and not having a good of this kind. You can only choose whether your absolute sphere will be inhabited by God, as the one good *commensurate* with the religious act, *or* an idol.[258]

Writing in "Problems of Religion" Scheler claims: "Looking through the web of relative being, thus of any relative non-entity, he looks *through,* but in the direction of the absolute entity."[259] Every human being has consciousness of an Absolute; however the potential for ambiguity in religious activity arises from the fact that the content of this sphere can be "filled" with something relative: "even relativism is an absolute." This raises the issue of the adequacy of the intentional object, namely the Divine Person as Absolute and Holy. Within human consciousness there exists the possibility of attaining an "inadequate" object by substituting a finite object or good for the Holy, with the accompanying experience of dissatisfaction and restlessness given the lack of proportion between the personal activity and the intentional object. In such circumstances a "good absolutized through delusion" is called an "idol."[260] Furthermore, while religious activity, such as acts of worship and adoration are directed to the value of the Holy, and the bearer of this value, the Divine Person,[261] this activity is characterized by the potential for confusion concerning the preferred value. In the act of love there is a movement from lower to higher values, which reflects the "*ordo amoris;*" however, given Scheler's directional understanding of love, the movement of value may be reversed in a form of disordered and confused "*pseudo* love" or "hate." The dilemma when approaching Scheler's understanding of religious activity is the deceptive ambiguity concealed within; namely, as a value orientated activity the potential exists for confusion or distortion concerning our loved religious object. Perhaps best illustrated by the reemergence of heretical sects around charismatic religious individuals, this reveals the potential for confusion which points to the distinctive vulnerability associated with religious activity, as Adso reflects: "there was little difference between Ubertino's mystic (and orthodox) faith and the distorted faith of the heretics."[262] This phenomenon of the loving displacement of our religious values was not only a feature of medieval times as brilliantly portrayed by Eco, but is also apparent in some current forms of malfeasance, especially the power related manipulative and predatory sexual activities, the blight of sexual abuse of minors, perpetrated by a minority of religious officials, whether priests, vowed religious or ministers of religion. Common to all Christian denominations, this behavior not only calls forth justified public condemnation and demoralizes ecclesial communities, but also raises the broader philosophical question as to how those entrusted with the pastoral care of others, who espouse a public commitment to Christian love and its religious values, can devalue these by such reprehensible irreligious behavior? Perhaps the motivation lies in value confusion. How often do the perpetrators attempt to justify their actions by some well meaning value informed "*pseudo-* love"? More seriously, there appears some existential consistency in the recurrent movement between these patterns of behavior, often over many years. This "tragic situation," which characterizes the disordering of one's loved value of the Holy by the substitution of finite values is well portrayed in *The Name of the Rose;* where sexual gratification, intellectual pride, religious pride, the quest for knowledge at the cost of everything else, appear as "idols." Why would professed monks be prepared to murder, to forgo their religious let alone human respect for life if not for something valued as Absolute? Furthermore, Eco sets up an interesting point of comparison between two young novices who both break their religious vows through momentary sexual gratification, one commits suicide, the other lives to literally "tell the tale;" in view of the significance given to the religious "other" in community, how significant is the supportive presence of the elderly mentor William? While these serve as rather extreme instances, they are indicative of the human potential for "filling" the religious sphere with something relative, the potential to identify a relative entity with the Absolute, "surrogates for the Divine." Characterized as "infatuation," this situation was understood as, citing the old mystics, "a wall of illusions blocking the Divine."[263] The inherent possibility of value "confusion" within religious activity is highly suggestive of its vulnerability. Grounded in the highest of values, the Holy, this is most readily substituted by "idols;" as such religious activity can be deceptively ambiguous in concealing the potential for value confusion. This is the fragile nature of religious activity; illustrated by the further potential for tension between the individual believer and the religious community.

CONCLUSION

Conclusions always seem such an anti-climax; and often made in haste. Nowhere is this more apparent than in attempting to bring to some form of closure what is deliberately intended to open up; to attempt to summarize ideas and connections which emerge when revisiting the thought of a complex and unsystematic thinker like Scheler. Not surprisingly Scheler's quixotic expectations of a new age were not realized, and at the beginning of a new Millennium we find ourselves addressing the concerns of our fictional young monk, which not only remain valid, but assume a greater significance in light of contemporary global events: How do we discern the difference between religious fervor and fanaticism?

Notes

[1] Siri Hustvedt, *A Plea for Eros* (London: Sceptre, 2006) 58

[2] Max Scheler, "*Ordo Amoris,*" *Selected Philosophical Essays,* tr. David R. Lachterman (Evanston: Northwestern University Press, 1973), 110-111.

[3] Bernard I. Murstein, "A taxonomy of love," in *The Psychology of Love*, ed. Robert J. Sternberg and Michael L. Barnes (London: Unwin, 1988), 33.

[4] Jean-Luc Marion, *The Erotic Phenomenon,* tr. Stephen E. Lewis (Chicago: The University of Chicago Press, 2007), 1.

[5] Emmnauel Levinas, *Entre Nous. Thinking-of-the-other,* tr. Michael B. Smith and Barbara Harshav. (London: Continuum, 2006), 92.

[6] Friedrich Nietzsche, *Assorted Opinions and Maxims,* 95 in *A Nietzsche Reader,* tr. R.J. Hollingdale (London: Penguin Books, 1977), 172.

[7] Friedrich Nietzsche, *On the Genealogy of Morality,* II, 13, tr.Carol Diethe (Cambridge: Cambridge University Press, 1994), 57.

[8]William Johnston, *Mystical Theology. The Science of Love,* (London: HarperCollins*Publishers,* 1995), 44.

[9] See the classic work by the Swedish theologian Anders Nygen, *Agape and Eros,* tr. Philip Watson (London: S.P.C.K. 1932); also M.C. D'Arcy, *The Mind and Heart of Love* (London: Collins, 1945), C.S. Lewis, *The Four Loves* (London: Collins/Fontana Books, 1960) and Erasmo Leiva-Merikakis, *Love's Sacred Order. Four Meditations,* (San Francisco: Ignatius Press, 2000).

[10] Saint Augustine, *City of God* XIV, 7, tr. Henry Bettenson (London: Penguin Books, 1984), 558; concerning the issue of flexibility, see Etienne Gilson, *The Christian Philosophy of St. Augustine* (New York: Random House, 1960), 311 n.40.

[11] Saint Augustine, *Eighty-three Different Questions,* 35, 1and 2; cited in Hannah Arendt, *Love and Saint Augustine,* ed. Joanna Vecchiarelli Scott and Judith Chelius Stark (Chicago: The University of Chicago Press, 1996), 9;. also Tarsicius J. van Bavel, "Love," in *Augustine through the Ages: An Encyclopedia,* ed. Allan D. Fitzgerald, O.S.A. (Grand Rapids, Michigan: William B. Eerdmans Publishing Company, 1999),509.

[12] Max Scheler, "Love and Knowledge," in *Max Scheler. On feeling, Knowing and Valuing: Selected Writings,* ed. Harold J. Bershady (Chicago: The University of Chicago Press, 1992), 149.

[13] Countering any claim of phenomenalism or agnosticism, Scheler introduces the notion of "absolute being;" which exercises a pivotal role in his later phenomenology of religion. Max Scheler, "The Idols of Self-Knowledge," in *Selected Philosophical Essays,* 4.

[14] While a review of Scheler's Personal Library held in the Staatsbibliotek München reveals no publications by Saint Augustine, though several commentaries by W. Achelis, Johannes Hessen, Bernhard Legewie, and Johann Möhler; it does contain several well annotated works by Nietzsche: *Die Geburt der*

Tragödie oder Griechentum und Pessimus (1900), *Gedichte.* (1911), *Zur Genealogie der Moral. Eine Streitschrift* (1894), *Jenseits von Gut und Böse. Zur Genealogie der Moral. Aus dem Nachlass,*1885-1886 (1904), *Morgenröthe. Aus dem Nachlass,*1880-1881.(1876) and *Der Wille zur Macht. Eine Auslegung alles Geschehens* (1921).

[15] Ernest Troeltsch, *Der Historismus unde seine Probleme. Gesammelte Schriften,* Vol. 3, ed. J.C.B. Mohr (Tübingen: Paul Siebeck, 1922), 609.

[16] Martin Heidegger, "In memoriam Max Scheler," in *The Metaphysical Foundations of Logic,* tr. Michael Heim (Bloomington, Indiana: Indiana University Press, 1984), 51.

[17] While the Editor shorted this title to *"Ordo Amoris,"* the related issue of value confusion features prominently in Scheler's Catholic thought. See David R. Lachterman, "Translator's Introduction," in *Selected Philosophical Essays,* xxxi.

[18] Max Scheler, "Ordo Amoris," *Selected Philosophical Essays,* 126.

[19] Description offered by Steven Best and Douglas Kellner, *The Postmodern Theory: Critical Interrogations* (London: Macmillan, 1991), 174.

[20] Denis De Rougemont, *Love in the Western World,* tr. Montgomery Belgion (Princeton, NJ: Princeton University Press, 1983), 6-7

[21] Paul Gifford, *Love, Desire and Transcendence in French Literature. Deciphering Eros* (Aldershot, Hampshire: Ashgate, 2005), 329.

[22] Siri Hustvedt, *A Pleas for Eros,* 51. Recently the ambiguity in erotic sexual language has been taken up by Susan Ackerman, *When Heroes Love. The Ambiguity of Eros in the Stories of Gilgamesh and David* (New York: Columbia University Press), 2005.

[23] Max Scheler, "Problems of Religion," *On the Eternal in Man,* tr. Bernard Noble (London: SCM Press, 1960), 251. Omitting the verb "est" from this Augustinian phrase suggests a quote remembered by rote rather than an accurate reference. First used in his unpublished manuscript *"Ordo Amoris," Selected Philosophical Essays,* 114; the remaining references occur in published works on a religious theme: "Christian Love and the Twentieth Century,"(1917), *On the Eternal in Man,* 375 and *"Deutschlands Sendung und der katholische Gedanke,"*(1918) *Politisch-pädagogische Schriften,* ed. Manfred Frings (Bern: Francke Verlag, 1982), 528.

[24] Max Scheler, *Formalism in Ethics and Non-Formal Ethics of Values. A New Attempt toward the Foundation of an Ethical Personalism,* tr. Manfred S. Frings and Roger L. Funk (Evanston: Northwestern University Press, 1973), 505.

[25] Max Scheler, Preface to 2nd Edition, *Formalism in Ethics and Non-Formal Ethics of Values,* xxiv.

[26] Edith Stein. *Life in a Jewish Family 1891-1916. Her Unfinished Autobiographical Account,* tr. Josephine Koeppel (Washington, D.C.: ICS Publications, 1986), 260.

[27] I.M. Bocheński, *Contemporary European Philosophy,* tr. Donald Nicholl and Karl Aschenbrenner (Westport: Greenwood Press, 1982), 140.

[28] Manfred S. Frings, *Max Scheler: A Concise Introduction into the World of a Great Thinker* (Pittsburgh, PA: Duquesene University Press, 1965), 77.

[29] This expression denotes the faith and practice of Christians who are in communion with the Pope, and refers to Catholicism as it has existed since the Reformation, to be distinguished from Protestantism. See "Roman Catholicism," in *The Oxford Dictionary of the Christian Church*, third major new edition, ed. F.L Cross and E.A. Livingstone (Oxford: Oxford University Press, 1997), 1408-9.

[30] Expression used by Michael J. Scanlon, "Theology, Modern," in *Augustine through the Ages: An Encyclopdeia*, 825. Scanlon observes "one only has to read Vatican II's *Gaudium et Spes* to discover this orientation."

[31] Max Scheler, *Man's Place in Nature*, tr. Hans Meyerhoff (Boston: Beacon Press, 1961), 6. Opinion of Herbert Schnädelbach, *Philosophy in Germany: 1831-1933*, tr. Eric Matthews (Cambridge: Cambridge University Press, 1984), 219, 222.

[32] Max Scheler, "Christian Love and the Twentieth Century" and "Problems of Religion" in *On the Eternal in Man*, 399 and 276; also "Philosopher's Outlook" in *Philosophical Perspectives*, tr. Oscar A. Haac (Boston: Beacon Press, 1958), 3.

[33] This reputation was based on his 1959 *Art and Beauty in the Middle Ages* tr. Hugh Bredin (New Haven: Yale University Press, 1986) and his earlier first book (1956), an extension of his university study *The Aesthetics of Thomas Aquinas*, tr. Hugh Bredin (Cambridge, Massachusetts: Harvard University Press, 1988).

[34] Umberto Eco, *The Name of the Rose*, tr. Willia Weaver (London: Secker & Warburg, 1983), 60.

[35] Boethius, *The Consolation of Philosophy*, Book II, viii, The Loeb Classical Library, tr..H.F. Stewart, E.K. Rand and S.J. Tester (Cambridge, Massachusetts, 1973), 227.

[36] H.F. Stewart and E.K. Rand, "Life of Boethius," in *The Consolation of Philosophy*, xii.They expand on the Renaissance humanist Lorenzo Vallas famous assessement of Boethius: "Last of the Romans, first of the scholastics."

[37] Opinion of H. Chadwick cited by Anne-Marie Bowery, "Boethius," *Augustine through the Ages: An Encyclopedia*, 108.

[38] Especially the verse in Book II, viii and Book IV, vi.

[39] Boethius, *The Consolation of Philosophy*, Book V, i, 393.

[40] Boethius, *The Consolation of Philosophy*, Book IV, vi, 375.

[41] Richard of Saint-Victor, *Of the Four Degrees of Passionate Charity*, in *Richard of Saint-Victor: Selected Writings on Contemplation*, tr. Clare Kirchberger (London: Faber and Faber Ltd. 1957), 213.

[42] The expression comes from M. Corneille Halflants, "Introduction," in *Bernard of Clairvaux: On the Song of Songs I* (Spencer: Cistercian Publications, 1971), xxix.

[43] Clare Kirchberger, *Richard of Saint-Victor: Selected Writings on Contemplation*, 49.

[44] Steven Chase, *Contemplation and Compassion. The Victorine Tradition* (Maryknoll, New York: Orbis Books, 2003), 13.

[45] Max Scheler, "Love and Knowledge," in *Max Scheler. On Feeling, Knowing and Valuing. Selected Writings*, 147-165.

[46] Umberto Ecco, *The Name of the Rose*, 5.

[47] Umberto Eco, *The Name of the Rose,*230.

[48] Umberto Eco, *Art and Beauty in the Middle Ages,* 5.

[49] Rudolf Eucken, *The Truth of Religion,* tr. W. Tudor Jones (London: William & Norgate, 1913), 543.

[50] Umberto Eco, *The Aesthetics of Thomas Aquinas,* 6.

[51] Boethius, *The Consolation of Philosophy,* Book IV, i and Book V, i, 312 and 393..

[52] Boethius, *The Consolation of Philosophy,* Book II, viii, 227.

[53] For a discussion of this term see Karlfied Froehlich, "Pseudo-Dionysius and the Reformation of the Sixteenth Century," in *Pseudo-Dionysius. The Complete Works,* tr. Colm Luibheid (London: SPCK, 1987), 33-46.

[54] Erasmo Leiva-Merikakis, *Love's Sacred Order. The Four Loves Revisited* (San Francisco: Ignatius Press, 2000), 12-13.

[55] René Rogues, "Preface," *Pseudo-Dionysius. The Complete Works,* 5.

[56] Max Scheler, *Problems of a Sociology of Knowledge,* tr. Manfred S. Frings (London: Routledge & Kegan Paul, 1980), 124.

[57] Max Scheler, "Ordo Amoris," *Selected Philosophical Essays,*114.

[58] Umberto Eco, *The Name of the Rose,* 322.

[59] Devoted to the study of the Middle Ages, the Medieval Academy of America took *Speculum* as the title for its journal, published since 1926; Ritamary Bradley, "Backgrounds of the Title *Speculum* in Medieval Literature," *Speculum* 29.1 (January 1954) 100-115.

[60] Jean Leclercq, "Introduction," in *Bernard of Clairvaux: Selected Works,* tr. G.R. Evans (New York: Paulist Press, 1987), 13.

[61] Bernard McGinn, *The Growth of Mysticism .From Gregory the Great to the Twelfth 0Century,* Volume 2, *The Presence of God: A History of Western Christian Mysticism* (London: SCM Press, 1995), 153-55.

[62] Jean Leclercq, "Introduction," *Bernard of Clairvaux: On the Song of Songs I,* 14.

[63] Helen Waddell, *Mediaeval Latin Lyrics* (London: Constable & Co. Ltd., 1929), 341.

[64] Max Scheler, *Problems of a Sociology of Knowledge,* 122-123.

[65] *Contributions towards the Establishment of the Relationship between Logical and Ethical Principles.*

[66] *The Transcendental and Psychological Method: A Fundamental Discussion in Philosophical Method.*

[67] Given the attitude of openness to all kinds of experiences and phenomena, Spiegelberg observes Catholicism, and particularly Augustinianism with its emphasis on intuitive insight, had a distinct advantage over Protestantism. Herbert Spiegelberg, "Note: Phenomenology and Conversion,"in *The Phenomenological Movement. A Historical Introduction* Vol.1 (The Hague: Martinus

Nijhoff Publishers, 1962), 173. For no apparent reason this "Note" has been deleted from the recent Enlarged Edition (1982).

[68] Max Scheler, "Ordo Amoris," Selected Philosophical Essays,109.

[69] Opinion cited in the Preface, Hannah Arendt, Love and Saint Augustine, xv.

[70] Martin Heidegger, "Augustine and Neo-Platonism," in The Phenomenology of Religious Life, tr. Matthias Fritsch and Jennifer Anna Gosetti-Ferencei (Bloomington: Indiana University Press, 2004), 115.

[71] R.P. Russell, "Augustinianism," The New Catholic Encyclopedia, Vol.1, 1068

[72] Max Scheler, "The Reconstruction of European Culture, On the Eternal in Man. 423.

[73] Max Scheler, "Christian Love and the Twentieth Century," Eternal 368.

[74] Max Scheler, "Ordo Amoris," Selected Philosophical Essays, 98.

[75] John Oesterreicher, Walls are Crumbling. Seven Jewish Philosophers discover Christ (London: Hollis and Carter, 1953), 121.

[76] Published in the first volume of Husserl's Jahrbuch für Philosophy und phänomenologische Forschung; Scheler was a founding member of its editorial panel of four.

[77] Max Scheler, "On the Idea of Man," tr. Clyde Nabe, Journal of the British Society of Phenomenology 9:3 (October 1978) 185.

[78] Hans Meyerhoff, "Translator's Introduction," Man's Place in Nature, xi.

[79] Robert F. Harvanek, "The Philosophical Foundations of the Thought of John Paul II," in The Thought of Pope John Paul II, ed.John M.McDermott (Roma: Editrice Pontificia Università Gregoriana, 1993), 2.

[80] Carl Muth, "Begegnungen: Max Scheler," Hochland 46 (October 1953) 13-17.

[81] Helmut Walser Smith, German Nationalism and Religious Conflict. Culture, Ideology, Politics, 1870-1914 (Princeton, N.J.: Princeton University Press, 1995), 165.

[82] Owen Chadwick, The Secularization of the European Mind in the Nineteenth Century (Cambridge: Canto Edition, 1990), 124.

[83] Hans Rollman, "Troeltsch, von Hügel and Modernism," The Downside Review 96: 322 (January 1978) 35.

[84] Paul Sabatier, Modernism, tr.C.A. Miles (London: T. Fisher Unwin, 1908), 104.

[85] Maurice Blondel, "History and Dogma," in Maurice Blondel, The Letter on Apologetics and History and Dogma, tr. Alexander Dru and Illtyd Trethowan (London: Harvill Press, 1964), 221.

[86] Expression first employed through Josef Müller's programe Der Reformkatholizisimus (1899); See Oskar Schroeder, Aufbruch und Missverstandnis: Zur Geschichte der reformkatholischen Bewegung (Wien: Verlag Styria, 1969).

[87] Eucken's Letter to von Hügel, August 8, 1900; cited by Hans Rollman, "Von Hügel and Scheler," The Downside Review 101:342 (January 1983) 31.

88 Martin Heidegger. "In memoriam Max Scheler," *The Metaphysical Foundations of Logic,* tr. Michael Heim (Bloomington, Indiana: Indiana University Press, 1984), 51.

89 Theodore Kisiel, *The Genesis of Heidegger's Being and Time* (Berkerley: University of California Press, 1993), 192.

90 Herbert Spiegelberg, *The Phenomenological Movement,* enlarged edition (The Hague: Martinus Nijhoff, 1982), 303, n.14.

91Hans Rollman, "Von Hügel and Scheler," *The Downside Review* 101:342 (January 1983) 34,35.

92 Friedrich Nietzsche, *Ecce Homo: How One Becomes What One is,* tr. R.J. Hollingdale (London: Penguin Books, 1979), 51.

93 Max Scheler, "Problems of Religion," *On the Eternal in Man,* 264.

94 Ludwig Curtius, *Deutsche und antike Welt, Lebenserinnerungen* (Stuttgart: Deutsche Verlags-Anstalt, 1950), 375. See John Ralphael Staude, *Max Scheler 1874-1928. An Intellectual Portrait* (New York: The Free Press, 1967), 248.

95 John Raphael Staude, *Max Scheler,* 88.

96 John Raphael Staude,. *Max Scheler,* 4.

97 The significance of Beuron is discussed in the manuscript "Max Scheler. Eine Darstellung seiner nationalpolitischen Bedeutung von Dr. Herbert Rüssel" held in the Scheler Archives, Bavarian State Library, Munich.

98 John H. Nota, *Max Scheler. The Man and His Work,* tr. Theodore Plantinga and John H. Nota (Chicago: Franciscan Herald Press, 1983)103. For Heidegger's first hand description see Hugo Ott, *Martin Heidegger. A Political Life,* tr. Allan Blunden (London: Harper Collins, 1993), 377.

99 Johannes Schaber OSB, "Phänomenologie und Mönchtum. Max Scheler, Martin Heidegger, Edith Stein und die Erzabtei Beuron," in *Leben, Tod und Entscheidung. Studien zur Geistesgeschichte der Weimarer Republik,* ed. Stephan Loos and Holger Zaborowski (Berlin: Duncker & Humblot, 2003), 71-100.

100 Max Scheler, "Exemplars of Person and Leaders," in *Person and Self-Value. Three Essays,* tr. M.S.Frings (Dordrecht: Martinus Nijhoff Publishers. 1987), 127-198.

101Max Scheler, "The Forms of Knowledge and Culture," in *Philosophical Perspectives,* tr. Oscar A. Haac (Boston: Beacon Press, 1958), 16.

102 Herbert Spiegelberg, *The Phenomenological Movement,* Vol. 1, 237-238.

103 Max Scheler, "Christian Love and the Twentieth Century," *On the Eternal in Man,* 369.

104 Max Scheler, *Man's Place in Nature,* 92.

105 Max Scheler, Preface to Third Edition, *Formalism,* xxv.

106 John Raphael Staude, *Max Scheler,* 240.

107 Max Scheler, *Problems of a Sociology of Knowledge,* tr. Manfred Frings (London: Routledge & Kegan Paul Ltd., 1980), 224, n.34.

[108] John Raphael Staude, *Max Scheler*, 243. With the completion of Scheler's fifteen volume *Gesammelte Werke* (1954-1997) it is anticipated an authoritative biography may be undertaken.

[109] Hans Urs von Balthasar, *Love Alone: The Way of Revelation* (London: Sheed and Ward, 1968), 98. Reprinted as *Love Alone is Credible* (San Francisco: Ignatius Press, 2004).

[110] Max Scheler, *Ressentiment*, 125.

[111] Matthew 6.21; Friedrich Nietzsche, *On the Genealogy of Morality*, Preface 1, tr. Carol Diethe. (Cambridge: Cambridge University Press, 1994), 3.

[112] Friedrich Nietzsche, *On the Genealogy of Morality*, Preface 6, 8.

[113] Friedrich Nietzsche, *On The Genealogy of Morality*, 20-21

[114] Friedrich Nietzsche, *The Will to Power*, Outline Book 1, 1, tr. Walter Kaufmann and R.J. Hollingdale (New York: Vintage Books Edition, 1968), 7.

[115] Friedrich Nietzsche, *Human, All Too Human*, Preface 3, tr. R. J. Hollingdale (Cambridge: Cambridge University Press, 1996), 7.

[116] Friedrich Nietzsche, *On the Genealogy of Morality*. Preface, 1, 3.

[117] Richard Schacht, *Nietzsche* (London: Routledge & Kegan Paul, 1985), 341.

[118] Pope Benedict XVI, Encyclical Letter *Deus Caritas Est*, #4 (Strathfield: St. Pauls Publications, 2006), 9.

[119] Friedrich Nietzsche, "What I owe to the Ancients," 4, *Twilight of the Idols* in *Twilight of the Idols* and *The Anti-Christ*, tr. R.J. Hollingdale (London: Penguin Books, 1968), 110.

[120] Max Scheler, *Ressentiment*, 125.

[121] Manfred Frings, "Max Scheler Centennial 1874-1974," *Philosophy Today* 18:3/4 (1974) 215.

[122] Max Scheler, "*Ordo Amoris*," *Selected Philosophical Essays*, 118.

[123] Max Scheler, "*Ordo Amoris*," *Selected Philosophical Essays*,113.

[124] Max Scheler, *Ressentiment*, 84.-85.

[125] Max Scheler, *Ressentiment*, 86.

[126] Herbert Spiegelberg, *The Phenomenological Movement*, 296.

[127] Rainer R. A. Albana, "The Stratification of Emotional Life and the Problem of Other Minds According to Max Scheler," *International Philosophical Quarterly* 31:4 (December 1991) 461.

[128] Max Scheler, *Formalism*, 256.

[129] Personal report of Scheler's student, Herbert Leyendecker, "Vorlesungsnachschriften Max Scheler über Phänomenologie," *Nachlass Herbert Leyendecker* ANA 375: B I, 12. 72-73, Bavarian State Library, Munich.

[130] Max Scheler, *Formalism*, 332.

[131] Max Scheler, "*Ordo Amoris*" *Selected Philosophical Essays*, 119.

[132] Max Scheler, "*Ordo Amoris*," *Selected Philosophical Essays*, 117.

[133] Max Scheler, "Love and Knowledge," *Max Scheler. On feeling, Knowing, and Valuing*, 147,164.

[134] Max Scheler, "The Meaning of Suffering," *Max Scheler. On feeling, Knowing, and Valuing*. 96.

[135] Max Scheler, "Love and Knowledge," *Max Scheler. On feeling, Knowing, and Valuing*, 147.

[136] Scheler, "Love and Knowledge," *Max Scheler. On feeling, Knowing, and Valuing*, 158. I am indebted to Rev. Prof. Allan Fitzgerald, o.s.a, of Villanova University for his assistance in conducting a computer search for this expression in the Augustinian corpus, *Clavis Patrorum Latinorum* (the 1961 issue of *Sacris Erudin*), which indicates no evidence of Augustine's actual use of this expression. However Scheler uses this expression nine times; first in *The Nature of Sympathy* (1913), 102, 164, 168, in *Formalism* (1916), 212, 223, 368, 398; in "The Meaning of Suffering" (1923), 163, and "Forms of Knowledge and Culture" (1927), 31.

[137] Jean-Luc Marion, *The Erotic Phenomenon*, 92.

[138] John Raphael Staude, *Max Scheler*, 89.

[139] Schubert M Ogden, *The Reality of God* (New York: Harper and Row, 1966), 13.

[140] Max Scheler, Preface to the Second Edition (1921), *Formalism*, xxiii.

[141] Ludwig Feuerbach, *The Essence of Christianity*, tr. George Eliot (Buffalo, New York: Prometheus Books, 1989), 281.

[142] Michael J. Buckley, *At the Origins of Modern Atheism* (New Haven: Yale University Press, 1987), 27-28; See John Henry Cardinal Newman, *Apologia Pro Vita Sua* (New York: Norton, 1968), 188; Friedrich Nietzsche, *The Gay Science*,Book 5, 343, tr. Walter Kaufman (New York: Random House,1974), 279.

[143] Stanley J. Grenz, *A Prime on Postmodernism* (Grand Rapids, Michigan: William B. Eerdmans, 1996), 88.

[144] Nietzsche's letter to Pinder and Krug, April 27, 1862. See Thomas H. Brobjer, "Nietzsche's Changing Relation with Christianity: Nietzsche as Christian, Atheist, and Anticharist." in *Nietzsche and the Gods*, ed. Donna Santaniello (New York: State University of New York Press, 2001),140

[145] R.J. Hollingdale, *Nietzsche. The Man and His Philosophy*, revised edition (Cambridge: Cambridge University Press, 2001), 20.

[146] Ludwig Feuerbach, *The Essence of Christianity*, 184.

[147] Friedrich Nietzsche, "On Moods," in *Nietzsche. The Man and His Philosophy*, ed. R.J. Hollingdale (Cambridge: Cambridge University Press, 2001), 26.

[148] Richard Schacht, "Introduction," *Human, All Too Human*, xv.

[149] Friedrich Nietzsche, *On the Genealogy of Morality*. Preface 5, 7.

[150] Friedrich Nietzsche, *Human, All Too Human*, 62.

[151] Friedrich Nietzsche, *Ecce Homo*, 89.

[152] Friedrich Nietzsche, *Human, All Too Human*, Preface 6 -7, 9-10.

[153] Friedrich Nietsche. *On the Genealogy of Morals* 1:17, 34.

[154] Friedrich Nietsche. *On the Genealogy of Morals* 3:27, 118.

[155] R.J. Hollingdale, *Nietzsche. The Man and His Philosophy*, 217.

[156] Friedrich Nietzsche, *The Anti-Christ*, 47, 163.

[157] Friedrich Nietzsche, *Will to Power*, 254, 148.

[158] Martin Heidegger, "The Word of Nietzsche: 'God is Dead.'" in *The Question Concerning Technology and Other Essays*. tr. William Lovitt (New York: Harper & Row, Publishers, 1977), 67.

[159] Ronald Hayman, *Nietzsche. A Critical Life* (London: Quartet Books, 1980), 3. See Jacques Derrida, *Writing and Difference*, tr. Alan Bass (Chicago: The University of Chicago Press, 1978).

[160] Nietzsche, *Will to Power*, Preface, 4, 3.

[161] Friedrich Nietzsche, *Will to Power*, Book IV, 1007, 521.

[162] Friedrich Nietzsche, *The Will to Power*, Book 1, I, 2, 9; compiled from notes written between 1883-1888 assembled by his sister Elizabeth Förster-Nietzsche and posthumously published in 1901 as *The Will to Power: Studies and Fragments*.

[163] Friedrich Nietzsche, *Will to Power*. 979, 512.

[164] Blasé Pascal, *Gedanken, Fragmente und Briefe* (Leipzig, 1865).

[165] Thomas H. Brobjer, *Nietzsche's Philosophical Context. An Intellectual Biography* (Urbana: University of Illinois Press, 2008), 102-103. For a detailed discussion of Nietzsche's reading of Pascal see Brobjer's forthcoming *Nietzsche's Knowledge of Philosophy: A Study and Survey of Nietzsche's Reading of and Relation to German, British and French Philosophy*.

[166] Friedrich Nietzsche, *Beyond Good and Evil. Prelude to a Philosophy of the Future* 50, tr. Judith Norman (Cambridge: Cambridge University Press, 2002), 47. For a discussion of the four references to Augustine in Nietzsche's published writings, see Thomas Brobjer, *Nietzsche's Philosophical Context. An Intellectual Biography* (Urbana: University of Illinois Press, 2008), 99.

[167] Friedrich Nietzsche, Letter to Franz Overbeck, March 31, 1885. Thomas Brobjer, *Nietzsche's Philosophical Context*, 100.

[168] Friedrich Nietzsche, *On the Genealogy of Morals*, Book II, 11, 48-50; Thomas H. Brobjer, *Nietzsche's Philosophical Context*, 68.

[169] Max Scheler, *Ressentiment*, 45-46.

[170] Max Scheler, *Man's Place in Nature*, 3.

[171] Martin Heidegger, *Being and Time*, tr. John Macquarie and Edward Robinson. (New York: Harper & Row, 1962), 490, vii.

[172] Max Scheler, "Ordo Amoris," *Selected Philosophical Essays*, 100.

[173] John Macquarie, *Twentieth Century Religious Thought*, revised edition (London: SCM Press, 1983), 296.

[174]Anton Maxsein, *Philosophia Cordis: Das Wesen der Personalität bei Augustinus* (Salzburg: Otto Müller Verlag, 1966), 23; also "Philosophia Cordis bei Augustinus," *Augustinus Magister* 1(1954) 357-371.

[175] Saint Augustine, *Confessions*. Book 1, 5, tr. R.S. Pine-Coffin (London: Penguin Books, 1961), 24.

[176] Max Scheler, "*Ordo Amoris*," *Selected Philosophical Essays*, 112.

[177] Max Scheler, "*Ordo Amoris*," *Selected Philosophical Essays*, 113.

[178] Max Schelr, "*Ordo Amoris*," *Selected Philosophical Essays*, 114

[179] Max Scheler, "Repentance and Rebirth," *On the Eternal in Man*, 65.

[180] Max Scheler, "*Ordo Amoris*," *Selected Philosophical Essays*, 126.

[181] Max Scheler, "*Ordo Amoris*," *Selected Philosophical Essays*, 114.

[182] Max Scheler, *Formalism*, 288

[183] Max Scheler, "*Ordo Amoris*," *Selected Philosophical Essays*, 110-111.

[184] Max Scheler, *The Nature of Sympathy*, tr. Peter Heath (London: Routledge & Kegan Paul, 1954),103f.

[185] Max Scheler, "On the Idea of Man," tr. Clyde Nabe, *Journal of the Bristish Society for Phenomenology* 9:3 (October 1978) 192.

[186] Max Scheler, "On the Idea of Man," 192.

[187] Max Scheler, "On the Idea of Man," 195.

[188] Max Scheler, *Formalism*, 288.

[189] Max Scheler, "On the Idea of Man," 193.

[190] Max Scheler, "The Meaning of Suffering," 121.

[191] Max Scheler, *Formalism*, 332.

[192] Andrew Tallon, "The Concept of Heart in Strasser's *Phenomenology of Feeling*," *American Catholic Philosophical Quarterly* 66 (Summer 1992) 341.

[193] Max Scheler, "Love and Knowledge," 147.

[194] Max Scheler, Preface to First Edition, *On the Eternal in Man*, 10.

[195] Max Scheler, "Problems of Religion," *Eternal*, 257, 312-13; also *Problems of a Sociology of Knowledge*, tr. Manfred Frings (London: Routledge & Kegan Paul, 1980), 70ff; "Idealism-Realism," *Selected Philosophical Essays*, 300.

[196] Max Scheler, *Ressentiment*, 129.

[197] Max Scheler, "Problems of Religion," *Eternal*, 258.

[198] Max Scheler, "Christian Love and the Twentieth Century," *Eternal*, 374.

[199] Ferdinand Tönnies, *Community and Society*, tr. C.P. Loomis (East Lansing: Michigan State University, 1957).

[200] Rudolf Eucken, *The Truth of Religion*, tr. W. Tudor Jones (London: Williams & Norgate, 1913), 543.

[201] Ludwig Feuerbach, *The Essence of Christianity*, Appendix #8, 293.

[202] Jean-Luc Marion, *The Erotic Phenomenon*, 5.

[203] Pope Benedict XVI, *Deus Caritas Est*, #8, 17.

[204] Pope Benedict XVI, *Deus Caritas Est*, #1, 6.

[205] Max Scheler, *The Nature of Sympathy*, 164.

[206] Plato, *Laws*. X, 886A, Volume 2, Loeb Classical Library Vol. 11, tr.R.G.Bury (Cambridge Massachusetts: Harvard University Press, 1984), 301.

[207] Lewis A. Coser, "Max Scheler: An Introduction," *Ressentiment,*, 5.

[208] Max Scheler, "Problems of Religion," *Eternal*, 120.

[209] Max Scheler, "Problems of Religion," *Eternal*, 128.

[210] Max Scheler, Preface to the Second Edition, *Eternal*, 16.

[211] Especially Rudolf Otto's *Das Heilige* and K.T. Österreich's *Religionspsychologie* and his article "Über die religiöse Erfahrung;" also H. Scholz's *Religionsphilosophie*, I.K Girgensohn's *Der seelische Aufbau des religiösen Erlebens* and Josef Heiler's *Das Absolute*.

[212] Eugene Kelly, "Ethical Personalism and Unity of Person," in *Max Scheler's Acting Persons. New Perspectives*, ed. Stephen Schneck (Amsterdam: Editions Rodopi, 2002), 105.

[213] Alfred Schutz, "Max Scheler's Philosophy," *Collected Papers III: Studies in Phenomenological Philosophy* (The Hague: Martinus Nijhoff, 1970), 132.

[214] Letter written to his former wife Märit in 1926; John H. Nota, "The Development of Max Scheler's Philosophy of Religion," *The Papin Festschrift: Wisdom and Knowledge*. 2. ed. Joseph A.Rmendi. (Villanova: The Villanova University Press, 1976), 254

[215] Max Scheler. "Christian Love and the Twentieth Century," *Eternal*, 368.

[216] Max Scheler, "Problems of Religion," *Eternal*, 339.

[217] Joan Timmerman, *Max Scheler: An Inquiry into His Theory of God* (Ann Arbor, Michigan:U.M.I. Dissertation Service, 1974), 29.

[218] Blasé Pascal, *Pensées*, 173, also 183. tr. A.J. Krailsheimer (London: Penguin Books, 1966), 83, 85.

[219] William James, *The Varieties of Religious Experience. A Study in Human Nature*, ed. Martin E. Marty (New York: Penguin Books, 1985), 31.

[220] William James, *The Varieties of Religious Experience*, 46.

[221] Herbert Spiegelberg, "Towards a Phenomenology of Experience," *American Philosophical Quarterly* 1:4 (October 1964) 326.

[222] Max Scheler, "Problems of Religion," *Eternal*, 255.

[223] Max Scheler, "Problems of Religion," *Eternal*, 261.

[224] Max Scheler, *The Nature of Sympathy*, 231.

[225] John E. Smith, "Preface to the New Edition," *Experience and God* (New York: Fordham University Press, 1995), xvi .

[226] Max Scheler, "Problems of Religion," *Eternal*, 352.

[227] Max Scheler, "Problems of Religion," *Eternal*, 352.

[228] Max Scheler, "Problems of Religion," *Eternal*, 173.

[229] Max Scheler, "Love and Knowledge," 147.

[230] Max Scheler, "Problems of Religion," *Eternal*, 254.

[231] Max Scheler, "Problems of Religion," *Eternal*, 250f.

[232] Max Scheler, "Problems of Religion," *Eternal*, 266.

[233] Max Scheler, "Problems of Religion," *Eternal*, 251.

[234] Robert J. Vanden Burgt, *The Religious Philosophy of William James* (Chicago: Nelson-Hall, 1981), 1.

[235] Robert J. Roth, *American Religious Philosophy* (New York: Harcourt & Brace, 1967), 176.

[236] Max Scheler, "Problems of Religion," *Eternal*, 283.

[237] Max Scheler, "Problems of Religion," *Eternal*, 229.

[238] Michael Downey, "Mysticism," *The Modern Catholic Encyclopedia*, ed. Michael Glazier and Monika K. Hellwig (Collegeville, Minnesota: A Michael Glazier Book/The Liturgical Press, 1994), 595; also. *Understanding Christian Spirituality* (New York: Orbis Books, 1996).

[239] Max Scheler, *Problems of a Sociology of Knowledge*, 124-125.

[240] Max Scheler, *The Nature of Sympathy*, 34.

[241] Max Scheler, *Sympathy* 77-96.

[242] Max Scheler, *Sympathy* 87

[243] Max Scheler, *Sympathy* 88.

[244] Max Scheler, "Problems of Religion," *Eternal* 229.

[245] Blaise Pascal, *Pensées*, 314.

[246] Max Scheler, *The Nature of Sympathy*, 64.

[247] Arthur Schopenhauer, *The World As Will and Representation*, Vol.1. §66, tr. E.F.J. Payne (New York: Dover Publications, Inc. 1969), 374.

[248] Arthur Schopenhauer, *The World As Will and Representation*, Vol..1, §66, 374.

[249] Max Scheler, *The Nature of Sympathy*, 215.

[250] Max Scheler, *The Nature of Sympathy*, 18-36.

[251] Max Scheler, *The Nature of Sympathy*, 61.

[252] Max Scheler, *The Nature of Sympathy*, 64.

[253] Max Scheler, *The Nature of Sympathy*, 100.

[254] Max Scheler, "Problems of Religion" *Eternal* 337.

[255] Max Scheler, *Formalism*, 104f.

[256] Max Scheler, "Problems of Religion," *Eternal*, 283.

[257] Max Scheler, *The Nature of Sympathy*, 167.

[258] Max Scheler, "Problems of Religion," *Eternal*, 269.

[259] Max Scheler, "Problems of Religion," *Eternal*, 101.

[260] Max Scheler, "*Ordo Amoris*," *Selected Philosophical Essays*, 115.
[261] Max Scheler, *Formalism*, 94.
[262] Umberto Eco, *The Name of the Rose*, 123.
[263] Max Scheler, "The Reconstruction of European Culture," *Eternal*, 443.

A Mystagogical Ascent of Love: A Spiritual Reflection on the Sensuality of the Byzantine Divine Liturgy

Craig J. N. de Paulo
Gwynedd Mercy College

I n a sense, all love is mystical; and this is particularly true in our relations with the Divine who mysteriously reaches out to us from His Eternity *and* also from the depths of our own interiority in our soul. According to many of the Fathers of the Church, we were created with a burning love, or desire, for the Creator; and this innate desire is, perhaps, the greatest evidence of our existential connection with God. As St. Augustine of Hippo has famously written, "our heart is restless until it rests in you,"[1] this desire is most certainly a deep and penetrating restlessness that points us, our hearts, in our loving, to the Creator, who is Love itself and who fashioned us by His divine love. So, we are linked to God by our love, and it is love that directs us to Him, our final end; and thus, it could be said, that our whole life, whether we know it or not, is simply a search for God. Now, aside from our living in the world, where we can surely come to know something of God from His creation, our ordinary religious encounter with God is usually made possible by simply entering His holy Temple, the Church, where we are immediately opened up to another world — the spiritual world — and its supernatural life powered by the fire of love ultimately made manifest to us in the Divine Liturgy.

Probably one of the earliest and certainly the most important commentary on the Byzantine (Greek) Divine Liturgy is that of St. Maximus the Confessor who composed his *Mystagogy* around the year AD 630. Highly influenced by the work of Pseudo-Dionysius, St. Maximus' work preserves an Alexandrian approach to understanding and interpreting the theology manifest in the orations, art and priestly gestures, movement and structure of the liturgy. According to Dionysian "*theoria*," our liturgical and (contemplative) perception is mysteriously converted, so to speak, to spiritual vision and ultimately pointing us to the spiritual realm.[2] Needless to say, this Christian neoplatonic interpretation provides the foundation for understanding the mystical depth as well as the intense eroticism and sensuality present in the Byzantine Rite.

SPIRITUAL PERCEPTION

In the Byzantine tradition, of course, we must address the significance of icons and their role liturgically and also in the life of faithful. First of all, it must be said that icons are not merely objects of sacred art. For the orthodox Christian, icons are the most important means of spiritualization and indeed an extension of the liturgy.[3] In fact, in the orthodox home, icons are always kept in a special place, often a corner or table, which becomes a sacred space, an extension of the Church, where daily prayers and devotions are performed with candles and even incense. For the orthodox Christian, there is really no place that is truly secular; and one's home is certainly holy since baptized Christians reside there and it could also be said that Christ, the Theotokos, the angels and saints also dwell there by their special presence through the icons. So, whether in church or at home, the byzantine icon provides the mortal person on earth with the ability to behold and adore the Divine presence and all of the saints as the individual performs prostrations, blessing himself or herself and reverencing Christ and the saints by their reverence of the icons that represent them. The icons provide a kind of "spiritual perception" whereby, it is believed, that the faithful can see and relate to spiritual realities that lie beyond the icon in the spiritual realm. The icons are like doors to the spiritual world, to heaven and therefore to the angels, saints, to Mary the Mother of God and even to God himself to some extent. So, in Byzantine spirituality, there is a real seamlessness of experience, of this world and the heavenly world in which the Christian spends his or her life, half in this world and half in the other. That is to say, that ideally speaking, the orthodox Christian lives a mystical life, always deeply aware that he or she is a soul that exists by God's grace, to be judged by God and desperately in need of mercy, constantly sighing "'Lord Jesus Christ, Son of God, have mercy upon me a sinner."

The Church and the Divine Liturgy make all of this possible as a spiritual bridge between heaven and earth. As the faithful walk through the doors of the church, he or she immediately becomes aware of leaving the material world and entering into the spiritual world, somewhere between heaven and earth, by encountering the darkness of the church and the holy icons glimmering by the light of hundreds of candles. This makes the faithful aware that one's ordinary vision and his or her physical eyes, so to speak, are of little use in this world. One must turn from his or her physical eyes and physical vision to use spiritual eyes and spiritual vision. In this way, one is not merely surrounded by two-dimensional depictions of Christ and the saints; but rather, with the assistance of our spiritual vision of faith, we can see that we are actually surrounded by the real presence of Christ, the Theotokos, and the entire celestial community of the angels and saints. In the Church, we walk and move, speak and even look, differently because we are now dwelling within a spiritual realm that provides us with an experience of the kingdom of God. Here, we find God not through reason and intellection, but through faith and *love*, moving from icon to icon, prostrating ourselves and kissing the hands and feet of Christ and the saints, displaying our right of citizenship by our devotion and praise. Meanwhile, the church becomes more and more clouded by the incense, reminding us again that we must not rely upon our physical senses to find God. Nevertheless, we can smell the perfumed fragrance of the incense, reminding us that this entire experience is a cosmic romance between the soul and God, as we prepare to receive the bridegroom in the Holy Eucharist, the divine kiss. The beautiful gold and white vestments of the priest, the deacons and sub-deacons also reminds us of the romantic aspects of the Divine Liturgy, all dressed exquisitely for the mystical banquet that is about to take place at the altar. Singing praises to God and to the Theotokos amidst the constant repetition of the *Kyrie eleison*, the faithful bow their heads at the mention of the blessed Trinity and bless themselves again and again, as they prepare themselves for the arrival of the King of Kings, first with the Little Entrance, then the Great Entrance and ultimately in the Chalice, the *mysterium tremendum*.

DIVINE LITURGY AS ASCENT OF THE SOUL TO GOD

Following neoplatonic insight, St. Maximus the Confessor instructs us that the rich and intense sensuality of the liturgy and of the sacred art is not intended to be enjoyed for its own sake. Rather, it is all meant to be a vehicle for spiritualization and ultimately the mystical ascent of the soul to the One, to God himself. All of the sacred images assist the faithful in their liturgical and spiritual conversion, directing them toward otherworldly relations with the angelic species and all of the holy men and women who surround them and now constitute heaven, all moving toward God in the experience of Holy Communion, where we are called to experience what Byzantine theology refers to as *"theosis."*[4] As St. Athanasius wrote, "God became man so that man can become God," and this is exactly what is intended to be experienced in the mystery of Holy Communion within the Divine Liturgy: divination. All of this takes place precisely because "God is love," as St. John the Evangelist proclaims.[5] Indeed, it is God's love that makes this mystical, Eucharistic union possible whereby the individual communicant is able to consume the divine presence in the Holy Eucharist. This "communion" with God is the liturgical journey of divination. But, the question is, what exactly *is* divination? What is meant by the words of St. Athanasius "so that man may become God?"

According to the acclaimed historian of liturgy, the Jesuit Father Robert Taft, who explains, that "The liturgy was perceived as an ascent into the Kingdom and as the image of the individual

soul's conversion and ascent to union with God, for which the incarnation served as a model."[6] By contrast, the ascent of the soul,
according to Plato and neoplatonists such as Plotinus, was essentially an intellectual conversion that leads to the contemplation
(*theoria*) of the Good.[7] Whereas, in Christianity, the conversion of
the soul involves more than the intellect alone, but the heart as
well—indeed, the whole life of the individual must turn to the
Lord in love. More importantly, however, is the fact that the
Christian ascent of the soul that is intended to take place within
and through what might be called the liturgical "exercises" of the
Divine Liturgy goes beyond platonic "*theoria*" to "*theosis.*" Now,
while both the platonic and Christian models of ascent involve
eros, the former ends in contemplation while the latter in communion, or mystical union. That is, the Divine Liturgy is *divine*
not only because it is the proper worship and praise of God, but
because it is where we can experience the Triune God in the ecstasy of Holy Communion. Thus, according to platonic ascent, the
golden soul can experience the contemplation of the Good, which
is quite significant; but, it is not union with the divine. Further, let
us not forget that this contemplation of God, despite what Aristotle will later rightly say that it is closely akin to the divine activity, is still only a human action. It is only the contemplation of an
ideal and not a divine person, which means that it is certainly not
divination. In the Divine Liturgy, it must equally be pointed out
that the experience of the ascent of the soul is only made possible
by the grace of God. For, unlike the platonic model, this ascent is
not possible by human means, and the experience is not merely
intellectual but ultimately mystical, involving the whole person.
As such, the faithful begin their journey by physical means, prostrations, bows, blessing oneself over and over again, reverencing
icons with devout kisses and the lighting of candles, to following
the liturgy and its movements with sincerity and even abandonment of self, giving oneself over to the liturgy, observing every
part with great devotion, seeing one's life and journey in terms of
Christ's life as seen through the liturgy, reciting "Lord, have
mercy" with profound passion over and over, until it is all interi-
orized and the meaning of one's life can no longer be understood
outside of the liturgy, then the soul is prepared for the final stage

of the ascent in the reception of Holy Communion. Thus, *eros* plays a vital role in both neoplatonic and Christian models of ascent since desire is the vehicle of ascent, moving the individual soul from its physical inclinations toward the spiritual, which is recognized and utilized by St. Maximus.

Nevertheless, this journey of ascent within the Divine Liturgy could take many years, even a lifetime for some. In fact, for the average Western Christian, byzantine Christianity could seem quite exotic and terribly foreign. But, in my opinion, this is an excellent beginning since we are all "strangers in a foreign land," as the Scriptures tell us. In a sense, we could say that this is also exactly what the byzantine liturgy is intended to do: make us feel at first confused, strange, and unable to orchestrate ourselves; and this is because, liturgically we have left the world, where we are at home, and now we must find God's way with a new language, a new physicality, new vision, walking by faith and love, not by reason alone. Thus, the liturgy is a kind of catechesis in itself since the faithful come to know and experience the Divine by the devout observance of it. Needless to say, the more one comes to know about the liturgy when he or she already has begun to live it, the more the individual is able to experience its powerful tug toward conversion and the possibility of mystical union. As St. Germanus of Constantinople among others have already shown, the faithful will move in their liturgical and mystical ascent also by turning away from the need to understanding things in the Church and in the liturgy in ordinary terms and spiritualizing them by way of allegory and allowing oneself in faith to experience all of these things mystically. That is, as Germanus, points out, "the discos represents the hands of Joseph and Nicodemus, who buried Christ,"[8] "the chalice corresponds to the vessel which received the mixture which poured out from the bloodied, undefiled side and from the hands and feet of Christ,"[9] the Little Entrance with the Gospel as "the coming of God, when He was seen by us,"[10] "the censor demonstrates the humanity of Christ, and the fire, His divinity. The sweet-smelling smoke reveals the fragrance of the Holy Spirit,"[11] to seeing Christ himself in the priest, and especially the Bishop when present, and in every liturgical action until the entire liturgy has been spiritualized and no longer understood in worldly ways. That is to say, in the Divine Liturgy, nothing is as it appears since we must seek to understand things with spiritual eyes and spiritual interpretation. All of this is directed toward preparing us for heaven where worldly perception, worldly knowledge and worldly customs will be useless.

MYSTICAL EROTICISM AND THE LITURGY

As I have attempted to describe and as anyone may easily observe in many Orthodox churches, the Byzantine liturgy is overflowing with sensuality and inviting the faithful not only to worship the Lord but to experience the Lord deeply and completely in what is sometimes referred to as mystical eroticism. At first glance, a Western Christian might be impressed with the glamour of Byzantine Christianity, but fail to see that all of the artistic, architectural and liturgical beauty not only reflects its imperial origins but more importantly its love for God. In fact, it is all the result of the love of God; and as I have already mentioned, all of the liturgical processions and indeed every action, icon and vestment is all to be spiritualized and understood through the Scriptures, the life of Christ and ultimately in our relation with God. The liturgy is a reflection of the Church's love for God as well as a revelation of God's love for us.

Moreover, participation in the Divine Liturgy has little to do with duty; it is a mystical participation in the Divine Life. From the point of view of faith, to miss it on Sunday is like missing one's invitation to eternity and its joy. It is a privilege of the baptized Christian to participate in the Divine Liturgy where we may stand upright in the Lord and feast on His love with the angels and the saints. Ideally, it is love that moves the faithful to participate in this mystical banquet — God Himself moves us since He is love and irresistible to those who know Him.[12] In fact, all of our relations derive from Him and His love: our parents, our spouses, our children, our friends are all the result of God's love and blessing to us. Thus, the Divine Liturgy permits us to praise and celebrate the Source of all love and to experience the divine love so that through love we may come to know God. "Purity of heart, love of God, desire for the sacrament, zeal for communion, a glowing ardour, a burning thirst," writes the famous medieval Byzantine commentator Nicholas Cabasilas, "These are the means by which we draw sanctification to ourselves; these are necessary if we are to partake of Christ; without them true communion is impossible."[13] Although many receive Holy Communion today, not all of the faithful experience "true communion," as Cabasilas puts it out because it requires true love, or "a burning thirst." Perhaps another way of saying this would be that the faithful must open him or herself up, open the heart, one's *eros* so he or she may truly participate in the liturgy as a *lover* but also as one who is loved; and in this way, find God and even a deeper and unknown understanding of oneself. But, to do this, one must put his or her whole heart into every action and allow the breathlessness of love to be experienced as with any love. That is to say, take nothing for granted in the Church and in the liturgy, enjoy the warm illumination of the candles, the brilliance of light against the icons, kiss the foot of Christ with love and devotion and imagine that your kiss reaches Christ Himself, kiss the hand of the Mother of God with the same passion and gratitude, light your candles with great love and affection for God and the saints, close your eyes in prayer, smell the fragrance of the incense and sense the presence of the Holy Spirit and begin to imagine that you are entering a world that permits you to experience the heavenly kingdom in a clouded vision filled with angels and saints welcoming you into the loving and merciful presence of God who Love itself. This mystical union of the soul with God, which is possible in the Divine Liturgy, is certainly erotic because it is love that makes it all possible: the love in us that desires the Creator as well as the reality that God, who is love, is our ultimate end. So, love is the principle of our movement and the source of our participation in the liturgy.

But, the question remains: is this love that moves us *eros* or *agape*? This apparent controversy of love persists because the New Testament only refers to God as *agape*, probably ignoring the term *eros* in order to distance the Christian revealed notion of God from the minor pagan god known by the same name. Further, despite what the protestant theologian Anders Nygren has stated on the distinctions between *eros* and *agape*, classical and patristic scholarship has shown that both of these Greek terms could be applied to God.[14] In fact, in his first encyclical *Deus Caritas Est*, Pope Benedict XVI boldly states, that "God is *eros* as much as *agape*." Although Latin Christianity in the Western Church began to translate *agape* as *caritas* and *eros* as *libido* or *concupiscentia* and thus create a division between these two loves, the former good and the latter evil, the Early Church shows that there is no such distinction in the Greek Fathers. Perhaps, the earliest example of the use of both of these terms to describe God appears in the third century writings of the Alexandrian monk, Origen, who argued that all Greek words for love are equivocal and can be applied to God. Plotinus was one of the first neoplatonic thinkers to state unequivocally that "God is *eros*,"[15] and Pseudo-Dionysius followed the position of Plotinus, arguing that *eros* and *agape* can be used interchangeably.[16] Thus, the Western Church can benefit from the tradition of the East on this matter of divine love, which might resolve its debate over *eros* and *caritas*. In fact, greater exposure to the more mystical and sensual Orthodox liturgy might also contribute to the ongoing discussion in the West on the shortcomings of its modern liturgy. Further, in light of the *"lex orandi, lex credendi"* tradition, scholars must ask the difficult question of whether our worship (especially in the West) truly reveals our ancient beliefs? And, finally, we must ask if our worship truly reflects our love for God and God's love for us? For, in the end, our worship must always be a *school of love* for the Christian in his or her spiritual pilgrimage.

Notes

[1] St. Augustine, *Confessions*. I. 1.

[2] Generally, in Antiquity, there were two main schools of thought on the liturgy that corresponded to the two great centers of early Christian thought, namely, Antioch and Alexandria. The School of Antioch emphasized an historical understanding of the liturgy whereas Alexandria was far more philosophical, speculative and allegorical. The term "theoria" here represents the Alexandrian School, whence Pseudo-Dionysius derives his philosophical position. The reader should also be aware of the term "historia," which in this context represents the Antiochene School on liturgy.

[3] By Orthodox Christian, I am also referring to Greek Catholics.

4 The Greek term *"theosis"* is generally translated into English as divination or deification. It is a central concept in Byzantine theology.

5 *The First Letter of St. John.* 4:8.

6 Robert Taft, S.J., "The Liturgy of the Great Church: An Initial Synthesis of Structure and Interpretation on the Eve of Iconoclasm," *Dumbarton Oaks Papers*, 34-35 (1980-1981) 70-71.

7 Here, I am using the term *"theoria"* differently, referring simply to the ancient Greek notion of contemplation.

8 St. Germanus of Constantinople, *Ecclesiastical History and Mystical Contemplation* (trans. Paul Meyendorff, *St. Germanus of Constantinople: On the Divine Liturgy.* Crestwood, NJ: St. Vladimir's Seminary Press, 1984), paragraph 38.

9 St. Germanus, op. cit., paragraph 39.

10 St. Germanus, Ibid., paragraph 31.

11 St. Germanus, Ibid., paragraph 30

12 From the very beginning of the Divine Liturgy, we immediately encounter a great deal of mystical language from the priest's first prayer in which he states, "Lord, our God, whose power is beyond compare, and glory is beyond understanding; whose mercy is boundless, and love for us is ineffable..."(The Divine Liturgy of Saint John Chrysostom, trans. Holy Cross Faculty, Brookline: Holy Cross Orthodox press, 1985, 3-4.) Thus, we can see that that the Byzantine liturgy emphasizes the idea that the human intellect, in its finitude and with all of its imperfections, cannot truly comprehend the divine qualities; and it is only through the illumination of faith that we can aspire to God in prayer and ultimately come to know Him and His divine truth through participation in the liturgy.

In the priest's prayer of the faithful, for instance, we find a great deal of sensual language. It begins by stating "we bow before You and pray to you, O good and loving God," which shows the great depth of physicality that belongs to worship in the Byzantine Rite. In this prayer, the priest's mention of the "bow" is an exhortation to the people to remember our lowliness before the Creator and our fundamental physical position of penance and humility when addressing Him. The prayer continues, "cleanse our souls and bodies and from every defilement of flesh and spirit, and grant that we may stand before Your holy altar without blame or condemnation." The focus on our physicality and cleanliness here certainly makes this prayer rather sensual in nature, keeping in mind that we are not disembodied spirits, but a union of soul with body. The prayer also assumes that we are in need of "cleansing" from our sins, "from every defilement of flesh and spirit," taking into account St. Paul's wisdom that the "flesh lusts against the spirit, and the spirit against the flesh." Thus, from this cleansing and our disposition of humility before our "good and loving God," we may "stand before" God's holy altar "without blame or condemnation." This indicates the significance of the byzantine position that we may stand, as baptized Christians, justified by Christ, who has conquered death by His cross and redeemed us. The priest then prays for the "progress in life, faith and spiritual discernment" of the faithful that they may always worship God "with reverence and love, partake of Your Holy Mysteries without blame or condemnation, and become worthy of Your heavenly kingdom."(Ibid., Prayer of the Faithful, 12.) This is the entire purpose of the Divine Liturgy, spiritual progress so that the faithful will worship God with love (agape) and thereby "partake" of the holy Mystery (Holy Communion) without sin and thus spiritually advance, so to speak, toward the heavenly kingdom. As such, Holy Communion is directly connected to our salvation and our spiritual citizenship in the heavenly kingdom, which begins in this life and through our participation in the Divine Liturgy.

[13] Nicholas Cabasilas, *A Commentary on the Divine Liturgy* (trans. J. M. Hussey and P. A. McNulty. New York: St. Vladimir's Seminary Press, 2002), 96-97.

[14] See Anders Nygren, *Agape and Eros*, trans. Philip S. Watson (Philadelphia: Westminster, 1953).

[15] See Plotinus, *Ennead*.VI.8.15.

[16] See Pseudo-Dionysius, *Divine Names*. IV.III.

Eros' Ambiguity: A Philosophical History of Male Love

Pieter Adriaens
Catholic University of Leuven

INTRODUCTION

"[A]mbiguity is essentially a threat of disorder, and often provokes an intensification of the cultural struggle for order."[1]

In *The Metaphysics of Apes*, Raymond Corbey notes that cultural anthropologists have often considered non-human primates to be privileged figures of otherness, assisting articulations of human identity. Thus studying our animal cousins and ancestors served to screen man's unicity from the rest of the animal kingdom.[2] Moreover, non-human primates are profoundly ambiguous creatures, and one could say that the wide range of anthropological traditions reflects different ways of dealing with this ambiguity. Whereas cultural anthropologists resolutely relegated our hairy relatives to the animal kingdom by putting man on a pedestal, biological anthropologists have continually emphasized the many similarities between humans and (other) animals.

In this chapter, I argue that the history of homosexuality and bisexuality, and their tense romance with heterosexuality, provides us with a similar issue of ambiguity and identity.[3] For one thing, homosexuality and bisexuality are profoundly ambiguous phenomena. The ambiguity of bisexuals consists in their having sexual relationships with both men (mostly boys and adolescents, historically) *and* women. Current (effeminate) homosexuals, by contrast, are ambiguous in the sense that they display both masculine and feminine traits, even though they only feel attracted to other men. In addition, historians have hypothesized that these homosexuals may have served as a dividing wall between men and women, especially in times of growing equality between both sexes. Therefore, one could say that the identity of heterosexuals is crucially dependent on the presence of (effeminate) homosexuals. For reasons to be explored in this chapter, ambiguity has always met with resistance, whether in anthropology or in sex research. In the first section of my contribution, I will show that evolutionary psychologists have consistently disregarded the proportion of bisexuals in the homosexual population. Thus they simply ignore the fact that, historically, most men who engaged in same-sex sexual practices were simultaneously married, i.e. they had sexual relationships with men and women. In the next section, I'll discuss another example of our uneasiness with ambiguity: the relentless pursuit of homosexuals throughout the ages, as well as the continuing contempt they meet in today's society. I also argue that the effeminate kind of homosexuality is nonetheless a vital link in the sexual scenery of many contemporary societies. In the third section, I will discuss the question why we find it so difficult to confront ambiguity, using "biphobia" and homophobia as casestudies. The bench-mark of this final section is Mary Douglas' famous *Purity and Danger*.

EVOLUTION VERSUS HISTORY: THE CASE OF BISEXUALITY

AN EVOLUTIONARY PARADOX

One of the more striking examples of ignoring bisexuality is the current Darwinian thinking about homosexuality. Male love is usually considered to be a paradox or a puzzle for evolutionary theory. Being heritable – scientists speak of "gay genes,"[4] – homosexuality is much more prevalent than typical mutation-based traits, such as klinefelter's syndrome. Moreover, it seems obvious that homosexuals are at a high reproductive disadvantage, simply because they can't have children. Now if it is true that homosexuality is heritable and common, and if it is true that homosexuals do not reproduce, then we should expect natural selection to eliminate the so-called gay genes soon. Yet we know that homosexuality already existed in the Graeco-Roman world, and the abundant evidence on animal same-sex sexual practices[5] suggests our early ancestors probably engaged in male love, too. To account for this odd persistence, evolutionary psychologists have thought up a number of explanations.

One such hypothesis is based on a very famous principle of evolutionary theory, i.e. the principle of kin selection. Biologists have observed that some organisms tend to exhibit strategies that favor the reproductive success of their relatives, even at a cost to their own survival and reproduction. They explain the persistence of these strategies by indicating that some organisms "choose" to protect their close relatives, rather than raising children themselves. For these relatives share a significant number of genes with them, including, perhaps, the gay gene. Edward Wilson, the founder of sociobiology, suggested that homosexuality may have evolved by means of kin selection.[6] By taking care of their nephews and nieces, homosexuals would enable the gay gene to proliferate through collateral lines of descent, *even though they themselves do not reproduce at all.*

Another hypothesis goes that homosexuality could have been preserved by natural selection as a trade-off for another, highly adaptive trait – a trait that would somehow be biologically connected to the supposed gay gene. What trait? Well, Italian researchers recently found that, generally, mothers and aunts of homosexuals have more children than mothers and aunts of heterosexuals.[7] Thus they suggested that homosexuality may be a trade-off for the enhanced fecundity of female maternal relatives of homosexuals. Put otherwise: the high number of children being born to mothers and maternal relatives of homosexuals provides some kind of compensation for the fact that homosexuals themselves remain childless.

In their feverish search for hidden adaptive benefits, evolutionary psychologists invariably assume that data about the reproduction of contemporary North American and Western European homosexuals are representative of the entire evolutionary history of male love. In their view, homosexuality and heterosexuality are all-or-none traits: one is either homosexual or heterosexual, and if one is homosexual one cannot have children. They also claim that this dichotomy has been there from time immemorial. In short: evolutionary psychologists claim that sexual orientation has always been organized according to a disambiguated and dateless binary system without any transitional forms.[8]

HISTORY'S SOLUTION

Unfortunately, evolutionary psychologists are wrong. It may be true that contemporary homosexuals have only one tenth as many children as contemporary heterosexuals,[9] but there is no good reason to think that this has always been the case. For one of the most surprising findings of recent historical and anthropological research on homosexuality is that the bulk of men practicing same-sex sexuality were bisexual. Indeed, while being married and raising children, they had sex with other men, mostly boys or adolescents.[10]

As strange as the idea of a homosexual marrying a woman may seem to some of us today, such marriages not only occurred in many ancient societies, they continue to occur in many contemporary ones, including the United States.[11] Two examples illustrate this point. In Japan today, marriageable women often read gay magazines because they contain personal ads from homosexuals whose families and employers are urging them to marry and beget children: "So long as those obligations [marriage and parenthood] are met, one's sexual activity is not anyone else's legitimate concern."[12] And in ancient Greece, Spartan boys (*eromenoi*) were drilled under the eagle's eye of their older lovers (*erastai*), so as to become good warriors. Spartan soldiers are said to have sacrificed to *Eros* (originally the patron of male love) before entering the battlefield, in the belief that their fate was closely tied to the intimate relationship they had with their fellow warriors.[13] Most of the boys married, however, which amounted to having intercourse with their wives at least once a month. The remaining nights they spent with their *erastes* (who often acted as the newlyweds' Maecenas for some time after the marriage) or with their own *eromenos*. Indeed, only the *eromenoi* who married and raised children were allowed to become *erastai* themselves: "Exclusive pederasty was negatively sanctioned, but pederasty was expected."[14]

In short, recent historical and anthropological evidence suggests that male love frequently involved, and still involves, married men. For the majority of men engaging in same-sex sexual activities, such activities have always been complementary to, and not a replacement of, marital sexuality. Only recently has homosexuality been redefined as *exclusive* sexual activity with others of the same sex, which necessarily forecloses the biological possibility of having children. Today, (some) male homosexuals have sex only with men, and never with women, but such exclusivity is by no means representative of the history of male love.

On the contrary: homosexuality as we now know it is definitely a recent phenomenon. In Western Europe, the era of exclusive same-sex sexuality probably began in the early eighteenth century. Historian Randolph Trumbach, for example, has argued that before about 1700, many European men maintained sexual relationships with women as well as with younger boys: "Homosexual activity occurred between most men and boys. ... Sodomy was therefore so widespread as to be universal. But it was always structured by age."[15] Unlike today, bisexuals (e.g. married men having sex with adolescents) were the majority, and "heterosexuals" the minority. While the religious authorities disapproved of male same-sex sexuality, public opinion saw nothing wrong with it, provided the older lover played the active part. But around 1700, a major shift in sexual morays started to set in: older men, who were called (and called themselves) *mollies* or *sodomites*, shifted roles and began playing the passive part that had, traditionally, been reserved for the adolescent.[16] Moreover, some *mollies* and *sodomites* now desired *only* men: they neither married nor raised children. Such *exclusive* sexual preference is just one of the characteristics of this "wholly new" kind of male love.[17] Modern homosexual partners also lack significant status differences, and they identify themselves with a gender that combines characteristics of both femininity and masculinity. The combination of these three characteristics (exclusivity, equality, and gender ambiguity) is indeed quite new in the history of human same-sex sexuality.

The eighteenth-century change in sexual scenery started out in Western Europe, mainly in England and Italy. In the subsequent centuries, it gradually carved its way in other parts of the world. In some countries, however, the old sexual system (with a bisexual majority) continued to exist a little longer. In Japan, for example, the changeover only took place between 1900 and 1950. And in Latin America, age-structured same-sex sexuality occurred up till the last decade of the twentieth century. In fact the age-structured system still exists, for example, in a number of Islamic Mediterranean countries such as Turkey, Morocco, Iraq, Oman, Saudi Arabia, Pakistan and Northern India.[18]

That said, contemporary sexologists emphasize that even today, bisexuals outnumber exclusive homosexuals. When trying to map out male sexual behavior, pioneer sexologist Alfred Kinsey did not expect to find that at least 37 per cent of the male population had at least some same-sex sexual experience between the beginning of adolescence and old age. He also found that 18 per cent of his interviewees had at least as much same-sex sexual as heterosexual experiences in their lives, whereas only 4 percent of his population turned out to be exclusively homosexual.[19] The general conclusion of his impressive research was that nearly half of the male population engages in both heterosexual and same-sex sexual activities. As he concludes himself:

> Males do not represent two discrete populations, heterosexual and homosexual. The world is not to be divided into sheep and goats. Not all things are black nor all things white. It is a fundamental of taxonomy that nature rarely deals with discrete categories. Only the human mind invents categories and tries to force facts into separated pigeon-holes. The living world is a continuum in each and every one of its aspects. The sooner we learn this concerning human sexual behavior the sooner we shall reach a sound understanding of the realities of sex.[20]

So one could say that most of history's male lovers were in fact bisexuals, and that evolutionary psychologists have consistently failed to account for the widespread existence of bisexuality before *and* after 1700, believing the post-1700 exclusive homosexual to be representative of the entire evolutionary history of male love. In the next section, I will argue that, historically, bisexuals have as much been ignored as (effeminate) homosexuals have been despised. In the final section it will be argued that neglect and contempt can be considered as two different strategies to deal with ambiguity.

AMBIGUITY AND IDENTITY: THE CASE OF HOMOSEXUALITY

HISTORY'S OLDEST HATRED

It is perhaps unnecessary to demonstrate that homosexuals have never been society's sweethearts. Throughout history they have been humiliated and taunted, degraded and derided, blackmailed and banished, burnt and beheaded, drowned, hanged, castrated, and blamed for numerous diseases and disasters.[21] Even today, same-sex sexual contacts are punishable by law in more than eighty countries. In some of them, homosexuality is a capital offence. And the sad fate of several Iranian young men being hanged because of their sexual orientation shows that, unfortunately, these laws are still complied with.

The historical vicissitudes of homophobia have been documented quite well, yet few authors have asked themselves *why* homosexuals often had such a hard time holding their ground in society. Whence homophobia? Obviously, the three great Abrahamic religions (Christianity, Judaism and Islam) have always been less than favorable to male lovers. The author(s) of Leviticus, for example, fiercely denounced male homosexuality by claiming that "if a man also lie with mankind, as he lieth with a woman, both of them have committed an abomination: they shall surely be put to death; their blood shall be upon them" (*Leviticus* 20:13). According to Louis Crompton, this one verse has determined the fate of millions of male lovers. For Judaism turned out to be much more than the belief system of a tiny tribe in the eastern Mediterranean. It became the breeding ground and source of inspiration for one of the leading world religions: Christianity. As such, Crompton continues, "the Levitical statute became the model for laws decreeing capital punishment for homosexuality in Europe and in as much of the world as came under Europe's sway, down to the end of the eighteenth century. Indeed, the moral authority of Leviticus has been determinative even in this day; American courts routinely cited it as an argument for retaining state sodomy laws."[22]

However, claiming that one cruel verse is the sole responsible for history's homophobia is perhaps a little too easy. Crompton seems to forget that religious considerations are often used as a cover for plainly secular motives. In Daniel Dennett's vocabulary, religions are not constructed by means of skyhooks but by means of cranes.[23] They embody a distinctive historical mentality – the fears, desires and worries of ordinary people in a specific place and time. And seemingly some of the trials and tribulations of that tiny Mediterranean tribe proved to be more universal and more tenacious than others. Christianity did not adopt all Thoraic enactments, for example, but they did adopt the prohibition of male homosexuality. In other words: the Levitical ferocity towards male lovers apparently struck a powerful chord in the mind of many. So maybe we should inquire into the appeal and the persistence of homophobia, rather than into its origin.

At this point, a philosopher may come to our aid. In a late interview with *The Advocate*, Michel Foucault suggested that there is a sudden surge of homophobia at the beginning of the eighteenth century – a surge that, still according to Foucault, may be due to the decline of the *amicitia*. The *amicitia*, Foucault explains, was a particular, affective kind of friendship between males that often included same-sex sexual behavior. "Once [such] friendship had disappeared as a culturally accepted relationship, the question was raised: 'But what are these men doing together?' At that moment, the problem [of homophobia] made its first appearance."[24] Male love was seen as some sort of plot, and the inability to understand it, to place it, made the public at large fearful and repudiating. To avert the fear, Foucault contends, these men were tagged with a new identity based on their sexual activities: the homosexual identity. Therefore, in Foucault's view, the construction of the modern homosexual identity originated as a kind of social control.

Foucault's untimely death prevented him from elaborating on this hypothesis. Yet one wonders if the obscurity surrounding homosexuality, i.e. the fact that people are unable to place it, would not enable us to understand the *entire* history of homophobia, rather than just one of its sordid episodes. Obviously, saying that same-sex sexual behavior only became a problem in the eighteenth century would be a gross historical error. As I already indicated, same-sex sexual behavior had by then been commonplace for thousands of years, and that in spite of a fierce Inquisition that had first reared its head in the thirteenth century. So again: why was homosexuality so consistently, and with ever-increasing vehemence since the rise of Christianity, regarded as subversive?

Before answering this question a further distinction has to be made. Indeed: not all male lovers met with the same contempt. Generally and historically, there are in fact four different sexual roles for male individuals engaging in same-sex sexuality: a passive boy or adolescent, an active adult male (usually married while having sex with boys and adolescents, and perhaps also with passive adult males), a passive adult male (mostly married while having sex with active adult males), and a passive adult male acting as a itinerant transvestite prostitute.[25] Historians have demonstrated that the first two roles (boy and active adult male) were seldom considered as problematical. Quite the contrary: by penetrating adolescents and passive adult males, the active adult male in fact proved his masculine dominance. In ancient Rome, individuals adopting the latter two roles were known as *cinaedi* and *galli*, respectively. Originally, *galli* were itinerant religious devotees who survived by begging, foretelling the future, performing religious rituals, and offering sexual services to active adult males. Being "prostitutes", they cross-dressed and (sometimes) castrated themselves. *Galli* were at least tolerated, and probably even admired because of their religious role.[26] The role of the *cinaedus*, by contrast, has been taunted and despised since time immemorial. Roman *cinaedi* behaved very womanly: they cross-dressed, wore too much jewelry, and depilated and scented themselves. According to Clement of Alexandria, they even made typical noises: "a noise in their noses like a frog, just as if they kept their spleen stored up in their nostrils."[27] The sexual passivity and effeminacy of the *cinaedi* was a thorn in the side of the prototypical Roman patriarch. Thus passivity in a same-sex sexual relationship was punishable by law: pre-Christian Roman rules stipulated that it should entail a loss of civic rights.[28]

In fact the eighteenth-century English *mollies* and *sodomites* strongly resembled the ancient character of the *cinaedus*.[29] *Mollies*, too, got totally absorbed in their effeminate roles. "Modern sodomites or homosexuals were conceived to be men who really wanted to be women and took on many of the characteristics of women. They walked and spoke like women. They used women's names. They often dressed partly or entirely as women. But they did not desire women. Instead, they wished to have sexual relations entirely with males."[30] And *mollies*, too, were always held in contempt, the more so because their gatherings slowly started to take the size of a full-blown subculture.[31]

Thus it seems that it is mainly *passive* and *effeminate* adult homosexuals that have never been accepted in Western culture. They are men and yet they do not desire women. They desire men. They are men and yet they do not dress like men. They dress like women. In short, the prototypical passive effeminate homosexual seems to undermine our habitual ways of classifying the world. As such, he upsets our snug and secure worldview, "inevitably" eliciting public repudiation. Indeed: along with Foucault, one could say that it is precisely the ambiguity of the effeminate homosexual that doomed his fate by occasioning disrespect, disdain and discrimination.

HOMOSEXUALITY AND HETEROSEXUALITY

And yet one could say that effeminate homosexuals play an important part in the division of sexual roles in many contemporary societies. Their ambiguity in fact allowed them to take on a symbolic function in the changing landscape of sexual orientation in eighteenth-century Europe. In order to understand this symbolic function, we have to inquire into the reasons of that impressive eighteenth-century changeover – a changeover from a system of age-structured same-sex sexuality, to a rather new and uniquely human complex of desires, behaviors, and identities, which we now call "homosexuality."

Whence this recent, exclusive kind of same-sex sexuality? Historians and philosophers differ in opinion about this issue. According to Michel Foucault, for example, it is the nineteenth-century medicalisation of same-sex sexual behavior that explains the genesis (or rather: the construction) of a homosexual identity. In his *History of Sexuality*, Foucault claims that the then authorities came to see the control of sexuality as an instrument with which to reach their goals of economic efficiency and political conservatism. The sciences, mostly psychiatry and sexology, developed discourses to monitor sexuality, and these discourses in turn gave rise to the medicalization of sexuality in general and of homosexuality in particular.[32]

Many contemporary historians disagree with Foucault by pointing to a major anachronism in his hypothesis. While it is true, they argue, that the terms "homosexual" and "heterosexual" were coined by late nineteenth-century psychiatrists and sexologists, the shift to the current, modern kind of same-sex sexuality took place earlier, probably around the very beginning of the eighteenth century. Therefore, psychiatry and sexology cannot be held responsible for its existence. That said, it is not unlikely that they served to legitimate an already existing binary ontology of human sexual orientation. By setting up a thorough search for physical and hereditary causes of homosexuality – just like they did for other then modish "illnesses" such as neurasthenia and *railway spine*[33] – psychiatrists validated the view that homosexuality was a firm and stable disposition, rather than a flexible sexual strategy.[34]

But if psychiatry and sexology did not create the modern kind of homosexuality, what did? Society did, says sociologist Mary McIntosh in a seminal paper entitled "The homosexual role."[35] In her view, homosexuality is not a medical condition, as psychiatrists and sexologists have suggested. If it would be a condition, people would be either homosexual or heterosexual, and Kinsey's work has clearly shown that at nearly every age far more men have sex with both men and women, rather than with men only.

Conversely, McIntosh suggests to consider homosexuality as a specialized social role that has been designed by a number of societal expectations. As to her, society expects those engaging in same-sex sexuality to be *exclusively* attracted to men, to be effeminate in manner and personality, and to be keen on seducing boys and young men.[36] Such expectations often act like self-fulfilling prophecies, thus establishing a real polarization between homosexuality and heterosexuality.

But why would a society create a homosexual role? Why would a predominantly heterosexual society need a homosexual minority? McIntosh leaves this question unanswered, except for the rather enigmatic claim that "the creation of a specialized, despised, and punished role of homosexual keeps the bulk of society pure in rather the same way that the similar treatment of some kinds of criminals helps to keep the rest of society law-abiding."[37] Pure from what? McIntosh seems to suggest that the creation of "the homosexual" acted as a deterrent; it urged people to affirm their heterosexuality, just like the imprisonment of criminals should prevent people from doing wrong.

Historian Randolph Trumbach continued this line of thinking, particularly by concentrating on the issue of effeminacy. In his opinion, the early eigtheenth century witnessed the beginning of a major cultural shift "in which a patriarchal morality that allowed adult men to own and dominate their wives, children, servants and slaves, was gradually challenged and partially replaced by an egalitarian morality which proposed that all men were created equal, that slavery must therefore be abolished, democracy achieved, women made equal with men, and children with their parents."[38] Family structures changed from a system of patriarchy to a system of domesticity: forced marriages made way for companionate and romantic marriages, and brute offspring domination made way for a more tender care of children. Consequently, differences between men and women were gradually leveled, resulting in a completely new system of sexual interactions. And here the marginalized homosexual minority enters the game. According to Trumbach, *mollies* and *sodomites* appeared to facilitate the new relations of males with women and children – relations produced by a rising domesticity. They facilitated these new relations because they soothed the fears of the male "heterosexual" majority that the new intimacy might transform them into women or children. In short, society "invented" the homosexual as "a wall that guaranteed the permanent, lifelong separation of the majority of men and women, in societies where their relative equality must have been a perpetual danger to patriarchy."[39] In Trumbach's view, society created "the homosexual" in order to safeguard the masculine (sexual) identity of the male heterosexual majority.[40] Therefore, one could say that homosexuals are truly indispensable in today's society and that, ironically, homophobia threatens to mine the shaky structure of our sexual role-play.

CONFRONTING AMBIGUITY: MARY DOUGLAS' *PURITY AND DANGER*

In order to make sense of the way people, whether scientists or laymen, have dealt with, and continue to deal with, the phenomena of both bisexuality and (effeminate) homosexuality, it would be interesting to have a look at the work of ethnologist Mary Douglas. In *Purity and Danger*, for example, Douglas (1966) inquires into the origin and meaning of rituals and taboos. According to her, taboos are not solely to be accounted for in prosaic medical terms. They are not simply hygienic measures, even though some of them might have sanitary advantages. *Halal* or *kosjer* food may perhaps prove be less toxic, for example, but the rules regulating food consumption may have other origins as well. Put otherwise: "Even if some of Moses's dietary rules were hygienically beneficial, it is a pity to treat him as an enlightened public health administrator, rather than as a spiritual leader."[41]

According to Douglas, creating a taboo and the corresponding defilement rules and rituals, may be just one way to deal with ambiguity. Indeed: ambiguous entities or situations lend themselves easily to be transformed in powerful symbols. They are frightening and yet fascinating examples of the loopholes in our laws. Take faeces, for example. Like so many other bodily fluids, such as urine, menses, mucus and earwax, faeces are on the verge of the inside and the outside of the body. Hovering somewhere between our body and the world, they belong to neither of them.

As such, faeces attest to an awkward ambiguity that turns over the way we categorize our world. Faeces, then, are not *unclean* (at least not in the first place) because they contain lots of bacteria, but because they are *unclear*. They refuse to be fitted in our comfortable and familiar worldview. Therefore, one could say that the taboo on faeces and, in general, on ambiguous entities and situations, originates in the typically human "reaction which condemns any object or idea likely to confuse or contradict cherished classifications."[42]

Ambiguity is ubiquitous, so we should expect there to be lots of taboos. According to Douglas, however, there's a whole range of tactics to deal with ambiguity. Apart from subjecting the ambiguous entity or situation to rules of avoidance (and transforming it into a taboo), one can also reduce ambiguity by assigning the ambiguous to one of the two possible categories involved. For example: in trying to dispose of the ambiguity surrounding our phylogenetic family members, anthropologists have proposed either to range humans under primates (as *Pan Sapiens*) or to range primates under humans (*Homo Niger* and *Homo Gorilla* representing the chimpanzee and the gorilla, respectively).[43] Finally, one can also control ambiguity by branding it as dangerous or even by destroying it. Thus Douglas relates how "some West African tribes" kill twin siblings at birth because they hold that two humans cannot be born from the same womb at the same time.[44]

Douglas doesn't mention a word about male love, but it is obvious that bisexuals and effeminate homosexuals can be considered as profoundly ambiguous beings, too. In this capacity they toy with some of our most cherished sexual structures and distinctions – distinctions we neurotically hang on to because we created them ourselves.[45] I already quoted Alfred Kinsey saying that "it is a fundamental of taxonomy that nature rarely deals with discrete categories."[46] Unfortunately, our mind seems to be unable to work without such categories. And whatever does not match with them makes us restless. For some reason, confronting the ambiguous cannot but result in its avoidance, its reduction or its elimination.[47]

The history of male love testifies to this tactics. Effeminate homosexuals, for example, seem to defy one of our most evident and basal symbolical distinctions, i.e. the difference between man and woman. Effeminate homosexuals are men and yet they do not desire women; they are men and yet they do not act like men. Constituting some kind of "middlesex," a hybrid form between man and woman, they play the fool with our rigid classification systems. Historically, different strategies haven been adopted to deal with the ambiguity of these homosexuals. When they were thought to spoil the young, they were avoided; when they were thought to cause diseases and epidemics, they were branded; and when they were thought to break the law, they were persecuted and killed. To my knowledge, there are no societies that value effeminate homosexuals *because of* their sexual behavior or their sexual orientation. Of course, itinerant transvestite prostitutes, such as the ancient Roman *gallus*, the Turkish *köçek* and the Indian *hijra*, were often highly valued and needed in their respective societies. However, they were not valued because of the sexual services they rendered, but rather because of their religious position. Proof of this claim is that today's hijra's in India meet with more and more contempt as they cut back their religious (vis-à-vis their sexual) services.[48]

Bisexuals are ambiguous not so much because they defy the difference between man and woman, but rather because they undermine the ongoing polarisation between homosexuality and heterosexuality. It was Alfred Kinsey who challenged the widespread assumption that "there are persons who are 'heterosexual' and persons who are 'homosexual,' that these two types represent antitheses in the sexual world, and that there is only an insignificant class of 'bisexuals' who occupy an intermediate position between the other groups."[49] Both denominations, "homosexuality" and "heterosexuality," do not refer to discrete populations. They are not two fortresses in an otherwise dead and barren landscape. Rather, they are the tail ends of a colourful continuum of sexual orientation. Kinsey demonstrated that there are in fact more "bisexuals" than "homosexuals," thus turning this supposedly "insignificant class" into a powerful community. One could say that minimalization is perhaps a coping strategy that would deserve to be added to Douglas' list of strategies to deal with ambiguity.

The ambiguity of bisexuals has often been reduced, too, and particularly so by labelling them as "undecided". Implicitly and explicitly, bisexuals have often been conceptualised as those who just don't know yet what side to choose. Thus they were seen as either future homosexuals or future heterosexuals. Finally, one could also consider the (creation of the) concept of "bisexuality" *in se* as a coping strategy. As Mary McIntosh notes, "[sexologists] introduced the notion of a third type of person, the 'bisexual,' to handle the fact that behavior patterns cannot be conveniently dichotomized into heterosexual and homosexual."[50] By adding a third category ("a third fortress") to our classification, the ambiguity is neutralized and our serenity saved.

CONCLUSION

In this chapter, I attempted to bring Mary Douglas' analysis of ambiguity to bear to the history of male love. Douglas' analysis revealed that whatever does not harmonize with our cherished symbolic structures is doomed to be avoided, minimalized, ignored, or eliminated. Male love proved to be no exception to this rule. Before 1700, bisexuals definitely outnumbered "heterosexuals". Today, they still outnumber "homosexuals", and yet they continue to be ignored as a sexual population. In their turn, effeminate homosexuals have been avoided, branded, persecuted and even killed, even though they do hold an important symbolic position in many contemporary societies. Indeed: their ambiguity in fact allows them to act as a symbolic dividing line between man and woman, especially in cultures wherein the differences between both sexes increasingly fade away.

Notes

[1] R. Corbey, *The Metaphysics of Apes. Negotiating the Animal-Human Boundary*, (Cambridge: Cambridge University Press, 2005) 25.

[2] Corbey 2005.

[3] For reasons to be revealed, I consider *homosexuality* as a recent kind of *same-sex sexuality*. The latter simply refers to someone having sex with a person of the same sex. *Bisexuality* refers to someone having sex with persons of both sexes. *Male love* is a rather neutral denomination I use to refer to both same-sex sexuality (including homosexuality) and bisexuality.

[4] By "gay gene" they refer to a hypothetical hereditary character that, along with all the other genes and the experiences one goes through, will make someone somewhat more likely to become homosexual (A. De Block and P. Adriaens "Darwinizing Sexual Ambivalence. A New Evolutionary Hypothesis of Male Homosexuality," *Philosophical Psychology* 17, 1 [2004].)

[5] B. Bagemihl, *Biological Exuberance: Animal Homosexuality and Natural Diversity*, (New York: St. Martin's, 1999); V. Sommer and P. Vasey, eds. *Homosexual Behavior in Animals: Evolutionary Perspectives*, (Cambridge: Cambridge University Press, 2006).

[6] E. O. Wilson, *On Human Nature* (Cambridge: Harvard Univerisyt Press, 1978).

[7] A. Camperio-Ciani *et al* "Evidence for Maternally Inherited Factors Favouring Mle Homosexuality and Promoting Female Fecundity," *Proceedings of the Royal Society B: Biological Sciences* 271.

[8] For an extensive discussion of the history and evolution of same-sex sexuality, as well as an alternative evolutionary explanation of male love, see De Block & Adriaens, *ibid.*, (2004) and P. Adriaens and A. De Block "The Evolution of a Social Construction: The Case of Male Homosexuality," *Perspectives in Biology and Medicine* (2006) 49, 4.

[9] Miller 2000.

[10] S. Murray, *Homosexualities* (Chicago: University of Chicago Press, 2000).

[11] C. Bagley and P. Tremblay, "On the Prevalence of Homosexuality and Bisexuality in a Random Community Survey of 750 Men Aged 18 to 27," *Journal of Homosexuality* (1998) 36, 2.

[12] Murray *op cit.*, 398.

[13] Murray *ibid*, 40.

[14] Murray *ibid*, 40.

[15] R. Trumbach, *Sex and the Gender Revolution. Volume One: Heterosexuality and the Third Gender in Enlightenment London*, (Chicago: University of Chicago Press, 1998), 5.

[16] L. Crompton, *Homosexuality and Civilization* (Cambridge: The Belknap Press of Harvard University Press, 2003); Murray, *op cit*;Trumbach *op cit.*

[17] It was Foucault who claimed that the modern kind of homosexuality is a "wholly new" kind of male love. Historians now agree, however, that Foucault was wrong about this. As historian Louis Crompton notes: "[T]he idea of a sexual identity is not uniquely modern. Aristophanes expressed it plainly enough in the *Symposium*, and the Romans used it, in a limited sense, in their concept of the cinaedus ("faggot"), who was certainly a distinct sort of person. In Plutarch's philosophical debate, half the speakers share an identity as lovers of youths and the other half as heterosexuals, though they lacked the term, and the same dichotomy appears in a brilliant dialogue from seventeenth-century Japan. Even in medieval times, when the view of same-sex relations as sins and crimes predominated, a French poet could make his heroine speak of 'men of that sort' (de

ce métier), that is, of a certain kind of individual" (Crompton, *op cit.*, xiv). Thus one might argue that perhaps evolutionary psychologists are not chasing shadows after all. In fact it may not be unreasonable to assume that exclusive homosexuals have always existed, even though they have perhaps occupied wildly different niches throughout history. As such, exclusive homosexuality would still deserve an evolutionary explanation.

[18] For a short discussion of cross-cultural differences in systems of sexual orientation, see R. Trumbach "Renaissance Sodomy, 1500-1700," in *A Gay History of Britain: Love and Sex between Men since the Middle Ages*, ed, M. Cook: 45-75 (London: Greenwood World Publishing, 2007a), 45ff.

[19] A. Kinsey, *et al., Sexual Behavior in the Human Male* (Philadelphia: W.B. Saunders Company, 1948).

[20] Kinsey, *ibid.*, 639.

[21] For an extensive historical overview of homophobia, see Crompton, *op cit.*

[22] Crompton *ibid.*, 34.

[23] D. Dennett *Darwin's Dangerous Idea: Evolution and the Meaning of Life*, (New York: Simon & Schuster, 1995).

[24] M. Foucault "Michel Foucault, an interview. Sex, Power and the Politics of Identity" *The Advocate* (1984) 400, 29.

[25] Trumbach 2007a, *op cit.*, 46ff.

[26] Murray *op cit.*, 298ff.

[27] Quoted in L. Berman *The Puzzle: Exploring the Evolutionary Puzzle of Male Homosexualiry*, (Illinois: Godot Press, 2003), 173.

[28] Both sexual roles, i.e. *gallus* and *cinaedus*, still exist today, for example in Turkey and Northern India. The contemporary Turkish equivalent of the Roman *gallus*, i.e. the *köçek*, is admired, while the *Ibne*, the passive adult married male, is held in contempt.

[29] The likeness between the *cinaedus* and the modern homosexual is not just outward. In fact the cinaedus, too, was considered as a genuine identity, for instance in the Aristotelian physiognomony (Murray *op cit.*, 255).

[30] R. Trumbach "Modern Sodomy: The Origins of Homosexuality, 1700-1800" in *A Gay History of Britain: Love and Sex between Men since the Middle Ages*, ed. M. Cook (London: Greenwood World Publishing, 2007) 78. In a satirical book on the history of the London clubs, Edward Ward pictured the meeting place of some *mollies*. According to him, these men 'adopted all the small vanities natural to the feminine sex to such an extent that they try to speak, walk, chatter, shriek and scold as women do, aping them as well in other respects' (Ward 1709, quoted in M. McIntosh, "The Homosexual Role," *Social Problems* (1968) 16, 2; 188).

[31] For an extensive overview of homophobia in renaissance and enlightenment Europe, see Gerard & Hekma 1988.

[32] M. Foucault, *The History of Sexuality* (New York: Pantheon Books, 1978). The attentive reader has perhaps noticed that Foucault seems to endorse two differ-

ent views. In his *History of Sexuality* (Foucault 1978) he claims that *nineteenth-century* psychiatry and sexology invented the modern homosexual. Eight years later, in the already mentioned interview with *The Advocate* (Foucault 1984), he had changed his view. For now he states that the role of the modern homosexual originated in the *eighteenth*-century public feeling being uncomfortable with male friendships. What happened? Of course Foucault is known for his changing viewpoints; when confronted with similar antics, he once exclaimed: "Well, do you really think I have worked hard all those years to say the same thing and not be changed?" For this once, however, there might not be a contradiction. One could argue indeed that sexology and psychiatry simply reflected the public uneasiness about homosexuality. As such, these sciences served as an instrument of public opinion, rather than as an instrument of the authorities.

[33] C. Rosenberg, "Contested Boundaries: Psychiatry, Disease and Diagosis" *Perspectives in Biology and Medicine* (2006) 49, 3.

[34] De Block & Adriaens 2004; Adriaens & De Block 2006.

[35] McIntosh *op cit.*

[36] *Ibid.*, 185.

[37] *Ibid.*, 184.

[38] R. Trumbach, "Gender and the Homosexual Role in Modern Western Culture: The 18th and 19th Centuries Compared," in *Homosexuality, Which Homosexuality?* ed. D. Altman, *et al.* (London: GMP Publishers, 1989) 154.

[39] *Ibid.* 155.

[40] Psychiatrists and sexologists will probably take offence at the idea that homosexuality is a creation (or an invention) of society. Trumbach, for example, repeatedly claims that 'a minority of males were *socialized* as children into a role that was both male and female' (R. Trumbach "London," in *Queer Sites: Gay Urban Histories Since 1600*, ed. D. Higgs [London: Routledge, 1999] 91; italics mine). Such claim is square to the biologist's creed that the flexibility of human behavior is limited, in particular by our biological equipment. However, Trumbach's claim about the *etiology* of homosexuality is not central to his theory about the *social function* of homosexuality. One could meet the biological criticism by saying that society did perhaps not *create* the role of the homosexual. Rather, it simply *exploited* an already existing group of male lovers, and put them to use in order to demarcate the line between men and women.

[41] M. Douglas, *Purity and Danger: An Analysis of the Concepts of Pollution and Taboo,* (London: Routledge, 1966), 37.

[42] *Ibid.*, 45.

[43] Corbey, *op cit.*, 145ff.

[44] Douglas, *op cit.*, 49.

[45] We created them ourselves because in the end so-called *natural* distinctions are never as clear as we would want them to be. As Douglas notes: "[I]deas about separating, purifying, demarcating and punishing transgressions have as their

main function to impose system on an inherently untidy experience. It is only by exaggerating the difference between within and without, about and below, male and female, with and against, that a semblance of order is created" (Douglas, *ibid.*, 5). Some of our symbolic distinctions (man-woman, inside-outside,...) may have been preformed in the natural world, but then again the natural world does not tell us anything about *which* distinctions are important, let alone whether they are important at all. (I thank Paul Moyaert for this line of reasoning.)

[46] Kinsey *et al.* 1948, 639.

[47] There is one important lacuna in Douglas' account of the ambiguous. For Douglas never asks why we have so much difficulty confronting ambiguity. Granted, ambiguity disrupts the existing order. But then the question is why we are so fond of our classifications. A detailed answer to this question is outside the scope of the present chapter, but psychologists have noted that there are perhaps good evolutionary reasons to consider social categories as natural kinds (see e.g. C. Barrett, "On the Functional Origins of Essentialism," *Mind and Society* (2001) 3, 2).

[48] Murray, *op cit.*, 307-8.

[49] Kinsey *et al.* 1948, 637.

[50] McIntosh, *op cit.*, 182-3.

Index